Ambiguous
EMPOWERMENT

The Work

Narratives of

Women School

Superintendents

Ambiguous

EMPOWERMENT

Susan E. Chase

University

of Massachusetts

Press

Amherst

Copyright © 1995 by
The University of Massachusetts Press
All rights reserved
Printed in the United States of America
LC 94-16897
ISBN 0-87023-949-X (cloth); 950-3 (pbk.)
Designed by Kristina Kachele
Set in Aldus with Folio Bold Condensed display
Printed and bound by Braun-Brumfield, Inc.

Library of Congress Cataloging-in-Publication Data
Chase, Susan E., 1954–
Ambiguous empowerment : the work narratives of women school
superintendents / Susan E. Chase.
p. cm.
Includes bibliographical references (p.   ) and index.
ISBN 0-87023-949-X (alk. paper). — ISBN 0-87023-950-3 (pkb. : alk.
paper)
1. Women school administrators—United States—Social conditions—
Interviews.   2. Women school administrators—United States—
Attitudes—Interviews.   3. Sex discrimination in education—United
States—Interviews.   I. Title.
LB2831.82.C43   1994
371.2'0082—dc20   94-16897
                                                   CIP

British Library Cataloguing in Publication data are available.

In memory of

Adelia Chase and

Marie Olaussen

CONTENTS

CONTENTS

Preface

This book studies the work narratives of one group of successful professional women in the contemporary United States: women who lead the nation's public schools. I focus on their stories about professional power and achievement on the one hand, and their stories about discrimination encountered in a white- and male-dominated profession on the other. I heard these stories during interviews that Colleen Bell and I conducted with women superintendents of various racial and ethnic backgrounds in rural, small-town, and urban districts across the country.

Readers who have listened to any group of professional women talk about their work experiences will likely find these stories familiar. Like other successful women who work in male- and white-dominated professions, women superintendents have much to say about the way they managed to get into such positions despite the anomaly of their gender or race, how they developed confidence in their competence and authority, and what they have accomplished by exercising their professional power. They also talk about various forms of gender and race inequality that structure the profession and how they respond to discriminatory treatment.

Women superintendents' stories are compelling and moving, but they do not reveal new and unusual forms of power or discrimination. Indeed, it is their familiar character that interests me. In this book, I study these familiar stories in order to understand how professional women make sense of their contradictory experiences of power and subjection—their ambiguous empowerment—in the context of contemporary American culture. This means that I do not simply report women superintendents' stories or present them as if their meanings were self-evident. In my view, neither these nor any other narratives "speak for themselves," as some social scientists assert they do. Rather, I support the idea that *any* representation of another's speech or action is already an interpretation that reflects the choices and interests of the one presenting it. My interest lies in understanding relations among culture, narrative, and experience—in understanding how women make sense of their experiences by narrating them within a particular cultural context.

In other words, as I present and interpret women superintendents' narratives, I simultaneously develop a narrative of my own. My narrative shows that as women recount their experiences, they simultaneously draw on and struggle with various cultural discourses—networks of meanings—about individual achievement and inequality. Through that narrative process, women construct self-understandings that both shape and are shaped by those cultural discourses.

My narrative is also about the ways researchers elicit and interpret stories heard during interviews. In recent years, some social scientists have begun to study *how* interviewees tell their stories by attending to the cultural, linguistic, and interactional contexts and processes of storytelling. Most researchers usually ignore these contexts and processes and focus simply on *what* respondents say. I view the recent attention to context and process not as a passing fad but as an important development sturdily grounded in traditions of social theory such as symbolic interaction, phenomenology, and ethnomethodology.

Throughout this book, I argue that listening closely to how women narrate their experiences is necessary if we want to understand how culture and narrative shape experience, as well as understand what professional women are telling us about their power and subjection.

Generally speaking, I find that women superintendents embrace their professional competencies and success and develop a primary commitment to their professional work. This suggests that the narrative of the successful, ambitious woman has achieved a certain acceptance in contemporary American culture. I also find that women superintendents fully acknowledge their continuous subjection to gendered and racial inequalities in the profession, and that they construct *individual* solutions to that *collective* problem. Through these individual solutions, women seek integration into the professional community so that they can get on with their work. This finding suggests that women superintendents face squarely the discrimination they encounter, rather than deny or ignore it as professional women are often accused of doing. I argue, however, that structural and discursive conditions continue to discourage them from seeking collective solutions to the collective problem of inequality.

In part 1 of the book, I articulate the cultural and discursive contexts in which successful professional women make sense of their experiences of power and subjection. Chapter 1 focuses on the tension within American culture between the emphasis on individual achievement and success on the one hand, and the persistent debates over the causes and meanings of inequality on the other. I argue that one manifestation of that tension is a disjunction between taken-for-granted, gender- and race-neutral discourse about professional work, and contentious, gendered and racialized discourse about inequality. That *discursive disjunction,* as I call it, shapes how women superintendents talk about their experiences of achievement and subjection. (It also shapes how my coresearcher and I asked interview questions.) In addition, chapter 1 presents the theoretical commitments that ground my method of inquiry. The chapter closes with a brief description of the profession of the superintendency for readers unfamiliar with its history and current status.

Chapter 2 demonstrates the argument through examples culled from the interviews. I show how the taken-for-granted—or settled—discursive realm of professional work shapes talk in ways that we are unself-conscious about, and how the contentious—or unsettled—discursive realm of inequality shapes talk in ways that make us self-conscious about what we are saying and how our speech will be interpreted. Women superintendents draw easily on professional discourse to describe themselves as accomplished, successful individuals. They self-consciously use discourse about inequality to discuss whether and how they are subject to discrimination as persons who belong to certain gender and racial groups.

Part 2, "Narrative Strategies," demonstrates that women superintendents are not passive in the face of the disjunction between settled discourse about professional work and unsettled discourse about inequality. I use the term *narrative strategy* to capture a woman's specific orientation to that disjunction, how she wrestles with that disjunction as she narrates her power and subjection. I identify her narrative strategy by focusing on patterns across the various stories she tells over the course of the interview, patterns in her manner of speaking, and patterns in her use of specific discourses. Because I wanted to highlight women's narrative strategies, I decided to devote an entire chapter to each of four women's narratives. The titles of chapters 3 through 6 name their narrative strategies.

Ana Martinez and Denise Nelson, whose stories are the subject of chapters 3 and 4 respectively, employ narrative strategies that tend to accentuate or reinforce the discursive disjunction. Martinez continually highlights her professional competence and deliberately excludes stories about subjection she experiences as a Hispanic woman in a white-dominated profession. Nelson recasts past experience as sex discrimination only after she lets go of discourse about ambition. By contrast, Margaret Parker and Karen Rhodes, in chapters 5 and 6, integrate stories about professional work and inequality and develop narrative strategies that tend to undermine the disjunction between the two discursive realms. Parker constantly juxtaposes her professional success and her subjection to men's greater power, and over the course of the interview she slowly uncovers deeper layers of her personal strength and vulnerability. Rhodes uses discourse about professional power and individualism to describe how she overcomes sexist treatment and integrates herself into the professional community.

Part 3 focuses on the larger story communicated by these four women's narratives. In chapter 7, I argue that despite their diversity, a certain commonality collects the narratives: in varying degrees, all of these superintendents employ narrative strategies that partially dismantle *and* partially preserve the individualistic, gender- and race-neutral character of the discursive realm of professional work. Furthermore, that commonality conveys a larger story: women superintendents devote themselves primarily to their professional commitments and manage to deal with the persistent inequalities they face in ways that do not distract them from their work. In short, the larger story is about individual solutions to the collective problem of inequality. I argue that this story is distinct from both the co-optation story and the activist story that professional women sometimes tell. By examining how women superintendents talk about their relationships with women colleagues, I explore the structural and discursive conditions that make it difficult for them to develop collective solutions to the persistent problem of inequality in their profession.

The interview material I analyze in this book belongs to a collaborative research project Colleen Bell and I began in 1986. As I describe in the appendix—"The Research Project"—we started with an interest in women superintendents' work experiences and the processes that reproduce or challenge male and white dominance in the profession. In addition to women superintendents, we interviewed gatekeepers to the occupation (school board members, superintendency search consultants, and department of education officials representing various states).

In the course of this joint project, I developed a particular interest in the narrative process itself, in how these highly accomplished women develop understandings of themselves as successful and subjected persons. Although I am sole author of this book and solely responsible for the analyses presented within it, Colleen has a strong presence in the text. I frequently mention Colleen as my coresearcher and cointerviewer, and her words appear (as do mine) in the interview transcripts. Because I treat the research project and the interview interaction as important aspects of the context in which women narrate their stories, I have made our presence as interviewers visible to the reader, rather than concealing it as researchers often do.

In a long list of acknowledgments, then, my first thanks go to Colleen Bell. As coresearcher, colleague, and friend, she has accompanied me through the exciting and mundane tasks of research, encouraged me as my interest in narrative developed, and shared my professional and personal joys and crises along the way.

Without the enthusiastic participation of women superintendents across the country, neither the research project nor this book would have been possible. The women whose narratives are the subject of my study gave generously of their time, energy, and thoughtfulness during interviews that took them away from their work (and sometimes their families) for many hours. Their stories have become important to me not only as research data but also as guides for reflection on my own professional experiences.

Colleen and I depended on many people throughout the research project. Martina Thompson, Marilyn Livingston, and Mimi Schuttloffel assisted with the phone surveys that provided data on women in the superintendency in all fifty states (see the appendix). Leann Stephenson, Stacy Clettenberg, Holly Ewing, Linda Golden, and the late Margaret Nichols gave us excellent technical and clerical assistance with many tasks. Friends across the country offered us housing and hospitality as we visited interview sites. Allen Soltow, director of research at the University of Tulsa, supported and encouraged us all along.

Our joint research project was funded by grants from the American Association of University Women, the Office of Educational Research and Improvement at the U.S. Department of Education (Grant #R117E00147), the Oklahoma Commission for Educational Leadership, the Office of Research at the University of Tulsa, and the College of Arts and Sciences at the University of Tulsa. Of course, the ideas I develop in this book do not necessarily reflect positions taken by any of these organizations.

As I wrote this book over the last few years, several people gave me useful comments and criticisms on various drafts of one or more chapters: John Anderson, Colleen Bell, Robert Crowson, Jane Nicholson, Richard Martin, Laurel Richardson, Jessica Rowe, and Marlie Wasserman. Linda Lacey's reading of chapter 1 was especially fruitful in helping me to organize and tighten my argument. Marjorie DeVault and Jack Hewitt, who served as external readers for the manuscript, broadened my perspective on the study and provided strong suggestions for revision. Elizabeth Chase, Lillian Corti, and Susan Haworth-

Hoeppner helped me with interpretations of particularly complex parts of several stories.

In addition to reading various versions of the manuscript, Peter Stromberg and Tod Sloan engaged me in conversations about language and narrative that helped me to formulate and strengthen my ideas. I am grateful to Vibeke Petersen for her ongoing collegial and personal support, her careful readings of my work from a women's studies perspective, and our many conversations about the ups and downs of writing. My department chair, Jean Blocker, supported me through trying times and helped me as an untenured assistant professor to preserve my energy for writing. As my professional mentor and friend, Mary Rogers offered invaluable advice about the process of writing and publishing the book, as well as generous readings of several chapters. Clark Dougan, my editor at the University of Massachusetts Press, guided me patiently through the entire publishing process. I appreciate the careful attention Pam Wilkinson, managing editor, and Dawn Potter, copy editor, gave to my manuscript.

The influence of my teachers—Alan Blum, Peter McHugh, and the late Stephen Karatheodoris—runs deeply throughout this book. They have been my constant interlocutors as I struggled to articulate in my own way the theoretical commitments and methodological interests that serve as the foundation for this study.

Finally, I thank John Anderson for understanding and respecting the importance of work in my life.

Cultural and

Discursive

Contexts

Part
ONE

1

American

Culture,

Professional

Work, and

Inequality

Karen Rhodes[1] is a sixty-year-old white woman whose career in public education spans forty years. Like many educational leaders, she presents herself as strongly committed to children's educational needs. In addition, she calls herself "a mover and a shaker," noting that several school districts have sought her leadership because she has a reputation for taking risks and making changes. The following is an excerpt from the story Rhodes told about how, as a teacher and union activist, she decided to pursue a career in educational administration.

I began to think "well I could do this this and this." I wanted all these things for teachers. . . . [It was] *that perspective*, seeing how things were *working*, and that there was another *dimension* to the operation. And quite frankly the fact that there are so many *assholes doing* these things [laughs]. I kept thinking "*god* there's got to be a better way to do this. If *I* were doing it I'd do this this and this." And I began to think "I could do a better job quite frankly than some of them."

As she describes her desire to improve conditions for teachers and her ability to do a better job than others, Rhodes presents herself as a confident, efficacious individual, as an educator committed to and capable of doing the leadership work that needs to be done.

Karen Rhodes also told a story about a blatant case of sex discrimination. According to her account, she was first on the short list for a desirable superintendency, but the men who were in charge of the search shuffled the short list in order to give the job to one of their buddies, a man she described as a "good old guy." Rhodes filed a complaint with the Equal Employment Opportunity Commission (or EEOC, the federal agency responsible for investigating sex discrimination charges) and eventually won a substantial out-of-court settlement. In the following excerpt, she talks about how betrayed she felt when her former boss failed to come to her aid in this situation. Although he was not directly involved, he carried a great deal of influence in the profession and was close to those who discriminated against Rhodes.

> I *did* something I *never* should have done. I said to him "you *knew* what was going on and that hurt me more. *You* and I sat for many hours and talked about" you know, how *his* daughter who is in kind of a male-dominated thing too—she went into medicine—and how tough it was for *her* because of being a female in it. And I said "you *knew* what was going on. . . ." I shouldn't have bitched at *him* but it *hurt* me that he'd been my superintendent, I'd been his assistant superintendent. And he just wasn't *straight* up with me. . . . He just smoothed it *all* over and really was *very* evasive and didn't tell me anything and didn't help and *let* the system go on and *that* hurt me a lot.

As she recounts this conversation, Rhodes accuses her former boss of complicity with the powerful men who discriminated against her and who failed to treat her as the competent professional she is.

Like the other women superintendents my coresearcher and I interviewed, Karen Rhodes talks about herself both as a competent and committed educator who makes an important difference through her work and as a person who is subject to sexism in her male-dominated profession. These two experiences are related to women superintendents' position in the professional world. As public school leaders, they occupy the most powerful position in their local school districts and are influential persons in their communities. (Some of them are also important figures in education on the state and national levels.) As white, Black, and Hispanic women, they are subject to gender and racial or ethnic inequalities in an occupation that is more than 94 percent male and 96 percent white.[2]

Like much contemporary feminist research, my study focuses on the coexistence of power and subjection in women's lives—in this case, professional women's lives. This focus highlights the complexity of women's experience, the intersection of vulnerability and strength, and specifically the ambiguity of professional women's empowerment in a continually inequitable context. As others do, I turn to women's own accounts of their experiences in order to address this complexity and ambiguity, a turn aimed at remedying the long history of social scientists' neglect and distortion of women's experience.[3]

But this book addresses women's accounts of power and subjection in an unusual way—unusual, at least, for a sociological study based on intensive interviews. Many such studies document women's move into positions of power that have been (and continue to be) dominated by white men, and present women's accounts of the various forms of discrimination they face in those positions. These studies demonstrate clearly that even the most privileged women in the American work force are subject to institutionalized male and white dominance. Yet the place of language in constituting experiences of power and subjection remains undeveloped in most of these studies. In this book, then, I attend to what researchers usually take for granted when they gather women's accounts: the narrative process itself; *how* women tell their stories. This means that I treat narration as a form of social action that is itself worthy of study. My inquiry brings to light how professional women shape their self-understandings and how they make sense of their contradictory experiences of power and subjection.

The narrative process—making sense of experience and shaping self-understanding—is at once a personal and a cultural endeavor. Like all narratives about the self, professional women's stories display the culture in which the women live. When professional women narrate their experiences of power and subjection, they draw on meaning systems—discourses—that American culture provides for talking about professional achievement on the one hand and inequality on the other. By shifting my focus to narrative practices, then, my study deepens our comprehension of how American culture constrains professional women's self-understandings and how they struggle against those constraints. This dynamic relationship between culture and experience comes to light only when we attend to the narrative process itself.

Throughout this study, I pursue several aims and interests. On a substantive level, I seek to expose a particular tension within American culture: the tension between discourse about professional work (with its emphasis on gender- and race-neutral individuals) and discourse about inequality (with its emphasis on gendered and racialized groups). Because this cultural tension shapes how professional women perceive themselves (as well as how Americans in general perceive professional women), we need to grasp its character and import if we are to understand the stories women tell. Women superintendents' narratives simultaneously reflect that tension and exhibit various strategies for making sense of experience in the face of it. In theoretical and methodological terms, I aim to show that analysis of the relationship between culture and experience is best achieved through a focus on the embodiment of that relationship in actual practice—in this case, women's work narratives as recounted during in-depth interviews. Finally, I hope this study will teach us to listen more carefully to how professional women talk about their work experiences. Only by hearing the cultural constraint and the narrative struggle in the stories women tell can we understand clearly what they are telling us about themselves and their ambiguous empowerment in white- and male-dominated professions.

HAVING A STORY TO TELL:
PROFESSIONAL WOMEN'S NARRATIVES
IN CULTURAL CONTEXT

Over the last few decades, humanities and, more recently, social science scholars have debated the nature and significance of narrative in literature, historical writings, the popular media, personal documents such as diaries and letters, and oral stories of various kinds.[4] Despite disagreement concerning what constitutes narrative and whether story-telling is a crosscultural human practice, most scholars point to the ubiquity of narrative in Western societies and concur that all forms of narrative share a fundamental interest in making sense of experience, in constructing and communicating meaning.[5] Furthermore, scholars agree that narration is a cultural practice; in making sense of experience, any narrative draws on and is constrained by the culture in which it is embedded. As Jerome Bruner states about the stories people tell about themselves, "life narratives obviously reflect the prevailing theories about 'possible lives' that are part of one's culture."[6] Similarly, others suggest that those prevailing theories stand as a culture's meta-narratives or scripts. Carolyn G. Heilbrun writes:

> We can only retell and live by the stories we have read or heard. We live our lives through texts. They may be read, or chanted, or experienced electronically, or come to us, like the murmurings of our mothers, telling us what conventions demand. Whatever their form or medium, these stories have formed us all; they are what we must use to make new fictions, new narratives.[7]

Like many others, Heilbrun suggests not only that cultural texts shape the stories we tell about ourselves, but also that the stories we tell form who we are and how we live. Contrary to common sense, which assumes that our lives determine our stories, narrative scholars argue that our stories shape our lives and that narration makes self-understanding possible.

While people construct self-understanding by making use of available cultural resources, their life stories are also particular. This is true in two senses. First, cultural resources constrain but do not wholly determine their use. A narrator draws on cultural resources as she tells her *own* story, a story that is distinguishable, for example, from her mother's or father's or any other individual's story. At the same time, a life story is never wholly idiosyncratic; its particularity must be culturally intelligible. Second, even when one tells an often-told story, there is something unique about *this* occasion of its telling. Barbara Herrnstein Smith reminds us that this particularity is part of the social character of narration: "As in any social transaction, each party must be individually motivated to participate in it: in other words . . . each party must have some *interest* in telling or listening to that narrative."[8] In addition, then, to making herself intelligible within the cultural context, a narrator also makes her story meaningful in specific ways, on this occasion, to this audience. In these two senses, every storyteller tells her own story.

Successful Women's Unconventional Stories

Western culture's metanarratives about women—as communicated through literature, popular culture, the natural and social sciences— emphasize women's selflessness, orientation to and development through others, and preoccupation with family and domestic affairs.[9] Within the substantial body of research that has developed around women's written and oral narratives, a major focus is the disjunction between these metanarratives and women's actual lived experiences, a disjunction that is particularly evident in narratives by and about women who have been successful through paths traditionally reserved for men. For example, Nadya Aisenberg and Mona Harrington describe the tension produced by the conventional marriage plot when academic women narrate their career stories.

> And we would emphasize here that the marriage plot applies to *all* women, married and unmarried alike, because it defines what women *should* want, the way they *should* behave, and the choices they *should* make under the old norms. Women may follow the plot successfully, try to follow it and fail, or decide *not* to follow it. But because it has for centuries been the paradigm for women's lives, the one thing women cannot do is ignore or rid themselves of the marriage plot entirely as a guide for their proper conduct and a measure of their success.[10]

Aisenberg and Harrington show how academic women struggle to come to terms with the marriage plot even as the quest or adventure plot emerges in their stories.

Heilbrun argues that accomplished women's life narratives have been severely constricted by the cultural prohibition of women's desire

Cultural and Discursive Contexts

for power and control over their own lives. "Because [power] has been declared unwomanly . . . women have been deprived of the narratives, or the texts, plots, or examples, by which they might assume power over—take control of—their own lives."[11] Thus, accomplished women have often suppressed or disguised ambition and success in recounting their experiences. Even twentieth-century autobiographies mute success and pain, "as though the women were certain of nothing but the necessity of denying both accomplishment and suffering."[12] In her study of the autobiographies of Eleanor Roosevelt, Golda Meir, Dorothy Day, and Emmeline Pankhurst, Patricia Meyer Spacks concludes:

> In writing of themselves, these women of public accomplishment implicitly stress uncertainties of the personal, denying rather than glorifying ambition, evading rather than enlarging private selves. They use autobiography, paradoxically, partly as a mode of self-denial. Although they have functioned successfully in spheres rarely open to women, their accounts of this activity emphasize its hidden costs more than its rewards and draw back—as women have traditionally done—from making large claims of importance. Even as they tell of unusual accomplishment, in other words, they finally hide from self-assertion. Their strategies of narrative reflect both a female dilemma and a female solution to it.[13]

While the disjunction between Western culture's metanarratives about women and women's actual experience is a major theme in this body of research, my study focuses on a different kind of disjunction that is expressed in accomplished women's narratives. As I analyzed how women superintendents talk about their work experiences, I found that they do struggle to tell their unconventional stories but that the struggle does not lie where I had anticipated it. It is not the unwomanly character of their accomplishments that causes them the most narrative difficulty. While they are certainly aware that their success violates the persistent cultural expectation that men should hold positions of power, these successful women do not disguise or mute their accomplishments, at least not to the extent described in the literature I have discussed. While their narratives are gendered—for example, through attention to relations with others[14]—these successful women also speak forthrightly about their accomplishments. As they move through their work histories and talk about their current work situations, most women superintendents embrace their power, achievement, and success, and speak with genuine enjoyment about developing themselves as competent, committed, educational leaders. Women superintendents confidently produce what the Personal Narratives Group calls *counternarratives,* stories in which their self-images contrast with dominant cultural models for women.[15] Thus, the narratives of these accomplished women do not point to a dearth of texts for telling stories about themselves as powerful educators. Rather, their stories provide evidence that the counternarrative of the confident, accomplished, successful woman has found a place in late twentieth-century American culture.

Moreover, talking about discrimination is not the greatest narrative difficulty these women encounter. Their narratives indicate a variety of culturally available texts for describing themselves as white, Black, and Hispanic women who are subject to racial and gender inequalities in their profession. Although stories about discrimination have not achieved a prominent place in American culture, the legacies of the civil rights and women's movements have made such stories familiar by giving them at least some public currency. In addition, such stories flourish in the safe spaces created when people who share similar experiences come together.[16] In the context of our in-depth interviews, women educational leaders expressed consciousness of themselves as members of oppressed groups in American society and awareness of how gender, race, and ethnicity shape their life experiences. Importantly, in these women's stories—and I suspect this would be true of most Americans' accounts of discrimination—victimization is never the end of the story. In our culture, talk about discrimination almost always includes an account of how one responds to such treatment: the victim is rarely wholly a victim. Although there is a great range in how women superintendents talk about experiences of discrimination and much diversity in how they articulate their responses to such treatment, all of them acknowledge that such experience must be addressed within their work stories.

The narrative difficulty these successful women encounter, then, is not related to a dearth of texts about women's accomplishments or about women's subjection to inequality. Their stories are conscious and expressive of both kinds of experience. Rather, the narrative strug-gle they face has to do with what I call a *discursive disjunction* between these two kinds of experience. In contemporary American culture, talk about professional work and talk about inequality belong to two dif-ferent discursive realms, two conflicting vocabularies for articulating experience, two different ways of talking about oneself. When success-ful professional women narrate their work stories, they bring together two kinds of talk that generally do not belong together in American culture: talk about professional achievement and talk about subjection to gender and racial inequalities.

The difference between my focus on this discursive disjunction and others' focus on the disjunction between conventional metanarratives and women's lives is related to two contextual factors. The first is historical. When Heilbrun describes the dearth of narratives in which women assume power over their lives, she is speaking in broad terms about the nineteenth and twentieth centuries. While that long history certainly continues to exert weight, it makes sense that successful women in the late 1980s would not be as burdened by it as women would have been in earlier decades. Indeed, Heilbrun acknowledges that much has changed since 1970.

Second, intensive interviews create a particular context for narra-tion, a context that differs interactionally and linguistically from that in which written (and some kinds of oral) narratives are constructed. Unlike narratives publicized under one's name—such as autobiogra-phies, biographies, and, in some cases, oral histories—the conventions of intensive interviews allow for public expression with the protection of pseudonyms and other forms of disguise. That condition removes at least one layer of constraint on speech. Of course, narratives produced during interviews are as embedded in culture as any other narratives. Indeed, the idea that pseudonyms allow women to speak a little more freely shows, paradoxically, how weighty gendered conventions are. My point is simply that interviews invite accomplished women to claim their achievements more than other narrative contexts might. This is especially true given the general congruence between women superintendents' experiences and my coresearcher's and mine. Like the women we interviewed, Colleen Bell and I also work in a white- and male-dominated profession (academia) in which competence, commitment, achievement, and ambition are integral components. There was no reason for women superintendents to conceal from us their pleasure in accomplishment and success.[17]

The Cultural Tension between Individualism and Inequality

Before turning to the disjunction between discourse about professional work and inequality, I need to step back and examine the broader cultural tension that makes successful women's work stories culturally interesting—or storyworthy—in the first place.

While everyone has stories to tell about his or her life, some people's stories draw the attention of the general public, the popular media, and researchers because their experiences embody cultural contradictions or tensions. In American society, women who hold positions of power are one such group of people. Whether at the national, state, or local level, women attract notice when they achieve positions that are usually held by white men: Supreme Court justice, state governor, city mayor, college president, scientist, engineer, doctor, lawyer, clergy, corporate executive. Such women are at once powerful individuals and members of groups that have been subject to racism and sexism throughout American history. On the one hand, they represent the culture's traditional emphasis on individual achievement and success. On the other hand, their achievement arouses the culture's persistent ideological debates concerning inequality and social change. Anyone who reads a city newspaper or listens to radio or TV news has heard— and has probably participated in—debates about these familiar questions: Do the increasing numbers of women in powerful positions mean that gender equality has been achieved and that we are living in a postfeminist era? Should we celebrate individual women's success as representing success for women in general? Have successful women worked at changing the structures and practices of the white- and male-dominated institutions in which they work, or have they been co-opted by those institutions? Why has it taken so long for white women and even longer for women of color to break into the prestigious male- and white-dominated professions? Why are there still so few women? Is it because women do not want the responsibility that comes with power? Because women are not as good as men at exercising power? Or because women face glass ceilings, persistent discrimination, and other insurmountable obstacles along the way? Does the contemporary situation mean the women's movement has succeeded or failed?

In this cultural context, it is no surprise that the popular media pay much more attention to the relatively small and privileged group of women in high-paying, prestigious, male-dominated professions than to the majority of women who work in low-paying, female-dominated occupations.

Generally speaking, sociologists and other social scientists argue that structural and cultural barriers continue to impede women's integration into white- and male-dominated professions. Many of these researchers emphasize men's control of the formal and informal sites of hiring, decision making, power brokering, and sponsorship and argue that women, especially women of color, are rarely members of the inner circles that provide these resources and opportunities.[18] Others point to the particular pressures that women experience when most or all of their colleagues are men or white: greater performance expectations, exclusion from collegial groups, and stereotypical interpretations of their actions.[19] Some show that men's higher gender status and whites' higher race status reinforce the identification of masculinity and whiteness with highly valued professional traits.[20] Moreover, the timing of professional careers around the male life cycle fortifies the persistent assumption that women who have children are not committed professionals.[21]

These sociological studies deepen our understanding of professional women's experiences and help us to sort out the popular debates about the meaning of their success. Nonetheless, like the popular debates, these studies articulate professional women's experiences in terms provided by the broader cultural context. In contemporary American society, successful professional women are interesting to the general public and become objects of researchers' study within a cultural context that emphasizes individual success and power on the one hand, and continually debates issues of inequality on the other. *Any* talk about and *any* study of powerful women enters, in one way or another, the cultural arenas of individualism and inequality. This is not a criticism of the research I have cited but an observation—by now a commonplace one—that the social sciences themselves are rhetorical constructions of knowledge that are culturally and historically embedded.[22]

Taking for Granted
the Cultural Context

Let me explain by using my own study as an example. Colleen and I—and the women we interviewed—conceptualized the research project in ways that took for granted the significance of the cultural tension between individualism and inequality. Like other members of our society, we approached professional women's experiences from within this complex cultural milieu. Harold Garfinkel uses the term *background expectancies* to describe features of the social world that we take for granted in our everyday lives and that we become aware of only when they are violated.[23] The background expectancies embedded in this research project become readily apparent when we imagine what would have happened if we had called women superintendents across the country to ask for several hours of their time to discuss their experiences as anything other than school leaders—for example, as pet owners. Even if we had requested interviews on topics of obvious societal importance and personal interest—such as their experiences as mothers or intimates—I doubt we would have had much response. My guess is that they would have consented to interviews about motherhood or intimacy only if we had explicitly connected those experiences to their work as superintendents. In fact, that is exactly how we introduced questions about their private lives. The point is that we articulated our interest in and they consented to talk about their experiences as successful women in this particular white- and male-dominated profession. This articulation and consent make sense in terms of the cultural tension between individualism and inequality. Even before we began the interviews, then, we approached the research project in ways that took for granted the significance of that cultural tension.

Here it is worth noting that out of the thirty women superintendents we contacted in regions all over the country, almost all—twenty-seven—were pleased to offer several hours of their time for interviews.[24] Of the three we did not interview, one was interested but could not accommodate our schedule, and two had no interest in our project.

Despite the general congruence between their situation and ours—we also work in a white- and male-dominated profession—almost all of the women we interviewed were much older than we were, much further along in their careers, and held more powerful positions in their communities. (I should mention that Colleen and I are white, and a quarter of the women we interviewed are of color.) Generally speaking, as persons who occupy higher social status, women superintendents were doing *us* a favor by consenting to interviews. Furthermore, we knew none of the women before contacting them, although some had heard about our project from other participants.

Researchers usually explain people's willingness to give their time for in-depth interviews in terms of the therapeutic aspect of talk (how often does anyone really listen to you for several hours for free?) or the interest in contributing to projects that promise to increase social knowledge.[25] While these explanations make sense—many of our interviewees spontaneously mentioned one or the other or both—they are partial. They ignore the background expectancies embedded in a person's willingness to be interviewed at length on some subject. To consent to an in-depth interview is to acknowledge tacitly that whatever the interview is about already makes sense of one's experience. As phenomenologists and ethnomethodologists have argued, everyday practices and talk are reflexive; people take for granted the cultural context even as they make their speech and actions intelligible within that context.[26] That so many high-status women with overloaded schedules put aside afternoons and evenings to talk to strangers, in some cases for two or three interviewing sessions, suggests the significance of shared background expectancies—in this case, the significance of the tension between individualism and inequality in American culture.

This taken-for-granted aspect of the cultural context is also evident in how Colleen and I asked interview questions and how women superintendents responded. We organized the interviews around a set of questions about the tasks and problems women educational leaders face in their current positions, the professional and interpersonal contexts in which they work, their work histories, and the relationship between their personal and professional lives. We also asked what difference gender and race or ethnicity have made to their experiences. Not surprisingly, these questions made sense to women superintendents as questions worth thinking about and answering. Together we assumed that successful professional women have stories to tell that others want and need to hear; stories about how they rose to such influential leadership positions despite the anomaly of their gender and, in some cases, their race or ethnicity; stories about what it is like to work in such positions; stories about the inequalities they face and how they handle them.

The Discursive Disjunction: Talking about Professional Work and Inequality

While we took for granted that women educational leaders would have stories to tell about professional achievement and discrimination, we did not anticipate *how* the tension between individualism and inequality would shape their stories and the interview talk generally. Throughout the interviews, Colleen and I found that it was easy to ask questions about the work women superintendents do, and that they responded at length to such questions, talking unself-consciously and eagerly even when describing formidable tasks such as closing schools and resolving teacher strikes. By contrast, we felt much more self-conscious when asking about their experiences with gender, racial, or ethnic inequality, and they, too, exhibited various forms of self-consciousness when talking about such experiences. Sometimes self-consciousness was expressed in their manner of speaking—for example, in careful, distracted, or angry speech. These forms of talk exhibit awareness of possible reproach from others or imply criticism of how others speak about such topics. Sometimes self-consciousness was expressed in the content of their talk—for example, in referring to the injury and pain caused by experiences of subjection. As we conducted the interviews, Colleen and I observed the relative ease of talk about professional work and the relative difficulty of talk about inequality. At the time, we treated the difference as an incidental technical problem, and we tried to think of ways to minimize the self-consciousness that surrounded our talk about inequality. In the course of my analytical work, however, I decided to treat the difference between unself-conscious and self-conscious talk as central to women's stories about power and subjection. This lived experience provided the point of entry for my analyses. By listening to *how* we spoke during the interviews—by attending to the difference between our unself-conscious talk about professional work and our self-conscious talk about inequality—I developed the notion that two distinct discursive realms shaped both women superintendents' talk and our interview questions.

I use the term *discursive realm* to refer to the set of discourses—the network of meanings or ideas—that are culturally available for talking about professional work on the one hand and inequality on the other.[27] These two realms differ in the content of the ideas they make available for talking about experience. Equally important, they also differ in how they shape *forms* of talk. My focus on the content of discursive realms is not unusual; many researchers who study in-depth interviews interpret what people say in relation to culturally familiar discourse.[28] My interest, however, in the differing forms of talk related to these two discursive realms—in self-conscious and unself-conscious talk—*is* unusual. When I refer to the disjunction between these realms, I mean that they shape the content and forms of talk in distinct ways. One of my major arguments is that talk about professional work usually belongs to a settled, taken-for-granted discursive realm, while talk about inequality generally belongs to an unsettled, explicitly ideological discursive realm.

In order to articulate the disjunction between these discursive realms, I borrow (and transform for my own purposes) Ann Swidler's ideas about the traditional and ideological aspects of culture and about settled and unsettled cultural periods.[29] In so doing, I import Swidler's distinctions into the discursive arenas of contemporary American culture.

The Discursive Realm
of Professional Work

Discourse about professional work—what it is, its value to society, and the relationship between such work and a person's identity—belongs to what Swidler calls the traditional aspect of culture: beliefs and practices that are "taken for granted so that they seem inevitable parts of life."[30] In the contemporary United States, we take for granted that the professions are integral to society's functioning, that professional work is a sphere of achievement and competence based in specialized knowledge useful to society at large, that such work encourages professionals to develop identities based in their work, and that professionals enjoy stature in their communities because of their expertise and the perceived importance of the work they do. In addition, professionals in the public sector are expected to use their expertise to serve the public good.[31] Although the general public may express doubts about the competence, integrity, or motives of individuals or certain groups of professionals—lawyers are a typical target, and, as we will see, school superintendents are highly vulnerable to public scrutiny—cases of incompetence or lack of integrity are evaluated against persisting notions about what professional work is, what its place in society is, and what professionals are like.

While individualism figures prominently in American culture generally, it is particularly well developed and entwined with professional discourse.[32] In describing the development of the "culture of professionalism" during the 1800s in the United States, Burton J. Bledstein writes:

> The culture of professionalism emancipated the active ego of a sovereign person as he performed organized activities within comprehensive spaces. The culture of professionalism incarnated the radical idea of the independent democrat, a liberated person seeking to free the power of nature within every worldly sphere, a self-governing individual exercising his trained judgment in an open society. The Mid-Victorian as professional person strove to achieve a level of autonomous individualism, a position of unchallenged authority heretofore unknown in American life.[33]

In more general terms, professional discourse draws on what Robert N. Bellah and his associates describe as "utilitarian individualism," the idea that America provides the individual with the opportunity "to get ahead on his own initiative."[34] In contemporary everyday speech, we talk about a professional's success or failure as determined by his or her individual competence, efforts, and ambition. Furthermore, individualism undergirds professional structures. *Individuals* earn certification or degrees; *individuals* occupy positions and develop careers. Two people can not share a Ph.D., and it is rare to find two people sharing a job. A résumé cannot be shared because it records a career—by definition, an individual's career.

Like any discourse, discourse about professional work is historically and culturally situated; what we take for granted today has not always been and may not always be taken for granted.[35] For example, Bledstein points out that in the eighteenth and early nineteenth centuries, "competence, knowledge, and preparation were less important in evaluating the skills of the professional than were dedication to the community, sincerity, trust, permanence, honorable reputation and righteous behavior." By the end of the nineteenth century, however, individualism had achieved a firmer hold through the growing emphasis on career: "The new individual professional life had gained both an inward coherence and self-regulating standards that separated and defined it independently of the general community." At this point, a professional career was understood (and still is) as "a pre-established total pattern of organized professional activity, with upward movement through recognized preparatory stages, and advancement based on merit and bearing honor."[36]

As it is usually constituted in everyday talk, discourse about professional work purports to be neutral with respect to gender and race. Within this discursive realm, competent and ambitious persons achieve as individuals, not as men, women, whites, Hispanics, or Blacks. While feminist scholars have shown that seemingly neutral discourse is often gendered and racialized,[37] their criticisms do not necessarily transform the everyday use of professional discourse and the unquestioned sense that it is gender- and race-neutral. In my own research project, I found that Colleen and I and the women we interviewed often (but not always) continued to use discourse about professional work in conventional, individualistic, gender- and race-neutral ways.

Thus, as we interviewed women superintendents, we found it easy to ask about the work itself and they found it easy to offer such stories because both we and they drew in a relatively unproblematic way on taken-for-granted discourse about professional work. For example, in the quotation that opens this chapter, Karen Rhodes explains her interest in becoming an educational leader by pointing to her individual competence and her desire to improve conditions for teachers. This self-description reflects recognizable, conventional discourse about professional work. The discursive realm of professional work provides resources with which Rhodes and other women superintendents comfortably describe themselves as accomplished, committed, and successful individuals. In American society, this conception of self as a strong and efficacious individual is enjoyable to experience and pleasurable to tell stories about.

The Discursive Realm
of Inequality

Compared to discourse about professional work, discourse about inequality occupies an uneasy place in American culture. Talk about inequality belongs to what Swidler calls the ideological aspect of culture: "highly articulated, self-conscious belief . . . system[s], aspiring to offer a unified answer to problems of social action."[38] Ideological talk is self-conscious because it takes place within a continually contested terrain. Hence any talk about inequality arouses (either explicitly or implicitly) these familiar arguments: What are the sources of and who is to blame for inequality in American society? How should inequality be defined and what counts as an instance of inequality? How should victims of inequality respond? What is achieved by and what are the risks of various kinds of responses? Each of the possible answers to these familiar questions has a highly articulated or well-developed vocabulary upon which speakers can draw—for example, fascist, neoconservative, liberal, socialist, or feminist vocabularies. Because people cannot take for granted that others share their views on matters of inequality, except perhaps within their own circle (and even there matters of inequality often are debated passionately), people are self-conscious as they speak about inequality. Self-consciousness in this context does not mean hesitance or shyness but rather consciousness of possible objections to one's speech. In Bakhtin's words, the "dialogic overtones" of speech—how "thought . . . is born and shaped in the process of interaction and struggle with others' thought"—are much more audible when we talk about inequality than when we talk about professional work.[39]

While the individual is the focus in talk about professional work, persons are identified primarily as members of some race, class, or gender group in talk about inequality. For example, in order to claim that one is a victim of discrimination, one must argue that she or

CULTURAL AND DISCURSIVE CONTEXTS

he has been discriminated against by virtue of membership in some group. When we talk about inequality, then, our attention turns from individuals to groups.

Like the discursive realm of professional work, the discursive realm of inequality is historically and culturally situated. Changes in public discourse about inequality, for instance, are documented in the history of United States Supreme Court decisions about matters of race and gender.[40] Despite the changes, however, the highly contentious character of such discourse has persisted over the course of that history.

Thus, in our interviews with women superintendents, we found talk about inequality relatively difficult and self-conscious for two reasons. First, any such speech presupposes a stand on some ideological issue that immediately brings to mind a set of competing stands. As women described experiences of discrimination or talked generally about the position of women in the occupation or in society, they used one or another well-developed vocabulary of inequality and they expressed awareness that others think differently. This awareness was sometimes explicit, as when they criticized others' (including other women's) ways of dealing with such issues or when they anticipated how others might criticize their own position. For example, in describing her decision not to rehire a woman who had previously taught in the school district, one superintendent stated, "I'm beginning to sound like a male chauvinist myself now but half the time she was requesting to be home with her kids." This superintendent explicitly acknowledges that her decision not to rehire the teacher *could* be interpreted as sexist because it ignored the teacher's needs as a mother.

Second, talk about inequality was relatively difficult and self-conscious because conceiving of oneself as subject to inequality is often painful. As Marilyn Frye argues, any person's actions are always circumscribed by the actions of others, and people's efforts are often frustrated by social forces or events beyond their control. However, what is particular about the experience of subjection (or oppression, to use Frye's word) is being "confined and shaped by forces and barriers which are not accidental or occasional and hence avoidable, but are systematically related to each other in such a way as to catch one between and among them and restrict or penalize motion in any direction."[41] For example, no matter how a woman responds to discriminatory treatment, her actions risk penalty: her career may be dead-ended if she files a lawsuit, or she may be subject to similar treatment in the future if she keeps quiet. I suggest that the pain caused by discrimination is the experience of subjection itself, feeling and knowing one's vulnerability to others' abuse of their greater institutionalized power.

The excerpt from Karen Rhodes's story about the incident of job discrimination demonstrates these aspects of the discursive realm of inequality. Rhodes takes a stand on a contentious ideological issue by arguing that her former boss should have intervened on her behalf in a situation where his friends were discriminating against her. At the same time, by stating that she shouldn't have "bitched at him," Rhodes acknowledges that her own action is debatable. She knows that another woman in her place would have reacted differently, perhaps without angrily confronting the one who hurt her, perhaps without even holding him responsible in the first place. In another part of this story, Rhodes supports her stand, and particularly her decision to take legal action, by articulating the injustice she has suffered. In the context of contemporary American culture, where talk about inequality is highly contentious, Rhodes must argue that what has happened to her is sex discrimination, that she encountered discrimination because of her membership in the group *women*. And even if she convinces others that the treatment she received is discriminatory, she must also argue that seeking legal remedy is the best course of action in response. In addition, by describing how hurt she was by her former boss's failure to come to her aid, Rhodes shows that she experiences discriminatory treatment not only as unjust in an abstract sense, but also as personally injurious.

Swidler develops the distinction between *traditions* and *ideologies* in order to articulate two models of cultural influence. She differentiates settled cultural periods in which traditions guide action from unsettled periods of cultural transformation in which ideologies shape action. By contrast, I am interested in how culture shapes *discourses* differently within contemporary American society, resulting in some discursive realms that are settled and other discursive realms that are unsettled.[42] Colleen and I asked questions and women superintendents told their stories within the constraints and resources provided by the settled discursive realm of professional work on the one hand, and the unsettled discursive realm of inequality on the other. As a relatively settled, traditional part of American culture, the discursive realm of professional work shapes talk in ways that we take for granted. And as a relatively unsettled, explicitly ideological part of American culture, the discursive realm of inequality shapes talk in ways that make us self-conscious about what we are saying and how our speech will be interpreted. The disjunction between these two discursive realms is constituted by their settled and unsettled characters.

Narrative Strategies:
Wrestling with the
Discursive Disjunction

While analysis of the discursive disjunction conveys how American culture constrains talk about professional women's experiences, analysis of women's narrative strategies shifts our attention to how they struggle with those constraints. As I did with the idea of discursive disjunction, I developed the notion of narrative strategy in the course of my analytic work. In the early stages of analysis, as I coded the interview transcripts, I focused on themes about work (for example, aspiration, competence, confidence) and themes about inequality (for example, specific structural and cultural barriers women encounter and their various responses to them).[43] As I attempted to articulate the meanings expressed in specific examples of talk, however, I found that it was difficult to maintain the separateness of a woman's talk about work and her talk about inequality. My persistent attempts to separate them violated my growing sense of their connectedness. For instance, in her story about her successful EEOC complaint, Karen Rhodes presents herself not only as a woman subject to institutionalized male dominance, but also as a strong individual brave enough to fight unjust treatment. That presentation of her individual strength echoes her earlier description of herself as a competent educational leader who knows what needs to be done and sets out to do it. I began to realize that there is a relationship between a woman's construction of self in one story and her construction of self in others. Thus, I started to focus on patterns across the various stories a woman told over the course of the interview, patterns that connected her relatively settled talk about herself as an accomplished professional and her relatively unsettled talk about herself as a subjected person. When I conceptualized the women as narrators, I realized that they were not simply telling a set of contiguous stories about professional work and inequality. Rather, they were juxtaposing those stories in particular, meaningful ways.

I use the term *narrative strategy* to capture that particular, meaningful juxtaposition in each case, to identify a woman's specific orientation or approach to the disjunction between the discursive realms of professional work and inequality. For example, as I demonstrate in chapter 6, Karen Rhodes develops a narrative strategy of using discourse about professional power and individual strength to describe how she overcomes her subjection to sexism and how she integrates herself into the male-dominated professional community.

My interest in women's narrative strategies required alterations in my analytic procedures. I shifted from a focus on substantive themes across the entire set of interviews to a focus on patterns in both content and form *within* each woman's interview—patterns in her manner of speaking and in her use of various settled and unsettled discourses. Furthermore, in order to highlight women's narrative strategies—how they wrestle with the discursive disjunction—I decided to devote an entire chapter to each of four women's narratives. As I examined each superintendent's narrative, these questions guided my inquiry: How shall I characterize this woman's narrative strategy? How does her narrative strategy wrestle with the discursive disjunction? Does it reproduce or undermine that disjunction? Finally, how does her use of *this* narrative strategy shape her self-understanding and what does it communicate about her experience in this white- and male-dominated profession?[44] While chapters 3 through 6 offer four sets of answers based on differences among the four women's narratives, chapter 7 argues that a certain commonality collects all of them. To greater and lesser extents, each of these four women's narratives partially dismantles and partially preserves the taken-for-granted, individualistic, gender- and race-neutral character of the discursive realm of professional work.

At this point I need to clarify my use of the term *narrative.* I began to conceptualize the interviews as narratives when I shifted my attention to how each woman recounts her experiences of achievement and discrimination over the course of the entire interview. I use narrative, then, to describe something broad and deep: the entire linguistic event through which a woman constructs her self-understanding and makes her experiences meaningful. By defining narrative in this way, I high-light the active sense-making process as a whole, a process that would remain concealed if I limited my attention to decontextualized pieces of the interviews. Nonetheless, when I examine separate stories, I find useful William Labov's much narrower definition of narrative as a linguistically and structurally distinct form of speech that reconstructs past events in chronological order.[45]

THEORETICAL COMMITMENTS AND METHOD OF INQUIRY

As the reader may be well aware of by now, my procedures for inter-preting and presenting material collected during in-depth interviews depart in some ways from those that sociologists usually employ. The most obvious departures lie in my serious attention to differing forms of talk (the self-conscious and unself-conscious talk of both interview-ers and interviewees), my focus on narrative strategies that individual women develop in relation to the disjunction between discourse about professional work and inequality, and my subsequent decision to de-vote four chapters to specific narratives. Sociologists who base their research on intensive interviews usually present analyses drawn from themes in *what* people say about their experiences, and they present their findings with respect to the whole set of interviews, devoting rel-atively little attention to individuals.[46] Despite these departures from usual practice, my procedures are grounded in strong traditions of social theory. Specifically, two theoretical commitments anchor my method of inquiry: first, culture is manifest in the actual, particular practices of everyday life; and second, talk is a form of social action worthy of study in itself.

The Embodiment of Culture in Everyday Practice

Several theoretical traditions in sociology—symbolic interaction, phe-nomenology, ethnomethodology—advance the idea that individuals' practices embody what is general to the group or society of which they are members. Theorists explicate this idea in a variety of ways, depending on their interests. Alan Blum and Peter McHugh state that the " 'particular' is not equivalent to 'private' or 'personal' experience and so does not necessarily reference ineffability, because it points to something common."[47] George Herbert Mead articulates the idea in this way: "Our symbols are all universal. You cannot say anything that is absolutely particular; anything you say that has any meaning at all is universal."[48]

In other words, we recognize any instance of human action as what it is only insofar as we understand that it is oriented to some common social world. Furthermore, that any instance of human action is particular is part of what is general: the social is always particularized by its embodiment in practice. Because I ground my work in this theoretical commitment, I am not concerned with the question of whether my sample adequately represents some larger population. Rather, I am concerned with the questions of what members of a group have in common in the first place and of the possible orientations to that commonality. Answers to the latter questions arise from investigating particular practices. Thus, I focus on particular practices (women's narrative strategies) in order to analyze both an aspect of American culture (the disjunction between discourse about professional work and inequality) and the relation between culture and practice (how women's narratives are constrained by the discursive disjunction; how their narrative strategies reproduce or undermine the disjunction; how their narratives shape and communicate their experiences).

I have already introduced this method of inquiry in this chapter. As discussed earlier, I developed an understanding of the culturally interesting or storyworthy character of successful women's experiences by attending to our actual research practices: how my coresearcher and I as well as the women we interviewed conceptualized and participated in the research project. Our mutual assumptions about the stories professional women have to tell point to the tension in American culture between individualism and inequality. As McHugh and his colleagues would say, that cultural tension makes successful women's stories intelligible, interesting, and problematic.[49] In addition, by focusing on unself-conscious and self-conscious *talk* in the interviews, I characterized one manifestation of that cultural tension as a disjunction between discourse about professional work and discourse about inequality. This disjunction shapes the entire set of interviews we conducted (see chapter 2). Indeed, I claim that *any* woman who works in a male- and white-dominated profession in the United States—which means any of the prestigious, high-paying professions—confronts this discursive disjunction as she narrates her work experiences.

In chapters 3 through 6, I use this method of inquiry to explore the narrative strategies that four women superintendents employ in relation to the discursive disjunction. As those chapters demonstrate, these women develop a variety of narrative strategies, all of which represent culturally intelligible solutions to the culturally constituted problem of the discursive disjunction. Thus, while the four women's narratives are particular, they are not idiosyncratic; they represent several different ways that successful professional women might tell their stories about achievement and discrimination. Each woman's narrative can be heard as an example of one particular kind of story successful professional women might tell, a story they might tell in certain narrative contexts, at certain points in their careers, given certain kinds of work experiences and certain perceptions of their options.

My focus on specific narratives allows me to analyze closely how the discursive disjunction shapes women's self-understandings and how women struggle with that disjunction in order to make their experiences meaningful. Treating the four narratives analyzed in chapters 3 through 6 as examples means that I could have chosen different examples from the twenty-seven interviews Colleen and I conducted with women superintendents. Indeed, I did extensive narrative analyses of many of the interviews before selecting these four for the book. I chose them in part because I wanted to include women of different races and ethnicities. Ana Martinez is Hispanic; Margaret Parker is African American; Denise Nelson and Karen Rhodes are white. In addition, I chose these four because there was something about each that captured my interest. In Ana Martinez's case, it was the uncomfortable interaction surrounding my question about what difference ethnicity has made to her experience; in Denise Nelson's, the long story about her decision to leave the superintendency; in Margaret Parker's, her telling and retelling of a discrimination story; and in Karen Rhodes's, the story of her successful EEOC complaint. Although as I began I could not articulate how, I sensed in each case that this interesting feature was central to the woman's narrative about power and subjection. I chose these four narratives, then, not because they are analytically different from the others but because they promised to be good and interesting examples of what they all share.[50]

While all professional women confront the discursive disjunction as they recount their experiences, I do not claim that the four examples I chose exhaust the range of narrative strategies used by professional women generally. (I am confident, however, that these four reflect much of the diversity of narrative strategies among the women we interviewed.) Nor do I claim that the narrative strategy developed by Margaret Parker, for example, is employed by other African-American educational leaders. What Margaret Parker and other Black professional women share in narrating their work experiences is the need to take some stance in relation to discourse about racial inequality. A woman's race or ethnicity does not determine her narrative strategy.

What difference does it make that I based my analysis on interviews with women in this particular male- and white-dominated profession? How different would the narrative strategies of women doctors, lawyers, scientists, corporate executives, or politicians be? The school superintendency has particular features that certainly shape these women's narratives. It is possible that the professional training and actual work of educational leadership may socialize women superintendents into a world that is somewhat more rigid, bureaucratic, and technical than that of other male- and white-dominated professions. If so, then women superintendents may encounter the discursive disjunction more forcefully than some other professional women do because their work depends on discourse that makes it especially difficult for them to consider their own inequitous situations. In that case, women educational leaders' narratives provide a good opportunity to examine a cultural tension that all American professional women face in greater or lesser degrees. In chapter 7, when I explicate the larger story conveyed by the four narratives in chapters 3 through 6, I distinguish it from the co-optation story and the activist story that professional women sometimes tell. Using the example of academics in the field of women's studies, I show that some professional contexts provide greater access to activist discourse that undermines the disjunction between the discursive realms of professional work and inequality. Chapter 7 also addresses the structural and discursive conditions within the superintendency that encourage a story about individual rather than collective solutions to the collective problem of inequality.

Despite the particular characteristics of this male- and white-dominated profession, I expect that many readers will find women superintendents' stories about achievement and discrimination quite familiar. The easily recognizable character of their talk suggests that women superintendents' stories are not so very different from many other professional women's stories. Readers who are professional women themselves might find one woman's narrative more familiar than others, but they might also find that each woman's narrative speaks to their experiences at different points of their careers or in different narrative contexts.

Talk As Social Action

The second theoretical commitment anchoring my method of inquiry is the idea that talk is a form of social action worthy of study in itself, a well-established idea in several traditions of social theory. In its stronger manifestations, this idea belongs to a theory of language as constitutive of meaning, as grounding any understanding of the social world or human action. As Blum and McHugh state, "What we know of the world is possible only because we can speak meaningfully about the world."[51] In Hans-Georg Gadamer's words, "Language is not just one of man's possessions in the world, but on it depends the fact that man has a world at all."[52] These theorists, along with others in the traditions of symbolic interaction, phenomenology, and ethnomethodology, subsume *every* form of social action in the general realm of language. In other words, common sense distinctions between language and action and between speech and thought are spurious; insofar as we recognize any human endeavor as what it is, we constitute it as such in language. Thus, while we make distinctions among various practices (for example, lecturing, chatting, interviewing, arguing), those distinctions are intelligible because we are language users, because our conceptualization of any human practice depends on our capacity as language users.

According to this theoretical perspective, the relationship between language and speech (or between language and any human practice) is one of interdependence or embodiment. Gadamer explains that "language has its true being only in conversation, in the exercise of understanding between people. . . . Communication . . . is a living process in which a community of life is lived out."[53] Similarly, Blum and McHugh state, "Language stands to speech as unity or a limit relates to multiplicity, and yet it is through the multiplicity of different speaking practices that language itself becomes available as what it is, as such an essential limit or unity."[54] And Kenneth Burke describes the relationship in this way: "The ultimate *origins* of language seem to me as mysterious as the origins of the universe itself. One must view it, I feel, simply as the 'given.' But once an animal comes into being that does happen to have this particular aptitude, the various tribal idioms are unquestionably *developed* by their use as instruments in the tribe's way of living."[55]

Despite the centrality of language and speech in several traditions of social theory, and despite the fact that sociologists as diverse as C. Wright Mills, Peter L. Berger and Thomas Luckmann, and Harold Garfinkel have argued that talk itself must be taken seriously in any understanding of the social world,[56] social scientists whose research depends heavily on talk (whether in survey, intensive interview, or ethnographic work) usually ignore the fact that talk itself constitutes their data.[57] Typically, researchers treat speech as an incidental passive instrument for referring to events and experience external to the present interaction and, more significantly, external to language itself.[58] Thus, a commonsense assumption about the passive, referential character of language pervades social science research as much as it does our everyday lives.[59] This means that researchers, like people in the ordinary course of their lives, generally assume that telling a story is simply a matter of using the tools that language provides. We all know and take into account that people sometimes lie and often alter or conceal parts of their stories; yet we assume that if they so choose, they can produce stories that directly reflect their experience. We usually assume that experience determines the story rather than that the narrative process itself shapes the meaningful character of experience. As we listen to others talk, whether during interviews or in our everyday lives, we are concerned mainly with what *this* story is about, why we are hearing this story *now*, and how candid the speaker is being.[60] In our telling and listening, then, we usually take for granted the linguistic and narrative conventions, the cultural scripts, as well as the primacy of language itself that mediate our speech and our understanding of experience. When researchers take talk for granted in this way, they ignore that the recounting itself is a particular kind of social action, a process of constructing and communicating self-understanding, of making experience intelligible and meaningful. They also ignore that the events or experiences being described can be understood as what they are only insofar as they are constituted in language in the first place.

In recent years some social science researchers have turned with renewed interest to those theoretical traditions that make language central to our understanding of the social world. This is especially evident in the burgeoning field of narrative analysis in the social sciences. For example, David R. Maines argues for a "narrative sociology" on the grounds that "a substantial portion of sociology's phenomena is made up precisely of stories," and that sociologists themselves are "spinners of professional tales that we call theories."[61] Researchers within this developing field have a variety of interests in the stories people tell during research interviews (or other contexts); develop diverse procedures for presenting and interpreting those stories; and take different approaches to questions concerning the relation between story and culture, story and fiction/truth, story and subjectivity, and story and life.

Rather than offer an overview of these varying interests, procedures, and approaches, I want to clarify further two aspects of my own approach.[62] First, unlike some narrative researchers, I do not ask *why* each woman develops this or that narrative strategy in the sense of looking for clues in her psyche or personal background.[63] To the extent that we know about a person's psychological makeup or past experiences only through narration, the idea that these factors explain her narrative practices is problematic. In any case, that is not my interest here. Rather, I ask phenomenological questions: *What* is her narrative strategy? *How* does that narrative strategy make her contradictory experiences of achievement and discrimination intelligible and meaningful? These *what* and *how* questions highlight the relationship between culture and experience as that relationship is expressed in and shaped by the individual's narrative. Thus, I focus on narration itself as a significant life activity, as a sense-making and communicative practice that is at once cultural and personal.

Second, I need to say more about the idea that narration makes sense of experience and shapes self-understanding. In one sense, this idea is easily grasped. Any life story constructs experience and self by developing one orientation or another to discursive resources and constraints. But it is more difficult to grasp the theoretical upshot of this idea. Experience and self do not exist independently of language, of the multitudinous ways in which we shape them in the course of our everyday lives; yet, paradoxically, we speak of experience and self as existing independently of our efforts at describing them. I like the way Clifford Geertz discusses this dilemma. The term *experience,* he suggests, is one that many anthropologists are unhappy with but unable to do without: "Without it, or something like it, cultural analyses seem to float several feet above their human ground." Geertz concludes, "Experiences, like tales, fetes, potteries, rites, dramas, images, memoirs, ethnographies, and allegorical machineries, are made; and it is such made things that make them."[64] In terms of my study, the narrative process itself makes experience and self into the entities we recognize them to be. We make experience and self real (meaningful and intelligible) through a variety of human practices, among them narration.

One of my major arguments is that we understand more fully how a narrator shapes her self, and hear more clearly what she communicates about her experience, when we focus on her narrative strategy rather than limiting our attention to her words. Her narrative strategy forms and presents her experience in ways not captured by her words alone. To put this another way, in recounting their experiences, women superintendents do much more than tell us about this or that specific achievement or incident of discrimination. Women's narrative strategies tell us about how experiences of achievement and discrimination are articulable in the contemporary United States, how pulling these contradictory experiences together is culturally problematic, and how it is possible to do so anyway. As I argue in chapter 7, women superintendents' narrative strategies invite us to hear a story that generally goes unheard in public discussions about successful professional women. While such women are often accused of being co-opted by the white- and male-dominated systems in which they work, I argue that this accusation is unfair, at least in this case. When we listen carefully to how women superintendents tell their stories, we hear something quite distinct from co-optation. Their primary commitment lies in doing their work well, but they also struggle in various ways against discriminatory treatment. They know that other women encounter similar experiences of discrimination, but they seek *individual* solutions to the collective problem of inequality, solutions that make sense given the structural and discursive context of educational administration. In this profession, a lonely, isolated struggle against inequality is the requirement and cost of professional success.

Broader Implications of This Study

My analysis of women superintendents' work narratives contributes to our understanding of how general social processes—the reproduction of culture, the construction of self-understandings—are embodied in the actual practices of everyday life: in this case, in narration and talk produced during interviews. The cultural context provides the boundaries within which certain kinds of experiences become especially interesting or storyworthy at certain times. It also provides the range of settled and unsettled discursive resources through which experience can be articulated. But it is only by listening closely to how people tell their stories that we understand how culture is at once limiting and malleable. It is only by listening closely to how people tell their stories that we hear how narrators struggle with those limits, how they stretch and bend the available discursive resources in order to make sense of their own experiences.

These general social processes certainly play an important part in most life narratives. But the concepts of discursive disjunction and narrative strategy have significance for certain kinds of narratives. Although everyone has stories to tell, some people's experiences are culturally interesting because they bring together divergent strands of culture in a new way and promise to elicit new stories. The experiences of professionals in the United States who occupy positions of power previously held by white men are storyworthy in this way. Contemporary American culture simultaneously invites their stories and makes their telling problematic by virtue of the disjunction between the discursive realms of professional work and inequality. Narrative strategies produce solutions to this particular narrative difficulty.

Thus, the concept of discursive disjunction should help us to articulate the disjointedness of many different contemporary discourses, disjunctions that remain unproblematic until they achieve expression in the narratives of various groups of people. The concept of narrative strategy should help us to understand narratives about contradictory identities, experiences of social change, or experiences that cross the boundaries of settled and unsettled discursive realms. The life stories of several groups of people come easily to mind: activists who challenge the status quo; people in the midst of major life transitions such as divorce, grief, or the birth of a child;[65] and people of any social category (such as gender, race, ethnicity, nationality, social class, or sexual orientation) whose lives are significantly intertwined with the lives of those unlike themselves.

THE PUBLIC SCHOOL SUPERINTENDENCY

I close this chapter with a brief description of the superintendency for readers who may not be familiar with its history and contemporary status.[66] There are approximately 15,400 public school districts in the United States,[67] all of which are governed by boards of education, laypersons usually elected by the community but sometimes appointed by mayors. Today the primary responsibilities of school boards are appointing and evaluating the superintendent and formulating school policy. The occupation of superintendent (or district administrator) arose in the middle of the nineteenth century when city school boards "found the tasks of supervising teachers, examining students, and buying supplies too burdensome and thus began appointing superintendents to do these things."[68] Most rural school districts did not have superintendents until the twentieth century. Over the last 150 years, the superintendency—the top position in the local school district—has evolved from a position that included clerical as well as educational tasks, to one of business management, and finally to a position that integrates the tasks of chief executive officer and professional educational leader.[69] In the late twentieth century, the responsibilities of public school superintendents include guiding the school board in policy development, budgeting and finance, business management, personnel administration, curriculum and instruction, community relations, state and federal relations, and strategic planning.[70]

Research on the superintendency contains much discussion about the best way to characterize the job. Many writers emphasize its conflictual and political elements, as the titles of these books suggest: *The Besieged School Superintendent; Urban School Chiefs under Fire; The Black School Superintendent: Messiah or Scapegoat?*; and *The School Superintendent: Living with Conflict.*[71] The conflictual and political aspects of the job arise from struggles over increasingly scarce resources for public education. They are also related to local, state, and nationwide attention to questions of quality and equity in public schools, with ever-growing numbers of groups adding their voices to the fray.[72] Moreover, the importance of education in American society intensifies the politics and conflicts. Superintendents are charged with overseeing the education of the community's children and so are often perceived as "managers of virtue."[73]

As accessible and visible public servants, superintendents are vulnerable to incompatible demands from many quarters. They must be attentive to the diverse interests of students, teachers, staff, school board, parents, the press, and various other interest groups in the community. Among the particularly difficult tasks superintendents face are negotiating employee contracts, closing schools (when enrollments decline), increasing student achievement, and maneuvering tighter budgets. In addition to these more or less routine aspects of the job, superintendents sometimes find themselves in the middle of extraordinary or emergency events. For example, two of the women we interviewed had to handle situations surrounding the violent deaths of students on school grounds; one of these was a case of multiple murder. Another superintendent reported the problems created by death threats made by a school board member. Given these immense responsibilities, it is not surprising that the job is frequently described as highly stressful, that a superintendent's average length of tenure in any one job is between four and six years (much shorter than that of other school administrators, such as principals),[74] and that the median number of superintendencies held is 1.3.[75] David Tyack and Elisabeth Hansot suggest that "the leadership of big-city school systems may well be among the most demanding jobs in the United States today."[76]

The superintendency has become increasingly professionalized during the twentieth century. In his extensive discussion of how to define *profession* and how to decide which occupations belong in the category, Eliot Freidson includes school administrators because the requirement of higher education is central to their work.[77] Today superintendents need state certification, which generally requires at least a master's degree, completion of an administrative internship, and evidence of competent performance in some position of school administration.[78] In 1991, 44 percent of superintendents nationwide had earned doctorates.[79] (Two-thirds of the women we interviewed had doctorates.) In addition, educational administrators usually receive specific training at leadership academies that have sprung up throughout the United States in recent years.[80]

The educational system has undergone a great deal of change during the twentieth century, but the social characteristics of superintendents have not. Almost all superintendents have been "married white males . . . middle-aged, Protestant, upwardly mobile, from favored ethnic groups, native-born, and of rural origins."[81] In 1991, 94.4 percent of superintendents were men; in 1990, 96.6 percent were white. Of the 3.4 percent of the superintendents who were people of color, approximately 12 percent were women.[82] In other words, in 1991, 594 of the nation's 10,683 K–12 superintendents were women, and approximately 45 were women of color.[83] The male dominance of the occupation is striking because superintendents rise from the ranks of teachers, 70 percent of whom are women.[84] While the presence of women in the prestigious professions of medicine and law has increased slowly over the last twenty years, the superintendency has remained resistant to women's integration, despite the fact that half the graduate students in programs of educational administration are now women.[85] By contrast, people of color are underrepresented not only among educational leaders, but also among teachers. Approximately 80 percent of the United States population is white, and 70 percent of K–12 children are white; but 87 percent of all teachers are white.[86]

Enduring structural and cultural barriers block the movement of white women and people of color into educational administration. Researchers demonstrate that gender and racial stratification in schools is maintained by differential access to opportunities for advancement, subtle and blatant forms of sex and racial or ethnic discrimination, and white men's control over gatekeeping positions.[87] Gatekeepers to the superintendency—those who control access to the desirable jobs in the field—include superintendents who have clout at the local, state, and national levels; consultants who are hired by school boards to conduct superintendency searches; professors of educational administration who distribute internships and introduce people to informal networks; and school board members.[88] Superintendents of color tend to be hired in urban school districts that have a high percentage of minority students and that suffer from "the engrossing problems of cities" that white leaders choose not to take on.[89] This focus in the literature on structural and cultural obstacles to integration is supported by the broader sociological research on women in white- and male-dominated professions.

2

Settled and

Unsettled

Discursive

Realms

In this chapter I explore in greater detail the disjunction between the discursive realms of professional work and inequality. Through a series of examples drawn from my interviews with women school superintendents, I show how the relatively settled, traditional discursive realm of professional work shapes our talk in ways that we—interviewers and interviewees—take for granted, and how the relatively unsettled, explicitly ideological discursive realm of inequality constrains our talk in ways that make us self-conscious about what we are saying. This idea is based on my analysis of the entire set of interviews and provides the underpinning for my focus on four women's narratives in chapters 3 through 6.

Before turning to the analysis, I need to explain how I present material from the interviews. Sociologists and others who base their research on interviews typically edit respondents' talk when they present excerpts. They exclude what appears to be extraneous and distracting material: stutters, repetitions, asides and pauses, as well as the interviewer's questions, interruptions, and nonlexical utterances such as "hm hmm." The intention of such editing, of course, is to provide readers with the content of speech. Yet as many others have argued, such editing ignores that meaning is communicated through the complex practices of speech as well as through words and phrases.[1] Thus, my interview transcripts include material that some deem distracting. By listening carefully to *how* speakers express themselves, I can interpret more fully *what* they are saying and understand better how cultural processes are manifest in and shape their speech. When we allow ourselves to be distracted by material that appears at first to be extraneous, we realize the centrality of that material.

Researchers who share this interest in the complex nature of talk use a variety of transcribing techniques. The researcher's particular analytical interests determine which speech practices she or he attends to. I am interested in those practices that reveal an individual's speaking style, that capture the interview interaction, and that exhibit the settled character of the discursive realm of professional work and the unsettled character of the discursive realm of inequality. Thus, I have produced transcripts that highlight the flow and intensity of speech. Each line of a transcript represents what Wallace Chafe calls a "spurt of language."[2] I determine the boundaries of a spurt by listening to intonation, a rise or fall in pitch. When a spurt is longer than a line of text, I indent the subsequent lines to show that speech is continuous. Italics indicate emphasis; capital letters signify extra emphasis or loudness; and dashes (—) show a break-off of speech or interruption. When speakers talk simultaneously, I place their overlapping words within double lines (‖it's true‖ ‖oh no‖). I identify noticeable pauses of less than three seconds by [p] and pauses of more than three seconds by [P]. Laughter and other nonlexicals are noted in brackets, as are words I added to clarify meaning or to describe important aspects of speech such as slowness or softness. I use punctuation sparingly, only when intonation clearly indicates a full stop or question. Quotation marks show that a speaker is reporting someone else's (or her own) speech. A series of dots (. . . .) indicates that I have omitted part of the speech.[3]

As is customary, I assigned pseudonyms to women superintendents and changed the names of persons and places they mentioned. In addition, I altered details to protect their identities; some of these educational leaders are public figures nationally as well as within their local communities. Some researchers suggest that pseudonyms disempower interviewees who wish to be named. In this case, however, women superintendents expressed appreciation of attempts to disguise their identities.

Finally, the question of how to refer to the women as I discuss excerpts from the interviews presents a dilemma. The use of last names emphasizes their professional stature while the use of first names captures the informality of the interview context. In order to remind the reader of both, I use a woman's last name when referring to her narrative in general terms, and her first name when discussing her talk in specific terms. The upshot is that I use first names more than last names.

THE SETTLED DISCURSIVE REALM OF PROFESSIONAL WORK

In the interviews, Colleen and I asked about the work women educational leaders do, the professional and interpersonal contexts in which they work, their work histories, the relationship between their personal and professional lives, and what difference gender and race or ethnicity have made to their experiences. While we structured the interviews around these general topics, our questions were open ended.

In the course of an interview, a woman's particular experiences or interests would pull us toward some questions and away from others. But despite the flexibility of our interviewing style and the differences among women's interests and experiences, our request for a work history—in one form or another—was central to every interview. Both we and they treated this question as fundamental to what the interview was about. Together we assumed that in a world in which so few women have well-paid, prestigious, leadership positions, in an occupational field in which women dominate teaching positions and men dominate administrative positions, there must be a story about the way a woman acquires one of these jobs. Two-thirds of the women we interviewed described their youthful aspirations in terms of conventional female occupations: teacher, nurse, secretary, or mother and housewife. Of the remaining third, most expressed their aspirations in general terms such as wanting to be "something important" or "something other than what was around me." Furthermore, two-thirds of the women grew up in working-class families; for these women, work histories were not only about upward mobility into a male- and white-dominated occupation, but also about upward mobility from the working-class to the upper-middle-class professional world.[4]

We did not have to search for words in order to ask women about their work histories; likewise, they heard the question as an invitation to speak easily and at length. Both we and they took for granted that the concept of work history would organize their experiences.[5] Similarly, with regard to the work done by mothers of school-age children, Dorothy Smith describes how she, her coresearcher, and the mothers they interviewed "relied on the concept of the school day to organize women's accounts of their work." She writes, "The ways we . . . referenced the school day in our talk was governed by our tacit knowledge, as practitioners, of that social organization. It would be hard for someone to speak unmethodically in referencing social organization of which she is a competent practitioner."[6]

To demonstrate how the concept of work history organized our talk, I present excerpts from three interviews, limiting each excerpt to the work history request and the immediate response. I focus not only on the content of women's responses but also on how women shape their work histories into stories. Notice that in her immediate response each woman shows that she does have a story to tell, and that she *will* tell that story rather than simply offer a list or résumé of career moves. In William Labov's terms, each woman's initial response provides an "abstract" or summary of the story she will tell.[7]

Tanya Jones is an African American who described her family background as "economically poor with middle-class values" and her youthful aspiration as the desire to be a schoolteacher. She is currently superintendent in an ethnically diverse urban district.

SC: Um [p] we'd like to hear about some of the *highlights* of your work career.

I'm sure it's long and varied

but if if you could just kind of think about what have been for *you* the most important steps.

You *wanted* to be a teacher and you ended up as a superintendent. So how did that happen?

TJ: [very softly, whispering] I keep asking myself.

SC and CB: [laugh]

TJ: And and and and I I say that facetiously

but it's the truth because uh

when I started out being a teacher

as dumb as this sounds

the word superintendent wasn't a part of my vocabulary.

You know it never dawned on me that there's somebody up there who's orchestrating all this thing.

Notice that the idea of upward mobility is implicit in my question as well as in Tanya's response; both of us assume that her work history is about upward mobility. It bears emphasizing that interviews with women in a working-class occupation would require a different kind of work history request and that such a request might not occupy the central position it does in interviews with professional women.

Tanya's joke—"I keep asking myself"—invites us to laugh at the discrepancy between her youthful aspiration to be a schoolteacher and her current position as urban superintendent. By emphasizing the discrepancy, Tanya introduces her work history as a particular kind of story about upward mobility, a story about the transformation of her identity. Her statements here suggest that the transformation involved learning how schools are organized and run, as well as learning about her own competence to do that organizing and orchestrating.[8] The tone of Tanya's statements is expressed most clearly by "I keep asking myself" and "dumb as this sounds." With this tone of incredulity, Tanya underscores the radical nature of her upward mobility and of her transformation from schoolteacher to city superintendent.

Diane McCall, a white woman who grew up in a working-class family, spoke about the gendered character of her youthful expectations: "I probably would go be a mother and teach school so I could have time off with my children." She is now superintendent in a predominantly white suburban district.

SC: Okay um [p] uh you've talked about the fact that you've had a
    varied career in education. (DM: mm)
    Could you talk about some of the highlights of that?
    What were the big decisions for you the big moves?
DM: Oh gee umm [P]
    I don't know if to start in reverse chronological order or what uh
    I think they've been *conscious* decisions.
    I have tried to *plan* a career instead of just taking what happens.
    I always resent someone who says uh
    "I never interviewed for a job
    somebody asked me
    they recognized my talent and you know promoted me."
    I think you're letting somebody else control your career when
    that happens.

Diane introduces her work history as a chronologically ordered
story, one she could tell either by beginning in the past and moving to
the present, or the other way around. The temporal ordering of events
is a conventional form for remembering and recounting past experience,[9] and it certainly fits the notion of career as an orderly progression
of events. But before offering the specifics of her work history, Diane
characterizes it as a story about conscious plans and decisions. By
differentiating herself from those who wait for others to recognize and
promote them, Diane presents herself as a particular kind of person, as
one who is active and decisive. While it is unclear from this brief
excerpt why Diane resents those who tell stories about waiting for and
receiving recognition, it is clear that Diane's work history will highlight her decisiveness and plans.

The last example demonstrates that women offered a story in response to the work history request even in those instances when I
phrased my query in an awkward way. Lisa Hayes, a woman of Native
American ancestry, depicted her family background as "lower working
class" and her early aspiration as the desire to be a teacher. At the time
of our interview, she was superintendent in a predominantly white
suburban school district.

SC: We'd like to hear some about the history of your work life
    and I know that's hard and it's probably a long story

but maybe you could focus on the highlights of that—
I forgot to ask another question.
Do you have a résumé?

LH: Uh huh

SC: okay

LH: would you like a résumé?

SC: Yes

LH: okay

SC: yeah ‖that that just‖

LH: ‖remind me at the end‖

SC: okay

LH: and I'll give you a résumé

SC: we will.

LH: Okay I'll just block it down and I can chuck it down to you really quick.

By interrupting my request for her work history to ask for her résumé, I may have encouraged Lisa to offer a list of events rather than a story. Yet while she begins as though she will "just block it down," Lisa quickly turns her response into a story:

LH: I left home.
I wanted to be a teacher.
I knew I wanted to be a teacher there was no question.
Uh went to college graduated from [university] after kind of a circuitous route cause I had to earn my way through school I didn't have any way to get support from anybody so I had to earn my way through.
I graduated from [university].
I had done a uh uh believe it or not
I had done uh *three* internships.
'Cause I didn't know whether I wanted to be elementary middle school or high school.
I *knew* that I wanted to be special education
but I didn't know what level.
So I did an internship at three levels
and I was offered *two* positions.

Lisa includes a list of events as she begins her work history, but she also tells a story about her purposiveness and drive. This is evident in the content of her talk: her certainty about wanting to teach, her persistence in working her way through school, and her completion of three internships in order to make an informed career choice. In addition, Lisa expresses her purposiveness and drive in her manner of speaking: every statement begins with (or assumes) the "I" as an efficacious person in the world.

Although the content of their work histories differs, Tanya Jones, Diane McCall, and Lisa Hayes all take up the work history request as an invitation to tell a *story*—rather than to offer a *report*—about their experiences. Livia Polanyi articulates the difference between stories and reports in this way: "*Stories* are told to make a point, to transmit a message . . . about the world the teller shares with other people." In telling a story, the narrator takes on the responsibility "of making the relevance of the telling clear." By contrast, a report is "typically elicited by the recipient," and "the burden of assigning differential weighting to the various narrated propositions thus falls to the receiver of the report."[10] The three examples I have examined (and I could have included many others) show that women superintendents easily and eagerly take on the responsibility of telling a story in response to the work history request.

But *how* does this request evoke a story? How does this request lend itself to easy and eager storytelling? In spite of narrative analysts' assumption that interviewees will tell stories if interviewers encourage them to do so, interviewees do not tell stories in response to any and every request. While Elliot Mishler implores researchers to pay attention to stories that we are tempted to treat as irrelevant,[11] it is equally important to pay attention to stories that we take for granted as relevant.

The work history request invites easy and eager stories because it draws women educational leaders into the settled, traditional discursive realm of professional work. As I discussed in chapter 1, that realm consists of unquestioned ways of articulating the importance of work to professionals' identities and the value of professional work in American society. The discursive realm of professional work provides resources with which women superintendents develop understandings of themselves as accomplished, successful, and powerful individuals. Despite the differences among women's stories—Tanya Jones's transformation, Diane McCall's decisiveness, Lisa Hayes's drive—all of them present themselves as active and efficacious individuals by using discourse about professional work.

To demonstrate this idea more fully, I present another excerpt from Tanya Jones's interview. Toward the end of her work history, Tanya discussed why she decided to move from a job she enjoyed immensely—an assistant superintendency in a large, upper-middle-class, predominantly white, suburban community—to her current position as superintendent in a racially and ethnically diverse urban district. She spoke about having begun her career in an urban district, and about the "elitist," "critical," and "unsympathetic" attitudes her suburban colleagues displayed toward the problems that plague urban districts. She continued:

TJ: And there was a part of me that felt that um
      even from the time that I was doing my doctorate uh
      I said "I want somehow to be able to make a contribution that's
         going to be significant." . . .
      And so I said "well the future of our country really is going to
         rest in in the cities
      because that's where you have this *huge* population that's
      out there that needs to be educated (SC: hmm hmmm)
      and if *they* fail then *everybody* fails." (SC: hmm hm)
      And so it was that challenge and the call for the city
      and I think somewhere in my mind
      I probably always wanted to wind up my career in an urban
         setting. (SC: hm hmm)
      So that is what brought me back to the city.

Notice that by this point in her work history Tanya speaks confidently about her competence as an educational leader. She accounts for her decision to take on the urban superintendency by articulating her desire to make a significant contribution to the education of city children. In so doing, she uses discourse about commitment and contribution, discourse with a history in the professional world generally as well as in Black professional communities. Historians and sociologists have shown that Black professional women frequently express a commitment to "racial uplift."[12] While Tanya does not speak directly about race, she tacitly suggests that the social relations of race and class have shaped her professional commitment and the kind of educational contribution she seeks to make. This is evident when she compares her attitude toward urban districts to that of her suburban colleagues and when she describes the needs of children who attend city schools.[13]

Working-class people are unlikely to use discourse about commitment and contribution when speaking about their work, not because they lack commitment and make no contributions, but because their work environments are organized in ways that effectively exclude such discourse. American society does not usually recognize as such the contributions working-class people make through work. Not surprisingly, then, they often construct their identities through activities other than work. For example, Judith Rollins shows that Black women domestics define themselves in relation to their families, churches, and communities. "Like other blue-collar workers who consider their 'real' lives that part that is away from their jobs, domestics' 'real' identities come from other than work-related activities."[14]

By using discourse about commitment and contribution, Tanya Jones draws on a resource provided by the professional upper-middle-class world. She constructs herself as an individual who has the power to make a significant difference through her work. While Jones speaks about commitment and contribution, other women superintendents draw on discourse about competence, ambition, decisiveness, education, privilege, and individualism to narrate their work histories. In addition, some women integrate discourse about professional qualities with discourse about personal strengths or characteristics. For example, Margaret Parker, whose narrative is the subject of chapter 5, presents herself not only as a competent, successful educator, but also as a woman whose professional strengths are shaped by her gendered identity. Nonetheless, in every case, the request for a work history became an occasion for these upwardly mobile, successful women to understand and present themselves as powerful and accomplished educational leaders. The discursive realm of professional work provides resources through which women talk about developing professional identities and exercising individual competence, commitment, power, responsibility, and authority. Listening to women's work histories, I sensed the kind of power aptly described by Carolyn Heilbrun: "Power is the ability to take one's place in whatever discourse is essential to action and the right to have one's part matter."[15]

The discursive realm of professional work is a relatively settled part of American culture in the sense that Americans generally do not question that professional work requires certain individual qualities, that it provides resources for continuous development of competence and authority, and that it is valuable to society. The settled character of this discursive realm is evident in my interviews in the mutual assumption (of both interviewers and interviewees) that the concept of work history would organize women superintendents' experiences. It is also apparent in the ease and eagerness with which women transformed their work histories into stories.[16]

Yet traditionally, stories about power and accomplishment through professional work have been the prerogative of middle-class, or upwardly mobile, white men. Historically, women—particularly women of color and women raised in working-class families—have not had access to well-paid, prestigious, professional jobs and so have not had access to discourse that is culturally intelligible within that realm. While white working-class men's stories about upward mobility feature obstacles related to their social class origins,[17] professional women's stories also include barriers created by gender, race, and ethnic inequalities. Even the brief work history excerpts I examined show racial and gendered traces. Tanya Jones holds the most powerful educational position in her city and her actions affect tens of thousands of students and thousands of school employees. Yet her joke—"I keep asking myself [how I ended up as superintendent]"—suggests that even now she sometimes hesitates to speak directly about her success, as if to do so would violate cultural expectations for a Black woman. Diane McCall's resentment of those who say they wait for others to recognize and promote them may indicate her sense that as a woman she has been denied such support. Her resentment might also point to the cultural proscription of women's decisiveness and ambition. (Indeed, a close analysis of McCall's narrative supports both interpretations.)

A reminder is pertinent here: although the male-dominated occupation of superintendent is at the top of the occupational hierarchy in the public education system, that system itself is predominantly female. Educational leaders rise from the ranks of teachers, 70 percent of whom are women. Moreover, the public sector has been the primary realm of work and mobility for Black professionals throughout the twentieth century.[18] It is possible, then, that women superintendents' stories about power and accomplishment do not violate as seriously conventional race and gender expectations as do the stories of women who work in other prestigious male- and white-dominated professions. Doctors, lawyers, scientists, professors, and higher education administrators do not rise from predominantly female ranks. Significantly, many women superintendents use teaching metaphors to describe their work as educational leaders. For example, Tanya Jones states bluntly, "I'm a teacher. You know they call me superintendent but I'm a teacher. And if I ever cease to be a teacher then I'm retired because that's to me the way that organizations move." Women may use the teaching metaphor to smooth their transition from a female- to a male-dominated occupation as well as to challenge conventional authoritarian conceptions of educational leadership.[19]

Nonetheless, the discursive realm of professional work provides resources with which women superintendents narrate their work histories as various kinds of stories about power and accomplishment. This idea brings to light what many discussions of professional women neglect when they focus exclusively on women's experiences of discrimination. Professional women, like their male counterparts, *do* draw strength from professional discourse. While the social relations of gender, class, and race certainly shape how they use that discursive resource, all of these women—in their own ways—embrace that resource and present themselves as efficacious individuals who use their professional power to make a difference through their work.

THE UNSETTLED DISCURSIVE
REALM OF INEQUALITY

At certain points in the interviews, Colleen and I asked directly about the inequalities women superintendents have faced in their white- and male-dominated profession. They were not surprised by these questions because they know that their experiences are storyworthy in part because they have been upwardly mobile within an overwhelmingly male and white occupation. Yet even though we and they expected the topic of inequality to be part of the interviews, our questions and their responses exhibited various forms of self-consciousness that were generally absent from our requests for and their recounting of their work histories. Direct talk about gender, race, and ethnicity drew us into the relatively unsettled, explicitly ideological discursive realm of inequality.

While the work history question was unproblematic from the beginning, Colleen and I continuously struggled with our questions about the ways gender, race, and ethnicity shape women's experiences. In our earliest interviews (which were with white women in rural and small-town districts), we asked a set of questions about being one of a few women in a male-dominated context: Are you treated as a representative of women in general? As an exception? Do other women treat you as a role model? What are the effects of your visibility? Do you experience social awkwardness with male colleagues? Was there any particular point in your career when you began to think that being a woman might make some kind of difference? In one or two of the early interviews, these questions produced awkwardness for both us and the interviewees. Although we presented these questions in the spirit of checking out sociological understandings through the reality of women's experiences, the very fact that we were asking such questions seemed to imply that we were looking for certain kinds of answers—for example, that being a woman does make a difference.[20] In addition, some women answered these questions with reports rather than stories. For instance, in response to my query about whether she had ever felt that she was treated as a representative of women in general, one woman simply stated, "No I really haven't." When I proceeded to ask whether other women treat her as a role model, she responded, "Well I hope that I have been and I've had two people call me since I've been here to ask my help with them applying for a superintendency." These brief reports stand in sharp contrast to the lively, lengthy, and engrossing story this superintendent told about her upward mobility from secretary to superintendent.

We eventually dropped these questions because they were too sociological, too abstract, and too external to women's experiences.[21] We were more interested in hearing women's stories than their reports on or opinions about sociological findings concerning the difference race

CULTURAL AND DISCURSIVE CONTEXTS

and gender make. As a result, we limited our direct questions about gender, race, and ethnicity to just a few. If a woman did not talk specifically about discrimination as she related her work history, we asked directly, at some point after her work history, whether she felt she had experienced sex, race, or ethnic discrimination. By waiting in this way, we gave women a chance to bring up issues of inequality without prompting from us.[22] In the context of a broad question about whom she turns to for support, we asked about her involvement in formal organizations or informal groups for women educational leaders. In addition, toward the end of our three years of interviewing, we began to ask women of color a direct question about the ways race or ethnicity have shaped their work experiences. That we did not ask such a question of *white* women reflects the lack of discourse in American culture for talking about how being white shapes experience.[23] While some white women discussed race and ethnicity as work-related issues (for example, in relation to integration, busing, curriculum, or racial tensions among students), none of the white women talked about how whiteness has influenced their own professional experiences.

Many women superintendents did not limit their talk about experiences of inequality to their responses to these specific questions. They frequently spoke without prompting from us about the ways gender, race, and ethnic relations have shaped their experiences. Although there was a range in terms of how and how much they talked about inequalities, all exhibited consciousness of institutionalized gender and race asymmetries. Some women emphasized unequal access to mentors, fellowships, and jobs; others focused on how gender, racial, and ethnic stereotypes subtly pervade their work environments.

Although we—Colleen and I and the women we interviewed—mutually assumed that issues of inequality would organize (at least partially) women's talk about their work experiences, we could not take for granted *how* it would do so. Our talk about inequality was much more self-conscious and unsettled than our talk about work histories. While the work history request easily produced stories, questions about experiences of inequality sometimes produced stories, sometimes reports, and sometimes *disrupted talk*.[24] I use this term to describe linguistic phenomena, such as stumbling and stammering uncharacteristic of the speaker, and metastatements—that is, talk about how we are speaking or what we are saying.[25] The following excerpts demonstrate how the discursive realm of inequality shaped our talk about gender, race, and ethnicity.

Bernice Turner is a white superintendent in a predominantly white, middle-class, small-town school district. At various points throughout her interview, she spoke spontaneously about the way gender has shaped her experiences. For example, in describing the hiring process for her current superintendency, Turner reported that the school board offered her $4,000 less than her male predecessor's salary, despite the comparability of their qualifications. She also described the controversy that arose among school board members over their joint decision (with Turner) to hire a woman as high school principal. With that hire, women held the top three administrative posts in the district, a highly unusual situation given the male dominance of educational leadership. Turner was concerned that the school board and community would continue to focus on gender in their interpretations of the women administrators' actions: "As we sit here now we don't know what's down the road for us in terms of being able to operate. Are we going to be viewed for our competence or are we going to be viewed now as these three women?" In addition, Turner spoke passionately about the need for work institutions to pay attention to the needs of families, stating, "I think that oftentimes a woman has to choose [between family and work]. You can't do both. Men can do both but women can't." In this context she pointed to the painful "personal sacrifices" she has made in order to have an administrative career: giving up time with her children and divorcing a man who was disturbed by her primary commitment to career.

The following exchange occurred after Bernice Turner finished a long discussion of those personal sacrifices.

SC: Okay ummm [p] would you say you've ever experienced sex discrimination?

BT: [P] [haltingly] I I don't have any thing on my agenda
I can't list off these three times (SC: hm hmm)
I'm *sure* I was
but I don't know what (SC: hm hmm)
you know I I c— don't know what they were.

SC: [haltingly] So it's a subtle kind of thing—

BT: It probably was subtle (SC: hm hmm)
     yeah [p]
     no I don't—
     I uh [p]
     [louder, still haltingly] I guess I *never* I NEVER l— looked at
        gender [p]
     you know I never thought I couldn't do something (SC: hm
        hmm)
     and I think it went back to (SC: hm hmm)
     the the drive I had as a young child
     I *never ever* thought that I shouldn't do it (SC: hm hmm)
     [p] so [p]
     and I don't know that I ever applied for a job that I didn't get
     I can't ever recall [p] (SC: hm hmm)
     [p] y— you know [p]
     any job I've ever applied for I've I've gotten
     so [p] I don't know how I could have been discriminated against.
SC: [laughing] okay

I have labeled this an instance of disrupted talk because its stumbling and hesitant character is atypical of Bernice's speech. This dis-
ruptiveness draws attention to the unsettled content of her talk, to her
difficulty in articulating what she wants to say about discrimination.
Unlike the work history request, this question does not invite Bernice
to tell a story. And yet, equally significant, this question does not
evoke a simple no. Bernice treats this question as requiring a serious
and thoughtful answer about whether and how she thinks of her experiences in terms of discrimination. Her use of so many negative
constructions in this short excerpt—she uses words such as "don't,"
"can't," and "never" fifteen times—conveys that she finds it easier to
eliminate options than to articulate what she wants to say.

Bernice rejects two ways of talking about discrimination before set-
tling on discourse about ambition as appropriate for describing her
experience. When she states, "I don't have anything on my agenda,"
she implicitly separates herself from women who *do* have an agenda
when they talk about discrimination—for example, women who use an
explicitly political or feminist discourse. Such discourse presupposes a

conscious examination of one's past experiences for instances of discrimination. While Bernice has not conducted such an examination, she asserts, "I'm *sure* I was [discriminated against] / but I don't know what . . . they were." She briefly considers my suggestion that the discrimination she has experienced may have been subtle. That suggestion draws on a distinction between blatant discrimination that has been prohibited (if not eliminated) by law, and subtle but persistent forms of discrimination that cannot be regulated legally. Yet Bernice decisively rejects my suggestion and opts instead for discourse about ambition: "I guess I *never* . . . looked at gender . . . I never thought I couldn't do something . . . and I think it went back to . . . the drive I had as a young child." Although the examples I cited from earlier in her interview clearly show that Bernice *has* looked at gender, she is not thinking of those experiences here. Rather, she reaches back to her discussion (offered as part of her work history) of her childhood socialization and her early aspiration to be "something important." Somehow, Bernice's construction of herself as an ambitious, gender-neutral individual capable of achieving whatever she strives for allows her to decide she has not experienced discrimination. As evidence, she points out that she has been offered every job she has applied for.

My awkward laugh at the end of this excerpt expresses my uncertainty about how to respond to Bernice's statements. What I wanted to say was this: "Given that you have spoken so much about how gender has shaped your experiences, what is it about this question that makes you stumble? And what does your drive as a young child really have to do with your conclusion that you haven't experienced discrimination?" A close analysis of Bernice Turner's narrative as a whole would provide answers to these questions and a fuller interpretation of this excerpt. Such an analysis would include examining how Bernice uses discourse about ambition, individualism, and inequality throughout her narrative, as well as patterns in her manner of speaking.

My interest here, however, lies in explicating how the discursive realm of inequality invites disrupted talk. When she considers and then rejects two ways of talking about discrimination, Bernice shows her awareness that it is possible to talk about inequality in a number of different ways. She knows that however she chooses to speak about discrimination, her choice will conflict and compete with other possibilities. Thus, the discursive realm of inequality invites disrupted talk because of the perpetual contests among the range of discourses it provides. Disrupted talk is one way in which a speaker expresses awareness of the contentious and explicitly ideological character of discourse about inequality. About one-quarter of the interviews with women superintendents contain an obvious instance of disrupted talk in response to a question about gender, race, or ethnicity. As I analyzed specific narratives in depth, however, I realized that many subtle instances of disrupted talk are sprinkled throughout the interviews, both in Colleen's and my questions and in women superintendents' talk.[26]

The second example is another excerpt from Tanya Jones's interview. When she had finished narrating her work history, I asked the following question:

SC: Um just one last question before we move on to a different set of
        questions. [p]
        Throughout your work history
        and this is a very broad question (TJ: mmm)
        but I think it's important to ask it
        throughout your work history
        and all your different work experiences
        would you say you've experienced sex discrimination or race
        discrimination?

My short phrase—"I think it's important to ask it"—interrupts the flow of my question by offering an evaluation of the question itself. This metastatement—a subtle instance of disrupted talk—signals that we are moving into an explicitly ideological arena. By claiming that this question is important, I acknowledge that others might think otherwise. When requesting women's work histories I did not assert the importance of the request. In that case, I took for granted (as did women superintendents, as does American society generally) that professional women's work histories are significant. Here is Tanya Jones's response:

TJ: [p] Um [P]
        I would say that uh [p]
        the most *offensive* thing is for uh people to view me as an exception to the rule.

That's very offensive.
Even when I came to this city
the first newspaper article was
[words spoken emphatically, separately]
Black female superintendent.
And uh I was still in [another state] and I called back
and I said "that's totally unacceptable." (SC: hm hmm)
You know "I'm an educator (SC: hm hmm)
and that's the way I want to be viewed."
And so fortunately the reporters have not done that (CB: hm
    hmm) again. (SC: hmm)
But most recently in the [large corporation] Report
they did an article on on the school district and said
[words spoken emphatically, separately]
Black female superintendent
who it was felt would be able to uh
it didn't use the word relate to
but that's what they meant
you know to the large Black student population.
Most offensive. (CB: hmmm)
Uh went to a a leadership training program
where I was a presenter on a panel
introduced as you know "Dr. Tanya Jones da da da da da"
all these accolades uh but you know
"who will da da da with the Black students." (SC: hmm)
And I got up and I said to this group
which was uh mostly white and mostly male
with one or two Blacks in there
and I said "I'm the superintendent for *all* of the students in Bay
    City Public Schools." (CB and SC: hm hmmm)
So that kind of thing (CB: yeah) does occur.
Or people's oh I remember once a person saying
a woman [emphatically, in a dramatic voice]
"oh you're you must be a you are a real credit to your race!"
Uh another who said [emphatically, in a dramatic voice]
"oh gee you speak so well!" (CB and SC: hmm)
What am I supposed to do?
To me that's discrimination. (CB and SC: hm hmmm)

Tanya is offended when others view her as an exception to the rule. Her first few examples suggest that she is referring to the rule that guides the work of educational leadership: educational leaders are committed to educating *all* students. Tanya is angered by others' attempts to define her educational commitment in terms of her race. In her last examples, Tanya refers to another rule to which she is viewed as an exception, the rule that educational leaders are white men or, conversely, that Black women are not educational leaders. When others commend her for being a credit to her race or for speaking well, Tanya feels she is treated as an exceptional Black woman. The assumptions about Black women embedded in such statements are discriminatory: Black women are not capable of achieving positions of authority, responsibility, and public voice.

Thus, Tanya names as discrimination others' attempts to define her as an exception among educational leaders or as an exception among Black women. By refusing such definitions, Tanya claims her connection to both groups. This point needs to be emphasized. If I had isolated such statements as "I'm an educator . . . and that's the way I want to be viewed" from the context of her full response to the question, I might have been tempted to interpret her self-descriptions as simply ignoring or erasing race and gender. In making such statements, Tanya clearly presents her professional commitment as gender- and race-neutral, as she implies any educational leader would. When we listen to her full response, however, we hear that Tanya is angered not by consciousness of race and gender, but by the assumption that her commitments and actions are somehow different or exceptional *because* she is a Black woman educational leader. By insisting that she is an educator for all the students in Bay City, Tanya connects herself to educational leaders as a group. By refusing to think of herself as more of a credit to her race than other Black women, she connects herself to Black women as a group.

In this excerpt Tanya talks about more than the experience of discrimination; she also includes her method for resisting others' attempts to define her as an exception. Instead of letting these offenses go unnoticed, Tanya insists on her own construction of self. She phoned the newspaper editor and informed him that "I'm an educator and that's the way I want to be viewed." She countered the problematic introduction by publicly proclaiming that "I'm the superintendent for *all* of the students in Bay City Public Schools." Tanya's method of resistance is a matter of teaching others how she wants to be viewed. She not only claims that "I'm an educator," but she also acts as a teacher by making that claim.

Tanya Jones's response to my question about discrimination shows how speakers enter the discursive realm of inequality by taking one or another stand (or discourse) in order to reject competing stands (or discourses). Tanya implicitly argues that she, unlike her white male counterparts, is subject to discriminatory treatment in the form of others' focus on her race and gender; she resists those who would assert that such treatment is not discriminatory. In her account, Tanya shows why she thinks it *is* discrimination. In addition, Tanya's repeated use of the word *offensive* reveals that she experiences such treatment as personally injurious. In response to that treatment, Tanya draws on gender- and race-neutral discourse about educational commitment to contest publicly others' offensive interpretations of her actions and to reclaim her sense of herself as a powerful individual and educator for all the city's children. Of course, some women of color (like Ana Martinez in chapter 3) *do* choose to articulate a particular commitment to the needs of Black or Hispanic students. This difference among women of color is another indication of the continual ideological contests within the discursive realm of inequality. Finally, when Tanya resists statements about herself as a credit to her race, she implicitly rejects discourse about Black women in general as failures in favor of discourse through which she identifies herself with other Black women, regardless of their status in the occupational world.

The Disjunction between the Discursive Realms of Professional Work and Inequality

While the discursive realm of professional work provides resources that allow women superintendents to present themselves as powerful and accomplished individuals, the discursive realm of inequality provides resources that they use to construct themselves as persons who belong to one or another subjected group. When speaking of experiences of discrimination, women use words that signify pain or injury;

they feel compelled to consider the impact on the self as well as the implications of various ways of responding to such treatment.

Moreover, unlike talk about professional work, talk about inequality is unsettled and takes place within a continuously contested, explicitly ideological arena. While the discursive realm of professional work provides a range of related discourses for describing experience, a speaker can talk in one way without being compelled to acknowledge, consider, or dismiss other possibilities. For example, when Tanya Jones uses discourse about commitment to account for her choice to take on the urban superintendency, she does not comment on other possible interpretations of her actions—for example, that she was ambitious to move up the occupational ladder. It is conceivable, of course, that another person might make such comments in telling her story or might employ discourse about ambition and commitment simultaneously. But in comparison to the loose relationship among various discourses about professional work, the various ways of talking about discrimination compete directly with each other. When Jones claims that others' perceptions of her as exceptional constitute discrimination, she argues this point against other possible interpretations—for example, that her exceptionality is simply a fact and that pointing to it is not a discriminatory action. No matter what particular stand one takes, the discursive realm of inequality produces talk that is self-conscious about its place on that explicitly ideological terrain. In describing an experience of discrimination, a woman is aware of and either explicitly or implicitly argues against other ways of speaking, other possible interpretations of her experience. When women talk about discrimination they speak with "a sideward glance at the word of another," to use Jane Hill's paraphrase of Mikhail Bakhtin's notion about the dialogical character of speech.[27] This self-consciousness is evident in Colleen's and my continual reflections on how to ask questions about gender, race, and ethnicity; in Bernice Turner's stumbling response to the discrimination question; in Tanya Jones's description of the offense caused by discrimination and her public assertion of her self-definition against the definitions proffered by others.

Thus, the differences in how the two discursive realms organize our talk are reflected not only in terms of content, but also in how we speak, in our forms of talk. Our unself-conscious request for women's work histories and the ease with which women turn their work histories into stories show that we take for granted the significance of that request for professional women's lives. Our self-conscious talk about inequality shows that we do not take for granted how to talk about experiences of discrimination. While the work history request invites stories that women enjoy telling, questions about inequality produce responses that range from stories to reports to disrupted talk.

Articulating the disjunction between these two discursive realms—their distinct ways of shaping the content and forms of talk—opens the possibility of listening to professional women's narratives as at once constrained by and struggling with that discursive disjunction. In chapters 3 through 6, I turn to each of four women's narratives in order to identify and explicate her narrative strategy, how she makes sense of her contradictory experiences of power and subjection, how she approaches the disjunction between discourse about professional work and inequality.

In order to analyze these narrative strategies, I focus specifically on women's work histories and on the parts of the interviews where they talk directly about their own experiences of inequality. In each chapter, I begin with the woman's work history (which came early in the interviews) and move to later parts of her narrative. In other words, I have selected the parts of these four interviews—which ranged from two and a half to five hours, producing from 60 to 120 pages of single-spaced transcripts each—where women make the most concentrated use of discourse about professional work and inequality. Sometimes this direct talk occurs in response to specific questions, and sometimes it is unprompted. It is important for me to emphasize that I selected direct talk about their own experiences of discrimination because this directness becomes significant for my analysis in chapter 7.

I began the process of identifying a woman's narrative strategy by listening over and over to her interview tapes and by paying particularly close attention to her work history and her direct talk about her own experiences of inequality. Then I analyzed how she separates or connects those two kinds of talk over the course of the interview. I named a woman's narrative strategy by attending to patterns in the content and form of her speech across various stories and patterns in her use of settled discourse about professional work and unsettled discourse about inequality. In each of these four chapters, I aim to show the patterns that constitute a woman's narrative strategy, how her narrative strategy orients to the disjunction between the discursive realms of professional work and inequality, and what her narrative strategy tells us about her experience in a white- and male-dominated profession.

I want to add a few comments about the import of the interview interaction to my analyses. When qualitative methodologists discuss interaction, they are usually concerned about the potential tension between the researcher's and interviewee's interests and about problems that arise as rapport develops or fails to develop.[28] Feminist methodologists raise the related question of how control over the interview should be negotiated. They are particularly concerned that the interviewee will be dominated by the researcher's greater power in the interview situation.[29] I share this concern, although it is less problematic in interviews like mine where the interviewees are high-status persons accustomed to being interviewed (not only by researchers but also by TV, radio, and newspaper reporters) and who do not hesitate to assert their interests while being interviewed. But I also suggest that understanding the interaction in terms of narrating and listening— rather than simply asking and answering questions—transforms our conception of the interview interaction.[30] Martine Burgos writes: "A life story comes off successfully when its narrator exercises her power upon the person who is ostensibly conducting the interview by de-realizing his interventions; capturing his attention, neutralizing his will, arousing his desire to learn something else, or something more, than what would be allowed by the logic of the narrative itself."[31]

Burgos argues that when an interviewee is a strong narrator, a reversal of power occurs in the interview situation and, further, that this reversal is necessary to a successful life story. As a corollary, I suggest that an interviewer can facilitate this reversal by listening, which requires hearing the interviewee's talk as narration rather than as answers to questions. But I also want to push this idea into the realm of interpretation. When analysis of interview material is guided by the idea that a speaker is narrating her experiences, the interruptions Burgos describes happen in the interpretive process itself. In fact, my abandonment of attempts to isolate women's talk about work on the one hand and inequality on the other provides an example of such an interruption. *My* interventions were derealized, *my* will was neutralized, and *my* attention was captured when I finally acknowledged that women were connecting and separating their stories about power and subjection in meaningful ways. In short, the analytic focus on narration is itself a way of empowering those whose words we interpret.[32]

Although my focus in the next four chapters shifts from patterns exhibited in all of the interviews to patterns within four specific narratives, my method of inquiry remains the same. In this chapter, I used examples of actual practice (interview talk) to articulate the disjunction between settled discourse about professional work and unsettled discourse about inequality. In the following chapters, I focus on examples of actual practice (specific narratives) to show how women superintendents develop narrative strategies in relation to the discursive disjunction, narrative strategies that make their experiences meaningful to themselves and others.

Narrative

Strategies

Part
TWO

3

Highlighting Competence and Excluding Subjection: ANA MARTINEZ

Ana Martinez is a sixty-year-old Hispanic woman who grew up in a modest working-class family and who aspired in her youth to be a "teacher, nothing else."[1] At the time of our interview, Martinez's thirty-five-year career in public education included leadership positions in several ethnically diverse urban districts. In her narrative, she recounts how she developed an identity as a competent, committed, educational leader and how she continually exercises those professional strengths through various challenges in her work. At the same time, she deliberately excludes stories about her experiences of ethnic inequality in a white-dominated profession. This chapter shows how Martinez's narrative strategy—highlighting competence and excluding subjection—reinforces the disjunction between the discursive realms of professional work and inequality. In addition, her narrative strategy tells us about her isolation as a Hispanic woman professional in a way that her words alone do not.

After hearing about the problems that Ana Martinez handles in her current superintendency, I asked about her work history.

SC: Um we'd like to hear about some of the highlights of your work
        history [p]
        um [p] what the the points for *you* that seemed to be important
        or turning points
        and in particular how you ended up getting into administration.
AM: [p] Well I can tell you that I never wanted to be a superintendent.
        This is *not* a career goal. (SC: hm hmm)
        And that it was sheer circumstances that brought me to where I
        am today. [p]
        I can also tell you very frankly that if I had to do it over again
        knowing what I know today about the superintendency
        I would never have done it.

Like the work history excerpts in chapter 2, Ana's response is clearly recognizable as the beginning of a story, as an abstract that summarizes the whole story.[2] Here she promises to tell us about her initial lack of desire to be an educational administrator, how sheer circumstances led her to the superintendency, and what she now knows about the job that would have prevented her from taking such work in the first place.[3] Although this abstract hints that she has encountered many difficulties in the superintendency, Ana goes on to narrate her work history with ease; she speaks for forty-five minutes with minimal interruptions from us.

Developing a Professional Identity

Ana came by her first administrative job when she applied for a part-time teaching position in a bilingual Head Start Program in Urbantown, the city where she eventually held her first superintendency. Instead of a teaching job, Ana was offered the directorship of the program. She emphasized her surprise and delight at this opportunity by reconstructing a conversation with her husband concerning her capability for supervisory work.

AM: I have to put another piece of the puzzle into this picture by the
    way and that's my husband
    who's a very supportive man
    uh when I was first offered the job as supervisor
    I came home and he I said to him
    [dramatically] "can you *imagine* they offered me a job as *supervisor.*
    I've never supervised anybody in my life."
    He said "of course you are you're always supervising everybody." (SC and CB: [laughing softly])
    And he said "look if you [laughing]
    if you don't want the job (CB: [laughing])
    because you don't want to do it
    don't *take* the job.
    But *DON'T* refuse it because you *think* you can't supervise.
    That's nonsense. (CB: hmm hmm)
    You've I've never seen you
    I've never seen you fail at anything that you really made up your
        mind that you were going to do." (SC: hmm hmm)
    That's a supportive husband. (SC: hm hmm)
    But then I also tell him "you're to blame"
    (CB and SC: [laugh])
    [laughing] But anyway he encouraged me and I took the job.

Ana contrasts her own surprise about the offer with her husband's confidence in her abilities; she suggests that his supportiveness influenced her decision to take the job.

This story includes several recurrent features in Ana's account of her early work history. First, even though she had no intention of taking on the responsibility and authority of administrative work, she presents others as inviting her to do so. Second, like many other women who become educational leaders, she treats her husband as an especially supportive character in this regard.[4] Third, she delights in telling this story, reflecting her pleasure in being encouraged to imagine herself as an able administrator. And finally, she uses reported speech[5]—in this case, direct quotations from a conversation with her husband—to dramatize the importance of others in the development of her identity as an educational leader.

As she continues, Ana speaks of being "given promotions, increasing responsibilities" within the same urban district and of her pride in the various programs she developed. Eventually, she was elevated to the superintendent's cabinet, the first woman to hold such a position in that district. She reports that the superintendent "*really* counted on me for a lot of things," especially during the unrest of the 1960s and 1970s:

> AM: It was people like *me* you know who were minorities
> and in *that* community it was Hispanics (SC: hm hmm)
> and I could speak the language
> and you know so it just uh
> I became really well known uh by parents
> people in the community.

Ana's description of herself as both invaluable to the superintendent because of her ethnicity and as highly respected within the Hispanic community as an educational leader introduces the story of how she became superintendent in Urbantown. The consultant who was conducting a national search for the position—the incumbent had retired—approached Ana after he had been in the district for a few weeks.

> AM: He came up to me afterward and said
> "so you're Ana Martinez."
> I said yes
> and he said "well I've heard your name over and over"
> he said "have you applied for the position?" (SC: [chuckle])
> "Moi? (SC and CB: [laugh])
> No."
> And he said "well there are a lot of people in this community that
> feel that you're the [p] right person for the times." (SC: hm
> hmm)

NARRATIVE STRATEGIES

CB: Others had been telling him?

AM: Yeah
> and so uh he said "you know you ought to think about it."
> Well I didn't think about it
> and then I had one community group come
> and this was a minority community group
> and I thought "well they just they know me and that's why"
> but then I had *another* group come
> *non*-minority group of parents (SC: hm hmm)
> and ask me if I wouldn't
> throw my hat in the ring so to so to speak.
> [sigh] And I thought about it and thought
> "well maybe I [sigh] maybe I will
> I'm not going to get it anyway and you know these
> maybe that's a way to get everybody off my back [laugh]
> I'll just do it (SC: hm hmm) you know
> and it'll be a good experience for me. (SC: hm hmm)
> I always like challenging experiences." (SC: hm hmm)
> So I *did* it.

Once again Ana describes herself as surprised that others would encourage her to apply for, in this case, the superintendency. Clearly pleased with others' high regard for her competence, she tells the story in a way that invites us to laugh, to share her enjoyment.[6] Although Ana chooses to emphasize the contrast between her lack of interest and the breadth of others' endorsement of her candidacy, this story also echoes a common theme in the careers of Hispanic school administrators. The consultant's comment—"there are a lot of people in this community that feel that you're the right person for the times"— points to the expectation that a Hispanic superintendent would be concerned about ethnic tensions and problems that white administrators could not or would not deal with.[7] It is noteworthy that Ana was hired despite her lack of superintendency experience, and that the other four finalists for the job were white men who already had such experience.

The two stories I have examined so far exhibit themal coherence[8] not only with each other but also with Ana's immediate response to the work history request: "Well I can tell you that I never wanted to be a superintendent. / This is *not* a career goal." Ana ties these stories together thematically by highlighting the major role others have played in her career moves when they recognized her competence and encouraged her to take on leadership positions. At the same time, she consistently presents herself as surprised and hesitant, although ultimately acceding to their encouragement.

How am I to interpret this presentation of self? In her overview of the autobiographies of privileged twentieth-century American and English women, Carolyn Heilbrun describes the difficulties women have had "admit[ting] into their autobiographical narratives the claim of achievement, the admission of ambition, the recognition that accomplishment was neither luck nor the result of the efforts or generosity of others." Heilbrun explains that "the only script for women's life insisted that work discover and pursue them, like the conventional romantic lover."[9] Similarly, Jacquelyn Wiersma's life history interviews with women who have changed careers led her to analyze what she calls the "press release," the disavowal of responsibility for their career changes. Wiersma argues that women use this disavowal as protection against anticipated criticism for violating women's traditional roles.[10]

Is Ana Martinez offering us a press release? Is she having trouble admitting that she is ambitious? Does work pursue her like the conventional romantic lover because that is the only script available? Despite the apparent fit of these ideas, a significant difference between Ana's narrative and those studied by Wiersma and Heilbrun leads me to an alternative interpretation. For Wiersma and Heilbrun, the clue that something was amiss lay in the unconvincing nature of women's stories. Wiersma felt that women were offering "someone else's version of their actions and feelings" and that their stories were "empty, stereotyped, and implausible."[11] Citing a study by Jill Conway, Heilbrun comments on the "narrative flatness" of women's autobiographies about their exciting lives.[12] By contrast, Ana's stories are neither flat nor unconvincing. I suggest that her emphasis on others' encouragement represents not the concealment of ambition, but the process by which she developed a professional identity. As Howard Becker and James Carper argue, "the evaluative responses of important persons and groups" constitute one of the social-psychological mechanisms through which individuals acquire an occupational identity.[13] Ana's obvious enjoyment in telling these stories reflects her pleasure at being perceived by others as competent. Her use of reported speech makes others' encouraging words believable and reinforces the idea that she needed others' encouragement in order to imagine herself as an educational leader. By putting words about her competence in others' mouths, Ana dramatizes how external the notion of her competence was, at least initially.

This interpretation does not conflict with the idea that the encouragement theme in Ana's work history is gendered. Her emphasis on the importance of others in the development of her professional identity may exemplify what Mary Gergen found when she compared accomplished women's and men's autobiographies: women depend much more heavily on "affiliative relationships" than men do, and women express "more profound emotional interdependency" than men do.[14] At the same time, the encouragement theme may also be related to Ana's ethnic and class background. In an occupational context where white women and people of color teach while white men lead, it makes sense that women, especially women of color from working-class backgrounds, need strong encouragement to become educational leaders. Sociologists who study women in male-dominated occupations explain women's career moves in terms of the structure of opportunities rather than women's initial ambition or lack of ambition.[15] By portraying her professional identity as developing in the context of encouragement and opportunity, Ana's narrative reflects the social organization of her occupation.

Exercising Professional Competence and Commitment

When Ana turns to a description of her superintendency in Urbantown, her tone becomes more serious and her use of reported speech decreases. This shift reflects the difference between the pleasurable process of developing a professional identity and the difficulties she encountered in the actual work of the superintendency. As Ana reports, "You need to know that it was probably the toughest experience I've ever had." This statement introduces a series of stories about the seemingly endless problems Ana faced as superintendent in that city. She resigned from the position after several years, explaining, "After a strike, closing schools, and laying off people, and now a [serious crisis],

you have got to let that district start all over again with a new team."[16]
Although lauded by school administrators in other cities as a "brilliant
strategy," Ana's handling of the district's crisis made her unpopular
with many teachers and community members. She concludes her description of that crisis with these strongly worded and passionately
expressed statements:

AM: So I I recognized that that an action I took that *jeopardized my*
    position
    STILL was of *SIGNIFICANT* assistance to other school districts.
    And you know if you if I have a big
    if I have a big ego or if I had a big ego
    that would have been very damaging
    I wouldn't have I don't think I would have taken that risk. (SC
    and CB: hm hmm)
    But I think with the *support* system that I have
    from my family
    and with the *confidence* in myself that
    what I really want to do is make things better for kids
    improve our instructional program
    if if I keep that if I keep my eye on the prize
    then I can almost survive anything.
    I *really* feel that. (SC and CB: hm hmm)
    And so I can take I feel I can take the risks that need to be taken.

By this point in her work history, Ana no longer needs others'
encouragement to know that she is competent. This is shown by the
absence of others' words, by her direct description of her own accomplishments. Her problem here is sorting out the meanings and consequences, for herself and others, of her actions as an educational leader.
On the one hand, Ana's handling of the crisis jeopardized her position
by damaging her reputation with teachers and community members.
Even now she feels that many people in Urbantown still view her as
"this woman who got the district into trouble." On the other hand, she
presents her actions as benefiting other superintendents by setting a
precedent for solving similar crises.

In this part of her narrative, Ana uses discourse about professional
competence and commitment to explain her actions and to satisfy

herself that she has done a good job. She speaks of *"confidence* in myself that what I really want to do is make things better for kids." Along with support from her family, Ana's commitment to children's education—"keep[ing] my eye on the prize"—helps her to take necessary risks and to survive the negative fallout of her actions. Risking her job doesn't disrupt Ana's confidence because her identity as an educational leader is located in her commitment to the work in a broader sense. As Eliot Freidson states, professions are distinguished in part by "an occupational community that extends beyond any particular workplace . . . and a shared occupational identity."[17] At this point in Ana's work history, the judgment of other educational administrators matters more to her than that of teachers and people in the local community. Her actions are more comprehensible to those in positions similar to hers than to those over whom she exercises authority. Discourse about professional competence and commitment provides Ana with resources for maintaining her confidence in the face of teachers' and community members' perceptions that she has failed. As if speaking of Ana's situation, Everett Cherrington Hughes asks, "Who has the right to say what a mistake or failure is?" and answers, "A colleague-group (the people who consider themselves subject to the same work risks) will stubbornly defend its own right to define mistakes, and to say in the given case whether one has been made."[18]

This story about the difficulties Ana encountered in her first superintendency explains her earlier statement: "I can also tell you very frankly that if I had to do it over again / knowing what I know today about the superintendency / I would never have done it." With respect to the particular pressures of administrative work, Freidson observes that "administrators . . . must represent their organization's policies and interests, not only those of the practitioners [teachers]. . . . They must therefore assume the onus of creating some of the major work contingencies against which the rank and file may chafe." School administrators' work is further exacerbated by their vulnerability "to the pressure of public opinion."[19] Ana emphasizes the unusually rough time she had in Urbantown by citing her colleagues' comments: "The male superintendents tell me / 'Ana, in Urbantown you had more experiences in six years than most superintendents have in thirty years.' "[20]

In the following work history story, Ana tells how she came to take her second urban superintendency, even though she had resigned from the first intending to retire altogether.

AM: But then um [p]
    I was not going to be looking for another position
    and uh then [p] some board members from another district told the board members from Grandcity about me (SC: hm hmm)
    and uh [p] I was encouraged to apply for that position [in Grandcity] and I did. (SC: hm hmm) . . .
    They wanted somebody *tough*
    that's their word
    they wanted somebody to to do change to to execute or effect change (SC: hm hmm) in Grandcity.
    And they wanted someone who would have the courage to do that.
    And interestingly enough the very the very thing that the [teachers'] union in Urbantown had said to me that I would never be considered again was the very thing that they *looked* for. (SC: yeah)

Once again, through no intention of her own, Ana was recruited to a superintendency, this time by another school board that had heard about how tough she was in Urbantown.[21] Unlike her earlier encouragement stories, however, Ana does not express surprise at others' perceptions of her competence; this time she does not say "Moi?" or use reported speech. Rather, she confidently cites her competence as the reason that others seek her leadership. She also presents her success in landing this job as vindication of her controversial actions in Urbantown.

In sum, as she recounts her work history, Ana convinces us that being a superintendent was not a career goal by telling stories about how surprised she was when others encouraged her to do administrative work. And she persuades us that "knowing what I know today about the superintendency / I would never have done it" by describing the immense problems of the job. Unlike the unconvincing character of the narratives that Wiersma analyzed, Ana's work history is replete with stories about "exposure to new tasks, risks, and gratifications, about . . . growing confidence in [her] talents and skills."[22] She uses discursive resources that belong to the world of professional work—discourse about educational leaders' competencies and commitments—to narrate the development of her identity as an educational leader and to recount her handling of the difficult work of the superintendency.

A Disconnected Story about Sex Discrimination

In a number of places in her work history, unprompted by us, Ana briefly discussed how gender has shaped others' treatment of her. For example, about her candidacy for her first superintendency, she mentioned that "it was a shock [to some] to have a woman" and that "the [school] board asked me different questions because I am a woman." And in the midst of the crisis in Urbantown, the teachers' union leaders tried to intimidate her by claiming that a woman who took such actions would never get another job. However, Ana did not describe any discriminatory instances in detail, nor did she mention any experiences of inequality related to her ethnicity. Thus, when she finished her work history, I asked a direct question about sex and ethnic discrimination. (The first part of my question is missing because I began to speak as Colleen changed the tape.)

SC: all of the things that you've told us about
would you say that you've experienced discrimination because you're a woman or because of your ethnicity?
AM: Hm hmm uh you mean in my well I can tell you as a superintendent
for instance

After this halting beginning, Ana launches into three stories about discrimination. Notice that she does not offer an abstract to introduce and summarize what she will say, as she did in her response to the work history request. The difference between her initial response to the work history request and her initial response to this question provides a clue that Ana has constructed a fuller sense of self within the discursive realm of professional work than within the discursive realm of inequality (at least in the context of this interview).

She recounts the first two stories about discrimination in a manner that emphasizes their relatively inconsequential nature. One is about her husband's being mistaken for the superintendent when they travel together to her work-related meetings and his "great sense of humor" in handling those incidents. The second is about the way she dealt with being mistaken for a secretary when she became the first woman on the superintendent's cabinet in Urbantown. While Ana laughs heartily as she narrates these two stories, her tone becomes serious in the third one:

AM: I will say the biggest disappointment that I *ever* had
was the *only* time within the system of Urbantown that I applied for a position.
And everyone within the district thought that I was the most qualified person
there wasn't anybody who *knew* as much about federal and state programs as I did.
And they were forming a new department called the Department of Special Programs
and they were getting a a *director* of special programs
I applied for that job.
Now here's a person who has *administered* all the programs knew everything
and uh [p] *politically* it was not expedient for the district [to hire me].
So they hired a fellow from the community [p]
[slowly, emphatically] *who didn't even have certification*. (CB: hmmm)
They had to get an eminence credential from (SC: hmmm) the state for him.
He'd never *worked* in a public school system.
He was uh at the local university.
But never had worked in a
he was a social worker
he was *not* an educator.

By comparing her qualifications to the man's lack of them, Ana convincingly presents this situation as an instance of discrimination. In another passage, she specifically describes it as such: "There was discrimination to the nth degree / I mean there was blatant rejection of a very qualified person for political expediency." While she does not clarify the nature of the political expediency that led her superordinates to hire the man, she may mean that it was easier for them to hire a man than a woman into a position of leadership at that time (the early 1970s).

As she continues, Ana focuses on her response to the situation.

AM: They put him in charge and then the *challenge* for *me* was [p]
[softly, each word spoken separately, emphatically]
I had to teach him everything. (CB and SC: hmm hm hmmm)
And [p] *that* builds character let me tell you because I had to within my [p]
myself search for what *I* thought was most important to do.
And I told you my bottom line I always say
"keep my eye on the prize" (SC: hm hmm)
"keep my eye on the prize."
And if I can do that then then I can function.
So I thought "what's in the best interest of the kids? (SC: hm hmm)
What's in the best interest of the kids is that [enthusiastically] I teach him everything I know so he does a good job! (SC: hm hmm)
So that we have a good program!"
So I did!

Ana portrays her response as a matter of searching *within herself* for some principle to guide her actions. While her husband, family, and colleagues appeared as supportive interlocutors throughout her work history, here she struggles alone.[23] This absence of otherwise helpful others conveys Ana's sense of isolation in dealing with the experience of discrimination.

Ana draws on discourse about professional commitment to guide her actions in this situation, evoking the words she used when confronted by the crisis in Urbantown: "I always say 'keep my eye on the prize' . . . 'keep my eye on the prize.' " But in this case, Ana's rhetoric is unconvincing: "What's in the best interest of the kids is that [enthusiastically] I teach him everything I know so he does a good job!" Ana's forced enthusiasm indicates that she is offering something akin to the press release described by Wiersma.[24] As a listener, I am unpersuaded that Ana's strategy is really in the best interest of the kids. Wouldn't their best interest be served by having the most qualified person in the job in the first place? Ana's statements come off as an unsuccessful attempt to conceal her resignation to a bad situation. Moreover, as she continues, it is clear that more is at stake for Ana in this event than the best interest of the kids.

AM: Consequently that man is still my friend and supporter to this
      day.
      He realized that he liked social work better [small laugh] than
      education (SC: hmm)
      so he went back to the school of social work at the university [p]
      and uh [p]
      I was *glad* I was never the Department of Special Programs direc-
      tor because they *hated* it.
      The whole *district* hated it. (SC: hmm)
      They thought it was *oooh*
      so it was the best thing that happened to me!

Ana portrays her decision to teach the man everything she knew as having unanticipated but positive consequences: she gained a friend rather than an enemy, and she was spared the unpleasantness of directing an unpopular program. But her conclusion tests the listener's credulity: "So it was the best thing that happened to me!" This statement fails to persuade not only because it exaggerates the positive character of the outcome but also because it seems to use that outcome to cover the pain of the discriminatory event. Furthermore, Ana's emphasis on having avoided a difficult assignment belies what her work history suggests: she does not shirk risks and difficult decisions, even those that earn her enemies and jeopardize her job.

Although Ana convincingly presents this story as an instance of discrimination, the way she recounts her response indicates that she is having difficulty integrating this story into her broader narrative. There are several indications of this lack of integration, this disconnectedness. First, the supportive others who figured prominently in her work history are absent from this story. Where are her husband, family, and colleagues during this discriminatory event? Second, while Ana seems to tie this story to the earlier narrative through discourse about professional commitment, the unpersuasive rhetoric of that discourse in this context reinforces the disconnection. Furthermore, this story belongs chronologically to the part of Ana's work history where she speaks of being "given promotions, increasing responsibilities" in Urbantown, yet she gave no hint at all of this experience of discrimination as she narrated her work history. While she included in her work history the long story about the crisis in Urbantown ("the toughest experience I've ever had"), she excluded from her work history this story about discrimination ("the biggest disappointment that I *ever* had"). Including the discrimination story in her work history would have required introducing disappointment and discouragement into her smooth narrative about encouragement and increasing confidence in her professional competencies. A story about handling the toughest experience is easily integrated into a narrative in which the dominant discourse is professional competence and commitment. That story becomes another occasion in which Ana presents herself as a competent and committed educator. A story about subjection, however, is not so easily integrated because it requires a different construction of self, a construction of self as subjected.

Ana is not trying to be unconvincing when she states that the discriminatory event was the best thing that ever happened to her. Rather, her problematic rhetoric points to the disjunction between the discursive realms of professional work and inequality. Couching her work history in discourse about professional competence and commitment makes it difficult to include the experience of discrimination within that history. In response to a direct question about discrimination, Ana has no trouble describing her experience *as* discrimination; she does not deny that the treatment she received was discriminatory. Instead, the difficulty she encounters is a narrative difficulty: how can she connect this story about subjection to her broader story about professional competence and commitment? Her particular way of resolving this narrative problem is to exclude the discrimination story from her work history.

Finally, even though my question was about both sex and ethnic discrimination, all three of Ana's stories exclude any mention of ethnicity. By referring to the sex but not the race or ethnicity of the man who got the job as director of special programs, Ana creates the impression that she experienced the incident as a matter of sex rather than ethnic discrimination.

Excluding Subjection While Talking about Ethnicity

Disrupted Talk

Near the end of the interview, I invited Ana to talk about the place of ethnicity in her work experiences. This part of our interview was unique; both my question and Ana's immediate response are instances of disrupted talk.

SC: [slowly] Basically [p] [sigh] we're interested [p] in how gender
    and ethnicity play a part in people's lives
    and and what we noticed is that the white women [p]
    end up in very homogeneous basically white communities
    and um the women of color [p]
    not always but tend to be in districts that have a much more
    diverse ethnic [p] um [clears throat] [p] ‖population‖

AM: ‖population‖

SC: student population yeah
    and um [p] among the women of color in their talk
    there there would sometimes be quite a bit of talk about ethnicity
    their own and that of the school district (AM: uh huh) that
        they're in
    and among the white women it was an *invisible* phenomenon.
    I mean everybody *has* race but it wasn't talked about by the white
        women.
    And we're just *interested* in your perspective on the role that
        ethnicity has played
    in in your life in your work experiences
    and I know it's a very broad question but (AM: uh huh)
    if you have any thoughts about that
    things that you haven't already said or uh (AM: uh huh)
    you know a general kind of thing.

In comparison to my questions about work history and discrimination, my query about ethnicity is replete with qualifications and explanations. What I am asking is not clear and specific, but diffuse and broad; and I am trying to make *that* clear. At the same time, I am attempting to explain how the question arose for *us*, rather than presenting it as an abstract sociological question. Because Ana was one of the last women we interviewed, it was possible for me to describe some general observations based on our interviews: not only do white women and women of color end up in districts with different student populations,[25] but their talk also reflects the differential impact of race and ethnicity on their experiences.

I could have stated simply, "We'd like to hear more about the place of ethnicity in your work experiences." My qualifications and explanations indicate that my speech is an instance of disrupted talk. As I argued in chapter 2, disrupted talk is one way of entering the discursive realm of inequality, a realm characterized by overt ideological struggles. Although my question does not refer specifically to experiences of discrimination—it is broad enough to include other kinds of experiences related to ethnicity—it does take us into the discursive realm of inequality in another way. My question evokes the difficulties that sometimes arise when white women and women of color struggle to converse, particularly when racial or ethnic differences are the topic. Pat Parker captures the struggle in a poem titled "For the White Person Who Wants to Know How to Be My Friend," which begins:

The first thing you do is to forget that i'm Black.
Second, you must never forget that i'm Black.[26]

Although Parker is referring specifically to friendship, her recommendation is instructive with regard to the history of conflict and tension between white women and women of color in the United States. Frequently, white women have either ignored racial and ethnic differences or addressed them in ways that are as insensitive as blatant indifference.[27] The disrupted character of my talk reflects my awareness of that history and my attempt to produce an invitation within the context of such a history. But while an invitation can be taken for granted in other questions—such as the request for a work history—an invitation to talk about ethnicity cannot be assumed in either a simply worded question or in a more complex introduction such as the one I offered.

Here is Ana's immediate response:

AM: Well now as I talked with you did ethnicity enter into it outside of [p]
oh even that you wouldn't know it was ethnic but the uh
the minority population that came to see me first initially in (CB: uh huh) Urbantown and encouraged me (CB: right) to be superintendent (CB: uh huh)
I *did* interject that (SC: right CB: uh huh)
um but did it did it [p]
now *gender* did (SC: right CB: uh huh)
but did *ethnicity* anywhere along the way when I talked with you?
SC: Not in a major ‖way no‖
CB: ‖on only‖ the stuff about want wanting your children to be bilingual
AM: bilingual
SC: yes
CB: your own family experience
AM: yes
SC: uh huh things like that
CB: *there* it seems
AM: *there* it came uh through
SC: yeah yeah
AM: uh because [p]
although *I* recognize the inequities that exist
I don't dwell on them (SC: hm hmm)
I don't talk a lot about them.

This is a tense moment; I am worried that my attempt to invite Ana to talk about ethnicity has offended her. At no other point in the interview did Ana turn a question back to us. She responded comfortably to the work history request with a fully developed narrative; and while her answer to the discrimination question began with some hesitation, she easily related three separate stories in that context.

NARRATIVE STRATEGIES

By contrast, Ana's immediate reply here is an instance of disrupted talk in the sense that it consists of metastatements—talk about talk—and breaks the conventional interactional flow. She begins not with an answer (the expected response in an interview situation), but with a question: "Well now as I talked with you did ethnicity enter into it outside of . . .?" Just as my disrupted question indicates that talking about ethnicity is a matter that cannot be taken for granted, Ana's disrupted talk also represents struggles surrounding ethnicity.

Ana interrupts her own question to clarify the role of ethnicity in the story she told earlier about the minority community encouraging her to apply for the superintendency in Urbantown. (Contrary to her statement here—"you wouldn't know it [the minority population] was ethnic"—Ana did specify in her earlier account that she was speaking of Hispanics.) Before returning to her question, she also states that she did talk about gender issues, referring to the times she spoke of gender shaping her work experiences, including the instance of discrimination examined in the previous section. Then, in response to her question—"but did *ethnicity* [enter] anywhere along the way when I talked with you?"—Colleen and I reflect, and Ana offers comments, on whether and how her previous talk included ethnicity. Her reason for turning the question back to us is not clear until the last lines in the excerpt:

uh because [p]
although *I* recognize the inequities that exist
I don't dwell on them (SC: hm hmm)
I don't talk a lot about them.

In other words, the absence of talk about inequities related to ethnicity is no accident; Ana deliberately controls her talk about ethnicity. Here she tells us explicitly that her narrative strategy consists of excluding talk about inequities related to her ethnicity. She hears my question, then, not as an offense but as an occasion to clarify how she wants us to hear her talk.

Charles Briggs notes that in any verbal interaction "participants are constantly exchanging implicit messages as to how they perceive the speeech event and how they want their utterances to be interpreted" and are "continually checking to see if their perceptions are shared by the other participants."[28] Disrupted talk occurs when a speaker brings this implicit process to the surface. Ana's response to my question informs us that she *could* tell stories about subjection or inequities she has experienced due to her ethnicity, but that she chooses to exclude them from her narrative. She asks us to review the way she has talked about ethnicity because she wants to make sure that we have interpreted her talk correctly. Her request conveys how important it is to her that we understand her choice to exclude talk about subjection.

My disrupted questioning may have encouraged Ana's disrupted talk; nonetheless, her particular response needs to be understood not only in relation to my question but also in the context of what follows. Notice that she interprets my broad comments about ethnicity as a question about inequities. Unlike the question about sex and ethnic discrimination, however, this question is not specifically about experiences of subjection. Other interpretations of the question are possible. For example, another Hispanic woman superintendent we interviewed, Rose Farrell, responded to the same question by talking about community and solidarity as well as about inequities. Farrell spoke first about the political issues she confronts because her district is racially and ethnically diverse and then about the friendships she has developed with other women of color because of their shared experiences in a white- and male-dominated occupation.[29]

Professional Commitment to the Needs of Students of Color

The following comments come immediately after the previous excerpt:

AM: I'm I'm a *doer* (CB and SC: hm hmm)
    as you can probably guess
    and I feel that I've done a lot particularly in Grandcity with Hispanic youngsters to raise the level of achievement. (SC: hm hmm)
    Uh here [in her current school district] the minority community which is mainly Black
    the challenge *here* for *me* is
    can I do with Black students not being a Black myself (SC: hm hmm)
    can I do with Black students what I did with

what I was able to do with Hispanic students in Urbantown and
  Grandcity. (CB: hmm)
That is the biggest challenge to me here. (SC: hm hmm)
That's the drawing card that brought me here frankly. (CB: hm
  hmm)
I had two other job offers (SC: hmm) when I took this position
and uh one of them was uh something I always talked big about
"well I'm going to get myself a district where the majority of the
  kids go to college and there are no problems"
and here I got one you know
five thousand students six thousand students
uh 92 percent of the kids go to college
uh no major problems
a lot of money
more money than I would have made here (SC: hm hmm)
but I told my husband "what would I *do* there? (SC and CB: hm
  hmm [small laugh])
I think I'd *die* (SC and CB: hm hmm)
what would I *do* there?"
what you know I couldn't figure out *what* I could *do* there that
  would keep me interested and alive. (SC: hm hmm) . . .
So [p] I uh [P]
I haven't *dwelled* on ethnicity (SC: hm hmm)
but it's there (SC and CB: hm hmm)
it's in the background (SC and CB: hm hmm)
always.

Ana begins by differentiating talk and action; she implies that to talk
about inequities is to complain passively about them. By describing
herself as a doer who has contributed to the improvement of Hispanic
and Black students' educational experiences, she reintroduces discourse about professional competence and commitment. She highlights her commitment by asserting that she chose her current job in
an ethnically diverse urban community over a higher-paid job in a
wealthier suburban district.

Ana integrates ethnicity into this story, then, without dwelling
on inequities *she* has experienced. Rather, ethnicity is "in the background . . . always" in the sense that it shapes the kind of work that

keeps her interested and alive. This self-construction expands on that developed in her work history; Ana portrays herself here as a competent, committed, educational leader and further specifies her commitment to the educational needs of students of color. Although Ana does not speak of herself as subjected to inequities related to ethnicity, inequities are manifest in the social conditions that lead to low achievement by students of color and that differentiate suburban and urban school districts. (Note that Ana once again features her husband in direct dialogue. This time, however, she portrays him as a listener rather than an encourager.)

She continues in the same vein by discussing the changing racial and ethnic demographics in the United States and educators' responsibility to prepare students well. She concludes by referring explicitly to her own commitment:

AM: And so that's *I* feel [p] a a commitment (CB and SC: hm hmm)
   I think also you know if you want to know how I feel as a
      member of an ethnic group
   I feel if *I* don't care *who's* going to care
   I should care more than *anybody* (SC: hm hmm) what happens to
      minorities.

More directly than in any other part of her narrative, Ana presents her ethnicity as the source of her commitments as an educational leader. As a Hispanic school superintendent, she uses her position of power to do something about inequities experienced by students of color. The professional world provides her with the material resources to do something about what she cares about and the discursive resources to describe herself as a powerful leader in those efforts. This sense of responsibility to use acquired power for the good of the group is expressed frequently by upwardly mobile professionals of color.[30]

At this point, Ana's description of herself as a Hispanic educational leader seems seductively complete. She seems to explain her exclusion of stories about inequities she has experienced by focusing on herself as a Hispanic woman in a position of power. Why should she need to talk about—to complain about—her experiences of subjection when she occupies a position that allows her to do something about others' experiences of inequality? In her final two stories, however, Ana shows that the professional world that provides the privileges of exercising competence, commitment, power, and responsibility is itself structured by inequalities. Importantly, she offers this analysis without talking specifically about her subjection to those inequalities.

The Privilege of Light Skin

After the previous excerpt, Colleen invited Ana to say more about the role of ethnicity in her career in Urbantown.

CB: It also sounded to me like when you were describing your promotions in Urbantown
    that your *bilingualism* and your *experience* with kids from other cultures than white
    led them to *look* to you for leadership in those arenas.
AM: I think the other advantage that I have that probably a woman who is *significantly* of color
    visibly of color (SC: hm hmm)
    doesn't have
    what I have over them is that I *lived* in the Beverly Hills of Urbantown.
    See having come from a humble background (SC: hm hmm)
    you aspire to get nicer *home* nicer *this* nicer *that*
    and so *I* lived in a nicer that kind of neighborhood
    I told you 98 percent of the kids from my kids' high school went to college (SC: hm hmm)
    so a *down* side to that but I won't go into now
    if I had it to do over again I wouldn't have them
    I wouldn't live there and I wouldn't have gone to that
    but that's another conversation. (CB and SC: hm hmm)
    But [p] by the same token I was *bilingual*
    and I could *relate* to and *converse* in Spanish with the *humblest* Hispanic family (SC: hm hmm) that came into my office. (SC: hm hmm) [p]
    But I also was in that *other* group.

I had been *accepted* (SC: hm hmm) in a sense by the upper middle
    class (SC: hm hmm)
and was living and raising my kids in that kind of community
    having come from another. (SC: hm hmm)
So *that's* a unique position because ah remember
the first group that came to me was the minority group (CB and
    SC: hm hmm)
and I thought well that's 'cause they relate to me and they want
    (SC: right)
but then the other group that came to me
they were the (CB: hmmm) PTA Anglo middle class
in that urban community you know you have both extremes (CB
    and SC: hm hmm yes)
in according to the neighborhoods.
And that's when I realized that *I* had gained credibility with *both*
    (SC: yes)
which I don't know if I were a woman visibly of color
I could have gained honestly. (CB: hm hmm yeah)
SC: So you can move between different worlds
AM: between the two cultures
    I very I am *very* comfortable between the two cultures
    and I switch back and forth
    and it was a *definite advantage.*

In this multilayered excerpt—more than one story is being told—
Ana introduces discourse about privilege into her discussion of the
profession and her place within it. The story with which Ana begins
and ends concerns the advantage she feels she has over women who are
"significantly of color / *visibly* of color." Speaking again of her experience in applying for the superintendency in Urbantown, she describes
her realization that she had gained credibility with the Hispanic community and the "PTA Anglo middle class" when both encouraged her
candidacy. She presents her credibility with both groups, as well as her
comfort in moving "between the two cultures," as professional advantages.[31] That credibility and comfort have made working with different
groups possible and have aided her career moves. By attributing to the
lightness of her skin the ease of her movement between the two cul-

                                                       Narrative Strategies

tures, Ana acknowledges the privileged status of light skin in American society as well as in her occupational context.

The other story told here, and woven into the first, is about Ana's humble background, her aspiration for "a nicer *home* nicer *this* nicer *that,*" and her residence in the "Beverly Hills of Urbantown." Despite the professional advantage that accompanied her move into the upper middle class, Ana hints at but chooses not to tell a story about the down side of upward mobility. Nonetheless, it is not difficult to surmise that the down side has to do with conflicts a Hispanic woman from a working-class background experiences even if she is accepted by the Anglo middle class and respected by the community in which she grew up.[32] Ana's exclusion of this personal story about the down side of upward mobility makes sense in an interview concerned primarily with her work experiences. But her juxtaposition of the personal disadvantage to the professional advantage of moving between two cultures still excludes talk about her subjection to inequalities in the profession. She uses discourse about the privilege of light skin to show how racial inequality is built into the profession and to speak of herself as privileged relative to women who are visibly of color.

The following is the final story Ana told in response to my question about ethnicity.

AM: I have had people say to me
    "gee you know Ana I never thought of you as a minority"
    because the newspaper would bring it up every so often (SC and
       CB: hm hmm)
    well in fact do you know I don't know whether Chris [a school
       board member we interviewed[33]] if this came out in your con-
       versation with Chris but when they hired me they didn't know
       I was a minority (CB and SC: hmm) [p]
    they just never really noticed it.
    It was *there* (SC and CB: hm hmm) you know in *all* of my papers
       (SC and CB: hm hmm)
CB: but they didn't focus on it
AM: they didn't
    I think they interviewed me as a middle-class (SC and CB: hm
       hmm) you know [p] person

and I think that the only way the men accepted me was as a good old boy. (SC and CB: hmm huh)

They saw me as a good old boy.

CB: So it was perhaps better that that wasn't a focus.

AM: Yea they see you when they interview you they see in you what they are looking for what they want to see.

Among those in the professional world who do not notice that Ana is Hispanic are the school board members who hired her into her current position. Ana emphasizes that this perception coexisted with evidence to the contrary: her papers are filled with references to her identity and commitments as a Hispanic educator. Their failure to notice her ethnicity, however, does not mean that ethnicity was irrelevant during the hiring process. Rather, Ana suggests that ethnicity, as well as class and gender, were very relevant to their perceptions: "they didn't know I was a minority"; "they interviewed me as a middle-class . . . person"; and "[the men] saw me as a good old boy." Ana depicts others within the professional context as perceiving her as white, middle class, and a good old boy. Her tone—her attitude toward what she is saying—is reflected in Colleen's comment, "So it was perhaps better that that wasn't a focus." Ana suggests that others' perceptions of her as a white, middle-class, good old boy are advantageous to her professional work.

Although Ana once again excludes the down side of a professional advantage, it is possible to construct that down side from her account of others' perceptions. She is invisible in the professional world as a Hispanic woman from a working-class background, even though evidence of her identity is readily available. This invisibility reflects the segregation and stratification of the working-class Hispanic world in which she grew up and the white professional world in which she now works. School board members' perceptions of Ana as a white, middle-class, good old boy are dependent on simultaneous devalued constructions of people of color, the working class, and women. Ana presents her professional success as contingent upon her white, middle-class, good-old-boy appearance in the professional world as well as on her ability to move between the two cultures. Although she speaks of her competence in moving between the two cultures as a professional advantage, her need to develop this competence is predicated on the

Narrative Strategies

segregation and stratification of those cultures, on the devaluation of her gender, her social-class background, and her ethnicity.

ANA MARTINEZ'S NARRATIVE STRATEGY:
HIGHLIGHTING COMPETENCE AND EXCLUDING SUBJECTION

Like other women who work in white- and male-dominated professions, Ana Martinez encounters the problem of how to talk about herself both as a powerful, successful individual and as a woman who is subject to gender and ethnic inequalities in her occupation. She approaches the disjunction between the discursive realms of professional work and inequality by highlighting the individual strengths she has developed through her work and by choosing not to talk about subjection she experiences as a Hispanic woman.

Throughout her narrative, Martinez empowers herself through the settled discursive realm of professional work. As other professionals might, she draws on discourse about competence and commitment to talk about developing a professional identity, exercising her competence, handling the crisis in Urbantown, and committing herself to the educational needs of students of color. Her deliberate exclusion of stories about her subjection to ethnic inequalities signifies the stand she takes within the contentious discursive realm of inequality. She acknowledges her subjection but implicitly argues that such talk is inappropriate for *her*, for one of the few successful Hispanic women educational leaders. When she describes her success at improving the achievement levels of Hispanic students, she includes others' but not her own experiences of ethnic inequities. When she speaks about the privilege of light skin, she points to the racism other women of color experience and to her relative privilege as a light-skinned Hispanic. And when she describes her invisibility as a Hispanic, she presents this not as a form of subjection, but as a professional advantage that has aided her acceptance within the white-dominated profession.

What does this narrative strategy accomplish? What are its consequences? And what does it communicate about Martinez's experience as a Hispanic woman educational leader?

In comparison to the women educational leaders whose narratives are the subjects of chapters 4, 5, and 6, Martinez sharply separates talk about professional work from talk about inequality. This narrative strategy accentuates and reinforces the disjunction between the two discursive realms. She tacitly argues that she cannot integrate the two kinds of stories she has to tell. Thus, she conveys her sense that there is no room within the professional world for talk about inequities *she* experiences as a Hispanic woman. This narrative strategy subtly communicates the isolation she feels as a Hispanic woman in the professional world. When we focus on content, we hear Martinez speaking primarily about her professional power; but when we focus on narrative strategy, we hear that she is also expressing her subjection. In other words, the *exclusion* of stories about subjection tacitly communicates her subjection, her isolation. Paradoxically, then, Martinez's narrative strategy conveys that she is at once empowered and silenced by the discursive realm of professional work. The price of empowerment through discourse about competence and commitment is concealment of her subjection within the professional world. The price of professional success is isolation.

Thus, Martinez's narrative strategy reproduces the disjunction between discourse about professional work and discourse about inequality. By excluding subjection from her narrative about work experiences, she reinforces the settled, individualistic, gender- and race-neutral character of the discursive realm of professional work. And yet there are cracks in that reinforcement. When she tells us of her choice to exclude stories about subjection, she includes the exclusion within her narrative. And by including that exclusion, she hints that another way of telling her story might be possible in another context.

On another level, this narrative strategy also informs us about Martinez's experience of the interview itself. On the one hand, her exclusion of stories about subjection suggests that she did not experience the interview as a safe space in which she could speak freely about her own experiences of discrimination.[34] Our difference from Martinez is certainly relevant here; both Colleen and I are white and more than twenty years her junior. In addition, our interview took place in her office during the course of her work day, while most of our other interviews took place in a more relaxed setting. On the other hand, there is evidence that Martinez did not simply experience the interview as a constrained professional interaction. Her willingness to speak with us about how the school board members perceive her as a white, middle-class, good old boy suggests that she did not experience us as treating her in the same way. Although she did not talk directly about her experiences of subjection, she clearly communicated her sense that the white- and male-dominated professional world and the working-class Hispanic world are segregated and stratified.

Ana Martinez's narrative provides an example of one kind of story a successful professional woman might tell about her work experiences. A woman tells this story when she feels that her success—her ability to do her work well—is contingent upon fitting herself into the established patterns of the professional world and fitting her story to the settled patterns of professional discourse. This is the kind of story a woman tells when she feels isolated from the few others who might share not only her experience of professional power but also her experience of subjection.

4

Letting

Ambition Go and

Reconsidering

Discrimination:

DENISE

NELSON

At the time of our interview with Denise Nelson, a fifty-year-old white woman, she was in the midst of a major career change. She had just left a superintendency she had held for ten years in a predominantly white, suburban school district and was moving into a less demanding administrative job in another field. Nelson's decision to leave the superintendency was a major topic during the interview.

In her work history, Nelson presents herself as a very ambitious individual. But when she explains her decision to leave the superintendency, she exposes the costs and limits of ambition and slowly begins to redefine past experiences in terms of sex discrimination. By separating the story of ambition from the story of discrimination, Nelson, like Ana Martinez, reproduces the disjunction between the discursive realms of professional work and inequality. However, Nelson's narrative strategy—letting ambition go and recasting past events as discrimination—also begins to undermine that disjunction in subtle ways. In addition, this narrative strategy communicates how difficult it is for Nelson to separate herself from discourse about ambition, and how painful it is to include discourse about subjection in her self-understanding.

Work History: Pursuing Ambition

Denise Nelson grew up in a working-class family in a rural community. When I asked about her parents' occupations and education, she talked at length about her mother, "a housewife who was extremely frustrated," who had no more than an eighth-grade education but "an *awful* lot of drive." As an example, Denise described how her mother always volunteered to host foreigners who were visiting their church because she wanted to "get as much information from them as possible." In this context Denise declared, "I'm living the life that she would have loved / to be fulfilled. . . . I'm Adele Porter [her mother]."[1]

Denise's parents died when she was in her teens. They had encouraged her to pursue a college degree and had left a small amount of money that would help her to do so. Although Denise did start college after high school, she was most interested in the "security of a home and family" at the time of her parents' deaths. She married John, who had a stable working-class job, and within a few years they had three children. When I asked about her aspirations at that point in her life, Denise remarked, "I didn't know / I just knew I wanted to be something other than what was around me."[2] Shortly after this discussion, I asked Denise about her work history and how she had made her career decisions and moves.

DN: Um [p] it's *interesting* because
I think my mother's influence has been with me *all* the way.
And when I was hired for the teaching position
I remember uh and I was hired in March on a three-year teaching certificate and and teachers were rather hard to find at that time.

Um I said to the superintendent [p]
talked to him about the principalship or you know
what was the next step?
Whether whether I'd go into psychology or something but
[louder, exclaiming] *hadn't* even I didn't even have my *bachelor's* and I was thinking in terms of the next step. (SC: mmm)
And as I look back at that *every* step has been that way.

In this summary of her work history, Denise emphasizes her ambitiousness and echoes her earlier statement about living the life her mother would have loved to live. In addition to ambition, she introduces several less obvious themes that resurface throughout her work history. First, she describes herself as confident about her competence and her pursuit of opportunities for further self-development. Second, she looks back with amazement at how unabashedly she pursued her career. In this case, she was already looking toward a principalship as she began her first teaching job and before she had finished her bachelor's degree. Third, she suggests that cultivating the support of powerful people has been integral to her success. In this story, Denise solicited the advice of the superintendent in the district where she held her first teaching job. Each of these themes supports the primary message that she conveys as she narrates her work history: she has always been ambitious.

During her many years of high school teaching, Denise earned bachelor's and master's degrees as well as administrative credentials. In her first administrative job, she helped to develop a new method of teacher evaluation, a process that "was very humane and that gave responsibility back to the teacher."

DN: I found that [method] to be successful in in working with teachers.
The *administration* were impressed with it as *well.*
And when another administrative position came open in the district I was named to that position and I think it was basically because of the success in working with one on one with teachers with this process.

Unlike Ana Martinez, Denise is not surprised that others perceive her as capable of taking on increasing responsibility and authority. She knows that others offer her leadership positions because they recognize her competence. While Ana presents herself as pushed along by others' encouragement and as developing confidence and a professional identity in that process, Denise presents herself as pursuing opportunities that are offered in accordance with her developing abilities. Even when she talks about those whose support has been integral to her success, she focuses on how *she* cultivated that support, as the next story shows.

During her first week in her second administrative job, Denise wrote to a woman superintendent whom she had never met. As she tells this story, Denise mentions that there were only two women superintendents in the state at the time.

DN: I *wrote* to Barbara Croft and asked how one becomes a superintendent. (CB: mm hmm)
She wrote back
We *laugh* about this [laugh] (CB and SC: laugh)
We *laugh* about this now.
She wrote back and said you know
"the the experiences but to get the doctorate."
And and this was my *first* week
I mean you think about how *arrogant* [laugh]
it's real it's pretty arrogant of me to to write a letter [laugh] (SC: hm hmm) the very first week that I'm in a job where I don't know what's up [laugh] uh for such a thing.

By describing her action as arrogant, Denise suggests that she was reaching for too much too quickly, that she was overly self-confident, and that she did not know at the time how presumptuous her action was or might have appeared to others. As such, she presents herself as having been naive, as unself-conscious about her ambition.[3] By laughing now at what she did in all seriousness then, Denise underscores her ambitiousness and confidence in her competence. It is only in hindsight—from the perspective of maturity and greater knowledge about the field and careers generally—that Denise can see how ambitious she really was. The light-hearted tone of this story conveys her amazement at (rather than criticism of or regret about) her earlier actions. In fact, her letter-writing tactic worked: Barbara Croft, the superintendent, wrote back with advice and is now someone with whom Denise can laugh about this story. Denise continues:

DN: But in that in that interim then I started thinking in terms of of the superintendency.
[louder] I was able to observe firsthand the working of three superintendents.
And in a vicarious way put myself in the position of them as they make decisions and as I could see (SC: hm hmm) how decisions were being made (SC: hm hmm)
I became very *critical* and at the same time I think was telling myself "I could do that (SC: hm hmm)
I could make a *better* decision based on the same information as what *you* guys are doing." (SC: hm hmm)
Uh so all of that I think led to the next step.

Like many of the women Colleen and I interviewed, Denise recognized her competence to do the work of the superintendency as she watched how others did the job. Unlike other women, however, she does not present this recognition of her competence as new, as a revelation. Rather, she simply presents it as the next step in her progression to positions of increasing power and responsibility.

Although I could cite others, these few stories demonstrate sufficiently how Denise draws on discourse about ambition to narrate her work history. That discourse lodges comfortably within the professional world, but it also belongs to many other sites in American culture.[4] Denise's expression of ambition is typical in a hierarchical institution such as public education. Like other ambitious professionals, she desires to move up the occupational ladder in order to develop her competence, exercise increasing responsibility and authority, acquire status or recognition, and make a significant difference to public education.

Denise presents the professional world as a context in which her ambition flourished. It is noteworthy that in comparison to other women superintendents who spoke forthrightly about their ambition—such as Karen Rhodes in chapter 6—Denise gives no clue that ambition is a gendered discourse associated with masculinity and thus conventionally used by men but not by women. Rather, she unself-consciously embraces that discourse as her own. In addition, as she narrates her work history, Denise speaks less than other women superintendents do about gender inequalities that structure the professional world.[5] Significantly, her story about seeking advice from a woman superintendent alludes to gender inequality. By describing how she contacted one of the two women superintendents in the state (rather than any of the hundreds of male superintendents), Denise hints at a subtext that she waits until later to articulate: gender inequality has shaped her work experiences.

Letting Ambition Go

Inviting a Request for an Account
of Leaving the Superintendency

Within the professional world, any move down the occupational structure appears as a deviation from expected upward movement and calls for an account.[6] Furthermore, by narrating her work history through discourse about ambition, Denise invited a request for an account of her decision to take a less demanding administrative job. Significantly, she described her decision in terms of leaving the superintendency rather than in the more neutral terms of changing jobs.[7] By the time I asked for an explanation, she had already mentioned her decision in two different contexts without prompting from us. The way she raised the topic in these two places anticipates the fuller account she offered later in response to my direct question about it.

Denise first mentioned her decision near the beginning of the interview. In response to Colleen's opening questions about the community, the history of the school district, and the school board, Denise described the "traumatic times" of the past two years. One school board member, who was "simply a jackass" and who "didn't have a very high regard for women," made life difficult not only for Denise but also for the rest of the school board. (This passing reference to sexism becomes important later in her narrative.) According to Denise, this school board member repeatedly attempted to discredit her and the board at public meetings, accused Denise and the treasurer of misusing funds, worked aggressively (and successfully) against the school levy, led a campaign to fire Denise, influenced the local newspaper (which published "extremely derogatory" cartoons about Denise), and generally spoiled relations between the community and the schools. In response to this havoc, a nightmare for any school superintendent,[8] Denise hired a consultant to help the other board members understand and deal with such behavior. She also created an advisory committee composed of several community members whose charge was to "investigate everything" including the district's finances and staffing. As a result of the advisory committee's work, most people in the community began to see that the one board member was the source of much of the trouble. A grass-roots campaign arose to pass the school levy, and Denise's supporters rallied around her. As she related these traumas of the past two years, Denise emphasized that "I did not leave [the job] under duress." To the contrary, when she informed the school board of her decision to take a new job, all (except the "jackass") tried to convince her to stay by raising her salary.

Denise also broached the topic of leaving as she talked about how supportive her family has been throughout her career. Asking us to "indulge" her, she showed us family snapshots. In this context, she described her children as having offered encouragement and understanding "through this decision of leaving the superintendency." When she talked about her grandson (her daughter's physically disabled baby), Denise became teary: "He has really brought all of us up a bit short / and brought us really closer together / he's teaching us a lot."

Much later in the interview, after her work history, I asked Denise directly about her decision to leave the superintendency. As we shall see, both the work-related traumas of the last two years and family members (particularly her grandchild) figure prominently in the extended account she offers. She discusses how her desire shifted from work to family, whether she is letting other women down by leaving, and whether she has failed professionally by leaving. She also uncovers the costs to herself and her family of the demanding job of superintendent.

SC: Um would you talk some about why you've decided to leave the superintendency?
DN: [P] Yeah [slight sigh]
     [p] um [p] as I mentioned
     I I uh the past two years have been *extremely* difficult

and [louder] I *won't* say that it got at the heart of who *I* am and yet I would be lying if I said it wasn't painful.

Although I ask why—a question that seeks an explanation—Denise introduces her account in terms of how she feels and what her decision means. Rather than offering a list of reasons, she works at making sense of her decision.[9] She points to the pain caused by the work-related traumas as well as to a deeper sense of self that was not harmed by those traumas. By talking about the process of constructing her account and by using negative and hypothetical forms—"I won't say . . . I would be lying if I said"—Denise compares this account to others that she might have developed.[10] She conveys that she is speaking as honestly as she can, and thus implies that the process itself of making sense of her decision is difficult.

Denise's use of metastatements—her talk *about* her account—suggests that this is an instance of disrupted talk. Rather than simply telling the story of leaving (as she told the story of her career), she talks about the process involved in coming up with *this* account. Yet this disrupted talk does not introduce us to the discursive realm of inequality, at least not in any obvious sense. As I discussed in chapter 2, the self-consciousness associated with the discursive realm of inequality is sometimes expressed in disrupted talk: stuttering or stammering uncharacteristic of the speaker or metastatements that interrupt the flow of a story. How, then, am I to make sense of Denise's disrupted talk in this context? The simplest answer to this question is that her account of leaving the superintendency is about professional deviance, moving down rather than up the occupational ladder. The idea of professional failure lurks in the background; it is a possible charge that Denise must listen to and debunk. In this sense, talk about deviance or failure may be similar to talk about inequality. In both cases speakers are highly self-conscious and thus sometimes produce linguistic disruptions. At the same time, however, I suggest that Denise's disrupted talk, her metastatements, may also be related to her later recasting of the traumatic events of the last two years as a story about sex discrimination. Although it is not evident at this point, she finds the process of constructing an account of her decision difficult in part because she is still struggling to come to terms with the discriminatory character of her work experiences.

Shifting Desire from Work to Family

This excerpt directly follows the previous one:

DN: Because there were some mm
it was very traumatic.
And yet uh the *support* and the *kindnesses* and so forth
from many people in the community and the *staff*
and the other four board members
uh it's it's been *wonderful*. [p]
[voice trembling slightly] But I think that this little boy [her
grandson] (CB: hmm) [p]
had a lot to do with
stepping back and uh [p]
sort of trying to put your ego aside and say what's it all about.
(SC and CB: mm hmm)

Here Denise weighs different parts of her experience against each other. By comparing the traumas of the past two years to the support she received from staff, board members, and people in the community, she places those traumas in a broader perspective: they were certainly painful, but they do not constitute the whole story of the past two years at work. She then sets the entire work situation against her experience as a grandmother. In the face of her grandchild's needs, both the positive and negative aspects of the work situation (the pain and the support) come to light as matters of ego. By thinking about her grandson, Denise arrives at what is most important in her life now, or to use her earlier phrase, "the heart of who *I* am."

DN: I'm I'm fifty [years old] uh [p]
and as I analyzed [p]
where I am um [p]
I've always had another mountain to climb. (SC: hm hmmm)
It's always been that way.
And I didn't really see that I *needed* for my *own* benefit another
superintendency. (SC: hm hmm)
In fact with the *demands* and so forth
I was to the point where [p]
I wanted a life of my own.

And and these *these* are the kinds of things that I talked not only
with John [her husband] but with my daughter (CB and SC:
hm hmm)
uh that I *really* wanted some life back so that if I *wanted* to spend
more time with the family and and the support with him [her
grandson] it would be possible.

Through consistent use of *I*—making herself the subject of each
statement—Denise sorts out what *she* desires. Although her statements
point to the societal context in which professional and family commitments frequently conflict, she presents herself as actively rearranging
her desire within that context rather than as being forced to do so.

By using discourse about ambition to narrate her work history,
Denise portrayed her work as being as much for herself as for the
communities she served. In the past she eagerly pursued the career her
mother wanted but couldn't have, always preparing to climb the next
step, the next mountain. Now she feels her ambition has been satisfied:
"I didn't really see that I *needed* for my *own* benefit another superintendency." Moreover, she now experiences the superintendency, in
Lewis Coser's words, as a "greedy institution," one that makes too
many demands and saps her energy.[11] Now Denise defines "a life of my
own" in terms of spending time with her family and grandson. Although she clearly portrays her grandchild (and, in places not cited, the
child's parents) as needing support, she focuses on her desire to be with
them. Her account is about how she is shifting her investment of self
from work to family. In short, she conveys that she is choosing deliberately to leave the job of superintendent for reasons related to her
changing sense of what is important in her life.

Being Responsible to Other Ambitious Women

After describing her grandson's particular situation and needs, Denise
continues:

DN: On the *other* side [p]
um I *weighed* and thought um [p]
"you have *modeled* uh for *women*"
[quickly] I mean what's this going to do for other aspiring women?

CB: Hm hmm how will they see it
DN: how will they see it
> will they see [p] you know it as cope— copping out running whatever.

Here Denise considers the consequences and meaning of her decision for other women who aspire to leadership positions. At this point her account moves directly into the discursive realm of inequality. As one of the few women in her occupation, she has been a role model for other ambitious women and feels responsible toward them. Presupposed in this sense of obligation is her acknowledgment that women have been denied equal access to the professional world. Thus her comments point to gender inequalities that are structured into the professional world, inequalities that she barely mentioned as she recounted her work history.

Throughout her narrative, Denise never once worries that her ambitiousness has violated the conventional ideology that women are not suited to and should not aspire to positions of power.[12] She *is* concerned, however, that her decision to leave the superintendency might violate the contemporary ideology that women *should* seek positions of power. As long as Denise pursued her career ambitiously, she apparently felt no tension between her participation in the professional world and her commitment to a broader struggle for power for women. Here she asserts her responsibility to other women and at the same time opens up the question of how her actions should be interpreted (by herself as well as by others) in relation to that responsibility. She seems to ask, Can a woman leave a powerful position and still fulfill that responsibility? She knows that this is contested terrain and imagines different interpretations of her action. The word *cope*—which appears to be a slip—represents a more generous interpretation than "copping out" or "running."

Debunking the Idea of Professional Failure

Denise continues interpreting her decision:

DN: *Now* whether I would have had that *same* feeling [wanting to leave the superintendency]

had had the two years prior not been as traumatic
I don't know.
My *hunch* is and and John [her husband] tells me
I would I was getting itchy feet to do something else.
He could ‖see it coming‖
CB: ‖anyway‖
DN: any yeah
CB: ‖regardless‖
DN: ‖regardless‖
CB: of the local controversies
DN: exactly exactly
uh and it wasn't that I'd not been through controversy when I first the first year I was here we went through a reduction in force
and *that* became very traumatic
uh but it was a different kind it was *not* the nastiness and the underhandedness (SC: hmm) and the ugliness and so forth (SC: hm hmm) to that as there was to this and it was was not out in the public this is the thing the papers and so forth (SC: hmm) and the cartoons and so on.
Uh I don't know I I think John's probably right
I would have I would have wanted to do something else
and it it still might have been a similar position to what I've to what I've (SC and CB: hm hmm) taken.
Uh this [new job] meant about a $10,000 a year increase
plus the job itself is just ideal [description deleted]
And I *don't* feel I mean if I had gone a year ago I think people might have said "she's running (CB and SC: hmmm) from the situation."
That can't be said now because we're we're on and upward.
CB: That's right.

As if answering her own question—how should my leaving the superintendency be understood?—Denise mulls over and then rejects several possible interpretations of her decision, each of which amounts to the idea that she is running from a difficult situation. She considers whether the traumatic events were the determining factor in her decision and concludes that they were not. She brings in her husband's comment that she would have been ready for a new job anyway and she suggests that she might have sought the same kind of new job. She bolsters her argument by pointing out that prior to the events of the past two years she had successfully handled other traumas, including laying off teachers and staff (reduction in force).[13] Thus, she argues convincingly that her competence in handling controversies and difficulties is not at stake. Given this argument, however, her emphasis on the difference between the traumas of the past two years—nasty, ugly, underhanded, public—and those she had handled previously is puzzling. She seems to want to separate these recent traumas from those that test a superintendent's competence in the job. (Her interest in separating them becomes clear later.) Nonetheless, even as she acknowledges the ugliness of the traumas of the last two years, she resists the idea that they caused her to leave the job.

Furthermore, even though the job she is taking is a step down in terms of the occupational hierarchy (a less demanding job in a different field), Denise points out that it is highly desirable by other conventional standards: her salary will increase by $10,000. Finally, she further supports her argument that she is not running away by noting that the situation in the district has turned around for the better.

By debunking the notion that she has run from a bad situation, Denise undermines any hint of professional failure and cogently presents herself as successful according to the standards of the professional world. She asserts that she did not leave the superintendency because of difficult conditions she faced at work but because she *chose* to do so as a result of her own shifting desire.[14]

Uncovering the Costs of
the Job to Self and Family

Denise turns next to a discussion of the job of superintendent. She points out that the average term of office is only a few years, largely because of the political nature of the work, the difficulty of satisfying various constituencies within the school district.[15] That she has held this superintendency for ten years, Denise implies, is further evidence of her success.[16] She goes on to describe the superintendency as a "twenty-four-hour job" that makes private life nearly impossible. In this discussion, she reiterates and expands on her previous talk about shifting her center from work to family.

DN: We would go to the athletic events the music and sometimes
John would go sometimes not the the major sporting events he
would go with me and one night Friday night
we'd go down to a little local hamburger place here
for a sandwich before going to the basketball game
and we were going to do that first and I said "No, let's not.
Let's wait go to the basketball game and then go get a sandwich
late."
And he said "well all right but what's why why not just now?"
I said "cause I want to have a beer (SC: [small laugh]) with my
hamburger." (CB: hm hmm)
And John said [angrily] "that *damn* school just runs our life."
(CB: hmm)
I said "yeah." [small laugh, throws up her arms]

Like other superintendents, both men and women, Denise describes the job as requiring constant vigilance about her appearance and demeanor, even during supposedly private activities. As Blumberg states, superintendents are perceived by their communities as public property, both in the sense that "[they are] and ought to be accessible, regardless of time, place, or occasion," and in the sense that "[their] personal li[ves] should be above reproach."[17]

This is one of the few places in her account of leaving that Denise uses reported speech to recount a conversation. By doing so, she imports her husband's perspective into her account: "That *damn* school just runs our life." By acknowledging the truth of her husband's statement—"I said 'yeah' "—Denise legitimates his anger about how much the job controls their lives. Not surprisingly, his sentiment is shared by superintendents' spouses in general.[18]

In her work history, Denise used discourse about ambition to present herself as actively pursuing "the next step" throughout her career. Here she suggests that something is askew, even for the most ambitious person, when the job determines one's actions. By showing

how the job has begun to control her life, she makes intelligible her
decision to leave the superintendency and distances herself further
from discourse about ambition.

DN: When I think about my family and what they've done [p] to uh
     promote *my* ca—
     [words spoken emphatically, separately] *John* taught himself to
     type so that *he* could type my papers (SC: hmm)
     when I was going to school undergrad
     and and the *baby-sitting* and the *things* that *he* would do
     that *I* say to him is before his time uh as far as *men* (SC: hm
     hmm) playing Mr. Mom. (SC: hm hmm)
     Uh if I *don't* have to go if I don't have to put them in that position
     and *always* be on *call* to five board members and the commu-
     nity
     isn't it time that I do something now that
     that I can be with *them?* (C: hm hmm hm hmm)

Here Denise describes her family's and particularly her husband's
contributions to her professional success, contributions that are invisible in the professional world. It would be an exaggeration, however,
to hear this as an instance of the two-person career in which one
person, usually a husband, depends on a full-time wife to provide
social, personal, and emotional support for his work.[19] Unlike the full-
time homemaker wife in the two-person career, John Nelson has always worked outside the home. Furthermore, while the professional
man enjoys cultural acceptance of his primary commitment to work
and his wife's primary commitment to supporting him, Denise points
to the unusualness of John's support. Not only has he provided the
personal and professional assistance she needed to have a successful
career, but he also did this long before other men did, long before the
gendered character of the conventional arrangements became a cultural topic. In the "economy of gratitude"[20] that structures gender
relations, Denise is indebted to John for giving more than the culture
at large expects men to give. She is more grateful to him than the
professional man needs to be to his wife.
    When she describes the demands of the superintendency and ex-
presses gratitude toward her husband, Denise points to the broader

societal and cultural context in which she has made her decision to leave the superintendency. Sociologists articulate this context in their discussions of the greedy institutions of work and family and the cultural mandate that women owe their primary allegiance to family.[21] Denise, however, is less concerned about being the object of multiple demands than she is about the consequences and meaning of such demands for the quality of her life. It is not because she is grateful to John that she chooses to devote less of her energy to work. When she legitimates John's anger—"that *damn* school just runs our life"—she is not simply surrendering to his demand for more of her time. Rather, she describes how the job precludes personal life because *she* now desires work that makes room for time with family. She wants a job that is not as greedy of her time, attention, and commitment as the superintendency. She does not want a job that requires her to depend on her family's support while having no time to be supportive in return. When Denise poses the rhetorical question, "Isn't it time that I do something now that / that I can be with *them?*" she articulates a desire to be *with*, not simply *for*, her family.

In reflecting on the commitment to career and ambition that characterized her work life in the past, Denise hints at the detrimental effects of such a commitment, effects that Arlie Hochschild discusses in *The Second Shift.* Hochschild shows that many dual-career couples respond to the heavy demands of professional work by choosing to cut back on the time and energy they put into their families and home life. This choice is encouraged by the professional world, which requires unequivocal commitment, as well as by the culture at large, which accords more esteem to work achievements than family life. While Hochschild is particularly concerned about the effects on children of such a cultural emphasis on work, her argument and concerns also hold for family and personal relationships generally.[22] By deciding to take a less demanding job, Denise chooses to develop her intimate relationships more fully. Such a decision is difficult because it violates both the mandates of the professional world and of the culture at large. In addition, it is particularly difficult for Denise to relax her professional commitment because she has constructed herself and her responsibility to women through discourse about ambition. Her desire for more time with family expresses an interest that may be shared by many men and women professionals. But because there is no well-charted path or vocabulary for this desire, she experiences herself as alone in making this decision.

DN: And um [p] you know if that's if that's being less of a professional careerist [p]
I guess so be it and I guess that's why I was really curious to have [p] research done [p] from *other* women (CB: hm hmm) who would be very honest and candid about that [p] uh to really know (SC: hm hmm)
CB: about leaving the position
DN: hm hmm
CB: by choice
DN: yeah
CB: yeah
DN: in favor of uh *pulling* back a little bit. (CB: hm hmm)

As she concludes her account of her decision to leave the superintendency, Denise articulates her interest in how other women think about such issues. While ambitious men sometimes choose to reorganize their work and family commitments, Denise's curiosity about other women suggests that she is most interested in the gendered meanings and implications of her choice.

In sum, throughout her account, Denise distances herself from her earlier ambitiousness, asserting that she now has a stronger interest in family relationships. She also distances herself from the job, arguing that the superintendency is detrimental to self and family when it begins to control one's life. Moreover, by exposing the family arrangements and support upon which professionals depend for success, she suggests that the ambitious professional often takes from family without giving much in return. As a whole, this extended account explains her decision. She claims that she chose to leave the superintendency because she altered her commitments to work and family relationships. The process of making sense of her decision, then, is a process of articulating a changing sense of self. As she exposes the costs and limits of ambition, she recenters herself and seeks her strength in her intimate relationships.

Denise's account shows how difficult it is for a successful professional to let go of discourse about ambition in the absence of strong discursive alternatives. She must work at making sense of her decision within a cultural context that interprets such a decision as a sign of professional failure. While the discursive realm of professional work provides resources for developing and understanding oneself as ambitious and wholly committed to career, it does not provide a strong vocabulary for "pulling back," for articulating a balance between professional and family commitments. When she wonders how other women have thought about these issues, she conveys how isolated she feels in making this decision.

As Denise lets her ambition go, she also begins to uncover the gender inequalities that undergird the world of professional work, inequalities that generally were absent from her work history. When she worries that leaving a position of power will let other ambitious women down, she tacitly acknowledges that women have not had equal access to such positions. When she describes the unusualness of her husband's strong support for her career, she points to the gendered character of conventional family arrangements. And when she expresses her need for conversation with other women, she conveys her interest in the gendered meanings and implications of her decision. As she lets go of discourse about ambition, then, Denise begins to make use of discourse about inequality.

Despite the discursive difficulties Denise encounters as she makes sense of her decision, she presents herself as desiring and actively choosing a new course for her life. By portraying herself as choosing in accordance with her new desire, she makes this account cohere with her work history on a deeper level. Just as she once actively pursued each new step in her career, she now actively pursues a new course for her life. In both parts of her narrative, although in different ways, Denise presents herself as a strong individual in control of her life choices.

RECASTING THE TRAUMATIC EVENTS
AS DISCRIMINATION

Although Denise has hinted at gender inequality in the profession and in society at large, she has not yet broached directly the topic of sex discrimination. Hence, when she finished her account of leaving the superintendency, I asked a direct question about it.

SC: Just a couple more questions about work stuff uh
      then we'll move on to the next section.
      Um [P] would you say you've experienced sex discrimination
      subtly or overtly?
DN: [p] Till two years ago I would have said no
      and yet I *have*
      and some of it's been overt I've just chosen to put blinders on and
          and go on and not make issue. [p]
      But I think these past two years [p]
      it was so subtle and *ugly* [p]
      that it really hurt
      and you have to *acknowledge* that it was there.

This response echoes in both form and content the beginning of Denise's account of leaving the superintendency. She reproduces the form of that account by making sense of her experience and by talking about the process itself of constructing an account: "Till two years ago I would have said no." She connects the content of the two discussions by focusing on the events of the past two years, and particularly on the pain they caused her. What is new, however, is her description of that pain in terms of sex discrimination.

Denise describes the blinders she used for most of her career as a method of ignoring any discrimination she encountered. But she claims that the ugliness and subtlety of the sexist treatment she experienced in the past two years have made the blinders ineffective. Because she consistently used *I* throughout the earlier parts of her narrative, making herself the subject of her statements, it is noteworthy that she uses the impersonal *you* here: "You have to *acknowledge* that it was there." According to Suzanne Laberge and Gillian Sankoff, a speaker generally uses the impersonal *you* to "downgrad[e] [her] own experience to incidental status in the discourse, phrasing it as something that could or would be anybody's."[23] In Denise's statement, however, her own experience is not incidental; her own experience is the *focus*. Hence, she seems to use the impersonal *you* to place distance between

NARRATIVE STRATEGIES

herself and her statement. This suggests that she finds it painful or at least difficult to acknowledge discrimination.[24]

SC: You're talking about this one board member? [the "jackass" she had mentioned earlier]
DN: Right plus um [p]
    I think that *because* our city government is very closely aligned in many ways with the school
    I think that there were some things that happened through the *city* in the city administration
    that point to that as well.
    But it's nothing that you can be specific about or go put your finger (CB: hm hmm) in their face and accuse them of (CB: hm hmm) it's just been very very subtle. (SC: hmm)
    Um *I* would say that many of our astute [p] community members recognize that as well. [p]
    [louder] And I think that that was basically why many of them wished me well (SC: hmm)
    when I got took when I took another position and particularly an even higher-paying position. (SC and CB: hm hmm [soft laughter])
    It was sort of like uh "up yours" [laugh]
    (CB and SC: [laugh])
CB: yeah ‖yeah‖
DN: ‖it was sort of‖ (SC: hm hmm) um
CB: who needs this
DN: right.

In addition to the board member whose antics Denise described earlier, the city administrators have subjected her to discriminatory treatment of the sort that cannot be fought legally. As in her account of leaving the superintendency, she contrasts the painful events of the past two years with the support of community members who were astute enough to realize what was going on. She cites their support to corroborate and vindicate her perception of the situation.

As she shifts her discussion of the past two years to a focus on sex discrimination, Denise begins to modify her account of leaving the superintendency. Although she already mentioned the salary increase as one of several rebuttals to the charge that she ran from a difficult situation, she zeroes in on that fact here. "Up yours" signifies that taking a higher-paying job is a strong response to discriminatory treatment. Her tormenters will see that they failed to suppress her because she has gone on to a better situation. By laughing and offering supportive comments, Colleen and I bolster this interpretation. But how does this new interpretation fit into Denise's earlier account? If taking a new job is a strong response to sexist treatment, then it can also be interpreted as an action that other women might learn from and thus as fulfilling a responsibility to them. That Denise neither considered this interpretation earlier nor makes the connection here suggests that she has not fully integrated her thoughts about discrimination into her general story of the traumatic events of the past two years.

SC: Yeah are you saying you can't really be more specific about this the city government stuff?
DN: Well I don't know how far you want me to *go*
    uh it's sort of like if [p]
    it it was a lot of subtle stuff
    [quickly] but but I guess yeah uh to back up and give you a little more information some of the accusations uh were th— that *"she* couldn't manage the district" I mean there were there were accusations against the treasurer [a woman] and myself (SC: hmm) uh about finances (SC: hm hmm)
    that that we didn't know how to manage and and so forth and I mentioned the campaign to to uh (SC: right) have me resign.
    Um the implication was you know "because she's female" (SC: hmm)
    And and a lot of a *lot* of uh rumors got back to me about jealousies I mean it it you know it's the *typical* kinds of things. (SC: hmm)
    "Here *she's* making this much money" and uh [p]
    "she's got a *husband"* I mean that actually was some (SC: hmm) some things that that you thought went out a long *time* ago (CB: hm hmm) but was still there
    so all of this

all the problems that were happening then become focused on
    on the superintendent (SC: hm hmm) as a scapegoat (SC: hm
    hmm)
"that woman down there." (SC: hm hmm yeah)
I don't know uh [p]
other than to say
there was just some underhanded kinds of things in the city but
    from the city council president and the mayor
uh that I think helped feed that. (SC: hm hmm)

Here Denise explicitly recasts the traumatic events of the past two
years as a story about sex discrimination. Through this recasting, it
becomes clear why in her earlier account she separated these traumatic
events from those difficulties and controversies that are an inherent
part of the superintendency. (Note that she ties the two accounts together through the words *underhanded* and *ugly.*) While any superintendent could become a scapegoat for the district's problems, could be
accused of incompetence or of making too much money, a man would
not be subject to the accusation that his failures are due to his gender.
In light of this revised story, it is clear that Denise excluded a discussion of sexism from her earlier description of the traumatic events. It is
as if she put blinders on or chose to ignore the sexist treatment in her
first recounting of those events. That Denise does speak about sexism—she does take the blinders off—when asked a direct question
about discrimination suggests at once that she is now ready to look at
the sexism she has encountered *and* that it is not easy for her to do so.

SC: When you say that two years ago you wouldn't have said this
    that you felt you had blinders on
DN: right
SC: [p] why I mean what's ‖been the difference?‖
DN: ‖because it had become *overt*‖
SC: okay
DN: because it'd become *overt* and the fact that uh
    I became the *focus* of of a good bit of *hatred* (SC: hmmm)
    I *couldn't* deny it (SC: hm hmm)
    And uh putting the blinders on is simply a way of saying I'm sure

it was there *before* but it never affected me in a *personal* way
like this did

so I chose to ignore it. (SC: hm hmm)

CB: And this was very public

DN: right

CB: you ‖couldn't ignore it‖

DN: ‖you couldn't ignore it‖ (CB: hmm)

you couldn't ignore it. (SC: hm hmm) [p]

Um [p] and I guess that's why there would be a certain amount of
catharsis to bring together other women who've had ex— similar things happen (SC: hm hmm)

and jus— just to talk about it. (SC: hm hmm)

Denise claims that the blinders strategy failed when the discriminatory treatment became overt and personal, when it imposed itself on
her.[25] When she became the object of others' hatred, she could no
longer choose to ignore the sexism embodied in that treatment. By
using metaphors of force to describe how she came to "see" sexism,
Denise portrays the process itself of acknowledging sexism as painful.

While the *you* in Colleen's statement—"you couldn't ignore it"—
refers specifically to Denise, Denise's repetition of that statement uses
the impersonal *you*. In this case, the impersonal *you* clearly connects
her to other women; she implies that any woman in her place would
find it impossible to ignore such sexist treatment. She concludes by
expressing a desire for conversation with other women about such
experiences.

Denise's story about sex discrimination enters the discursive realm
of inequality in a very different way from her earlier talk about her responsibility to other ambitious women. In that earlier talk, she tacitly
acknowledged that women as a group have been subject to inequalities
structured into the professional world. But she concentrated on her
responsibility to other women in that regard rather than on her own
subjection. By contrast, here Denise presents a specific story about
herself as subject to discriminatory treatment, and she focuses on her
own vulnerability to men's greater power in a male-dominated context. By recasting the traumatic events as a story about sex discrimination, then, Denise reconsiders her conception of self. In both her work
history and her account of leaving the superintendency, she presented

NARRATIVE STRATEGIES

herself as an active agent, as choosing to pursue her career ambitiously, and then as choosing to spend more time with family. At this point, however, she confronts the limits of that understanding of self. She acknowledges that she has been subject to others' sexism and that she has been forced to consider the impact of that experience on her sense of self. Acknowledging subjection is painful not only because it is unjust but also because it disrupts her sense of herself as one who actively chooses and who controls her own life.

Denise Nelson's Narrative Strategy: Letting Ambition Go and Reconsidering Discrimination

Denise Nelson's interview is unusual in that it took place while she was in the midst of a major career change. Her narrative strategy—letting ambition go and recasting past events as discrimination—is certainly shaped by this important circumstance. Her narrative strategy, more than those of the other three women superintendents whose narratives I analyze closely, reflects a changing sense of self. It also suggests that the interview situation itself became an occasion for Nelson to make new sense of her divergent experiences as a successful educational leader and as a woman subject to gender inequality.

In some ways, Denise Nelson's narrative strategy, like Ana Martinez's, reinforces the disjunction between the discursive realms of professional work and inequality. Both women empower themselves through professional discourse and narrate their work histories with little mention of inequalities to which they have been subject during their careers. While Martinez uses discourse about competence and commitment, Nelson draws on discourse about ambition to present herself as a successful professional. It is significant that Nelson is comfortable narrating her work history through this discourse even though at the time of the interview she did not think of herself primarily as ambitious and most of her narrative is devoted to dismantling that discourse. Her comfort in this regard is evidence of the settled and taken-for-granted character of the discursive realm of professional work.

Ana Martinez underscores the disjunction between discourse about professional work and inequality by consistently highlighting her competence and excluding stories about subjection. By contrast, Nelson dramatizes the disjunction by moving from one discursive realm to the other over the course of the interview. As she accounts for her career change, Nelson slowly distances herself from discourse about ambition. And as she loosens her attachment to that discourse, she begins to consider how she has been subject to discrimination. While Martinez excludes stories about her own subjection because she experiences the discursive realm of professional work as making no room for such talk, Nelson includes stories about her own subjection only when she is ready to give up professional discourse as the primary resource for her self-understanding.

By offering an extended account of her decision to leave the superintendency—rather than a brief explanation—Nelson conveys how difficult it is for a successful professional woman to let go of discourse about ambition in the absence of well-developed, culturally supported discourse about balancing work and family commitments. Confronting that lacuna, she slowly unravels discourse about ambition by articulating the limits of a life devoted wholly to career and the costs of a job that impoverishes family life. Through this unraveling, Nelson alters her understanding of the source of her strength and desire, the center of her sense of self. Although she states that she has her family's support for her decision, she also conveys a deeper sense of being alone in her decision. The culture at large, the professional world, and some forms of feminism construct the choice to relax ambition as deviating from their mandates. Nelson wonders how other women would think about the meaning and consequences of her decision.

While the narrative process of unraveling ambition conveys how difficult it is for a successful professional woman to let go of ambition in contemporary American society, the narrative process of redefining past experiences as discrimination communicates how painful it is for a successful professional woman to introduce subjection into her narrative. Acknowledging subjection interrupts her conception of self as actively choosing the course of her life. Denise communicates the pain of this acknowledgment most clearly when she describes not only the sexist treatment, but also the process of seeing it as such, as forced upon her. According to her story, Denise did not choose to acknowledge the sexism she encountered; she wore blinders until they were torn away.

Nelson's narrative strategy reinforces the disjunction between discourse about professional work and inequality in the sense that she talks freely about discrimination only after she has detached herself from discourse about ambition. Yet her narrative also begins to undermine that disjunction in two ways. First, the process of unraveling discourse about ambition shakes its settled, taken-for-granted character. Nelson shows that the individualistic stance embedded in that discourse conceals the family supports upon which most successful professionals depend. And she argues that the strong sense of self embedded in that discursive realm is countered by hidden costs to the professional's self and family. Second, as Nelson considers discrimination she has experienced as a successful professional woman and begins the process of revising earlier stories, she shows how she might integrate stories about professional work and inequality. For example, when she recasts the story of the traumatic events of the last two years as a story about sex discrimination, Nelson clearly presents discourse about professional work as gendered. She acknowledges that others attacked her competence as a *woman* educational leader. A similar attack on a man's competence as a *male* superintendent would be culturally unintelligible. Nonetheless, Nelson does not complete her revisions of earlier stories during the interview. We are left wondering, for instance, how she would revise her work history in light of her present acknowledgment of sexism.

Denise Nelson's narrative is a story in transition. This is the kind of story a professional woman tells when she begins to acknowledge the constraints under which she has told her story in the past, and when she is ready to take the risk of facing (and telling others about) what she will uncover as she revises her story (for example, the pain of understanding the self as subjected). While Ana Martinez's story is told when a professional woman feels isolated from others who might share her experiences, Denise Nelson's story is told when a woman actively seeks others who might share her experiences.

5

Uncovering

Layers of

Vulnerability

and Strength:

MARGARET

PARKER

Margaret Parker is an African-American woman in her late fifties and is currently superintendent in a predominantly Black, working-class, urban school district. Her long career in public education includes teaching and administrative positions in cities across the United States. Unlike Ana Martinez and Denise Nelson, who develop narrative strategies that separate professional accomplishment and discrimination, Parker continually juxtaposes her professional success with her vulnerability as an African-American woman in a white- and male-dominated profession.

In her work history, Parker credits her success to the continuous support she has received from powerful men, and she contrasts that support with one instance of job discrimination she encountered. Over the course of her narrative, she retells the job discrimination story several times; and in these retellings, she slowly uncovers deeper layers of her vulnerability and strength. Parker's narrative strategy of juxtaposing professional success and discrimination undermines in important ways the disjunction between the discursive realms of professional work and inequality. At the same time, however, I suggest that her strategy of slowly uncovering a deeper story about vulnerability and strength represents that discursive disjunction on another level. Overall, Parker's narrative communicates the pervasiveness and depth of her subjection as an African-American woman in this profession, as well as the pervasiveness and depth of the personal strength she summons to deal with that subjection.

WORK HISTORY:
JUXTAPOSING MENTORSHIP
AND DISCRIMINATION

When I asked for her work history, Margaret began by talking about her desire to be a school secretary, a realistic ambition for a Black working-class girl in the 1940s. She described how her mother, two teachers, and the pastor's wife found scholarships and pushed her to attend college where she studied to become a teacher. Margaret's emphasis on the prominent role others played in making her education and upward mobility possible reflects the importance of education to Black working-class families and communities.[1] This emphasis also anticipates the theme of mentorship in her work history.

In addition to teaching, Margaret's early work history included secretarial work (in a city where she was told they "have all the Black teachers they need") and several years in other occupational fields. In describing how she returned to teaching, she used one of a set of expressions that appears throughout her work history: "He just *paved* the way for me."

MP: And then finally decided um
    well I didn't decide truly
    somebody who knew me when I was teaching before said to
    me
    "you need to be in education

you need to get out of that [job]."
And he just *paved* the way for me to go back into education.

This passage captures a primary theme in Margaret's work history: powerful men opened doors and made opportunities available to her. They removed obstacles to upward mobility that Margaret could not remove for herself. Although ostensibly similar to the encouragement theme in Ana Martinez's work history, Margaret's talk about mentorship is distinct. Ana discusses others' encouragement as the context in which she developed a professional identity. By contrast, Margaret talks about others' mentorship as the means through which she gained access to opportunities for increased responsibility and authority.

In addition, notice Margaret's "self-initiated repair":[2] "And then finally decided um / well I didn't decide truly / somebody who knew me . . . just *paved* the way." As we shall see, Margaret is interested in getting the story straight about whose actions—her own or another's—were most crucial in any particular instance.

In what follows, I focus on five nearly contiguous excerpts in which Margaret juxtaposes the support she has received from powerful men with the discrimination story that stands as an exception to that pattern. At this point, Margaret has already recounted her movement through various administrative positions in urban districts across the country.

Asymmetrical Gender Relations and Mentorship

MP: And then there I sat in Lake City
      assistant superintendent
      and *people PEOPLE* began telling me
      that I needed to be a superintendent.
      I didn't tell myself that.
      I *did* tell myself that I needed to be an *assistant* superintendent
      but I did not tell myself I needed to be a principal
      nor an elementary director.
      I didn't tell myself that.
      Other people *people pushed* me into all those positions. (SC: hm
          hmm)

Okay?

But I *did* tell myself I needed to be an assistant superintendent.

SC: Hm hmm you mean other administrators ‖tried to push you into‖

MP: ‖ other administrators‖ would *encourage* me to go for it. (SC: hm hmm)

Somebody was always *pivoting* me to the next place.

SC: Were they mentors?

MP: Oh yes

I had uh I had *great great* mentors yes.

Margaret conveys in several ways that encouragement from others has been a general pattern in her career. She lists the positions that "other people *people pushed* me into." She repeats words and phrases—a constant feature of her narrative style—to emphasize the persistence of others' support.[3] In addition, she shifts from the simple past tense to the conditional and continuous past tenses (as indicated by *would* and *was always*): "Other administrators would *encourage* me to go for it. . . . Somebody was always *pivoting* me to the next place." This shift signifies what Catherine Kohler Riessman calls "the habitual narrative genre" in which "events are not unique to a particular moment in time but instead stand for classes of events that happen over and over again."[4] Margaret also includes one instance in which *she* initiated a job change. By carefully distinguishing her own effective actions in that instance from others' persistently supportive actions, Margaret convinces the listener that mentorship has been a general pattern in her career. Finally, in response to my direct question, Margaret affirms that these supportive people are mentors. She goes on to describe her relationships with three male urban superintendents— one African-American, two white. Then she concludes:

MP: So I had *very* good support

all men (SC: hm hmm)

all men *VERY very* good support. (SC: hm hmm)

And even now and of course the network is much *stronger* now

I can pick up the phone and there are women now we can talk to like [names of three Black women educators].

There are peo—women now that we can call and talk to also. (SC: hm hmm)
But the *men* are the ones who can pivot you into the jobs
'cause they've got all the jobs. (CB: right SC: hm hmm)
And if you don't understand that you don't understand anything you un you see. (CB: yeah)
So uh this is not a situation where women need to try to block out that ma male support (SC: hm hmm)
'cause that's where it is. (SC: hm hmm)
You can't get nothing from nothing. [laugh]

Margaret ends the story about her mentors by discussing how gender structures the field of educational administration. Although she can call on some women now for support, men still occupy and control positions of power. Margaret claims that understanding the fact of men's greater power and accepting men's support are crucial to women's success in the field. Notice that a trace of another way of dealing with asymmetrical gender relations is evident in her statements: she hints that some women *do* block out men's support.

By including one African-American male superintendent among her mentors, Margaret suggests that some Black men belong to the powerful circle in the occupation. That all three women whom Margaret mentions when she speaks about those "we can call and talk to" are Black implies that her strongest same-sex relationships are with other Black women. (Margaret does not state that these three women are Black, but I know that they are because they are well-known educators.) Whatever support she receives from African-American women colleagues, however, is outweighed by the asymmetry of gender relations: "But the *men* are the ones who can pivot you into the jobs / 'cause they've got all the jobs."

Margaret's story about mentors is at once a story about her professional success and a story about asymmetrical gender relations. While Ana Martinez and Denise Nelson limit themselves to discourse about professional work when narrating their work histories, Margaret draws simultaneously on the discursive realms of professional work and inequality. The vocabulary of mentorship belongs to the professional world generally; any professional person's success is facilitated by sponsorship from powerful others. But when Margaret argues that success for professional women resides in cultivating relationships with powerful men, she also draws on discourse concerning the unequal distribution of power and opportunities. This discourse is often used by sociologists who study women in male-dominated professions. For example, Rosabeth Moss Kanter observes that "if sponsors are important for the success of men in organizations, they seem absolutely essential for women."[5] Although Margaret explicitly discusses only gender relations here, race and class relations get implicit acknowledgment. An African-American woman from a working-class family is more likely than others to be excluded from opportunities for mentorship in a predominantly white profession because of "the tendency to offer opportunities for advancement to those most similar in background to the members of already established inner circles."[6] While many professionals depend on mentors for success, Margaret's focus on mentorship suggests that she does not take such sponsorship for granted.

Asymmetrical Gender Relations and Discrimination

At this point I prompted Margaret to talk about her pursuit of the job of assistant superintendent in Lake City. (Recall that she said, "I *did* tell myself that I needed to be an *assistant* superintendent.") This story is an exception to her career pattern in two senses: she went after the job herself, and she encountered discrimination in doing so. At the time, the school administration in Lake City was predominantly white; both the superintendent who discriminated against Margaret and the man he hired instead are white.

SC: But you said you *did* feel you needed the assistant superintendency
MP: yes
SC: and you wanted that
MP: yes
SC: and but why?
MP: Because I was doing the work.
Um I was in the system
I had been watching the system for a long time.
I *recognized* the support that I was giving to the superintendent.

I *recognized* the support I was giving to the school board.
I *recognized* the support that I was giving to the community.
And it was clear to me
that uh there was *nothing* in the role of an assistant superintendent that I could not handle
'cause I was doing it anyway. (SC: hmm)
And so I I *consciously* applied (SC: hm hmm)
and interviewed
seriously interviewed [laugh] for the position of assistant superintendent. (SC: hm hmm)
And truth of the matter is
the superintendent *chose* to not give me the job.

By repeating the phrase, "I *recognized* the support I was giving to,"
Margaret portrays confidence in her ability to do the job; she pursued
the job because she felt she was already doing the work. This is a
familiar story. Many women superintendents reported that they applied for an administrative position when they realized that they were
already doing the work of the position without the title. As she continues, Margaret explains that even though the school board pressured
the superintendent to hire her, he chose instead to hire an old friend.
Here she describes how she responded to the situation:

MP: But I just sat back and let those people do what they wanted to do
      and I always do that.
      I work very hard not to enter into other people's battles (SC:
         hmm) you know (CB: hm hmm)
      I may be at war within myself but I'll keep that within myself
         you know. (SC and CB: hm hmm)

For the first time in the excerpts I have examined, Margaret uses the
phrase "you know." Marjorie DeVault points out that these words
"signal a request for understanding" and "occur in places where they
are consequential for the joint production" of talk in interviews.[7] Although it is easy to infer that Margaret stepped aside and let the superintendent and school board fight over whom to hire, the deeper meanings of these statements are unclear. How can Margaret think that
being denied a job she felt she deserved is an example of "other peo-

ple's battles"? Why does she work hard at not getting involved in that battle? And what is the "war within myself"? With the words "you know," Margaret acknowledges that what she is saying is unclear and asks us to work at understanding her meanings. When she retells this story later in the interview, what she is saying is easier to interpret.

After several months, the superintendent responded to the school board's (and others') pressure by creating an assistant superintendency for Margaret. Thus, she eventually got the job she wanted. Here she recounts how she handled the situation during the interim.

MP: When the guy [who got the job] came on I told him
"I'll do everything I can to help you"
although I knew he had the job I was supposed to have had
he told me the *day* [slaps table] he came to work
he said "I thought I was coming here to be the assistant superin-
tendent for administration
I don't know a thing about running schools
so I'm going to be really relying on you" (SC: [soft laugh])
I said "if there's any way to help you I will." (CB: uh huh)
That's what happens to women. (CB: uh huh SC: yeah)
That's what happens to women you know.
Uh and that's what we do.
Most women
just by the nature of ourselves
we will say
"we'll let this work itself out" you know.
CB: [whispering] It'll work itself out.
MP: And it did it did. (SC and CB: hm hmm)

Margaret's account discloses two senses in which gender shaped the entire situation. First, she describes herself as subject to gender inequality in the occupation: "That's what happens to women you know." Although she does not use the word *discrimination*, the context, along with her use of "you know," invites us to interpret her statement as one that is about discrimination. She suggests that men who lack competence end up in positions that entitle them to exercise power over competent women. Margaret's use of discourse about asymmetrical gender relations exhibits feminist consciousness as Judith Gerson and Kathy Peiss define it: "a highly articulated challenge to . . . the system of gender relations in the form of ideology, as well as a shared group identity."[8] Margaret expresses that shared group identity by subsuming her own experience in that of women in general ("That's what happens to women") and by shifting from *I* to *we* ("*Most* women / just by the nature of ourselves / we will say"). Margaret's use of *we*, here as well as later in her narrative, is striking because most women superintendents did not express their collective identity as explicitly.

Second, Margaret suggests that gender shaped her response to such discriminatory treatment. She understands her generosity toward the man who got the job, as well as her decision to "let this work itself out," as instances of women's nature. Gerson and Peiss describe such an understanding as "gender awareness"—that is, "a non-critical description of the existing system of gender relations, whereby people accept the current social definitions of gender as natural and inevitable."[9] Margaret's use of discourse about unequal power, then, coexists in this story with discourse about gendered natures or identities.

In sum, although Margaret presents this discrimination story as an exception within her work history, she connects the two through discourse about asymmetrical gender relations. In both the discrimination story and her general work history, she proclaims that men have more power than women and that they can use it either to pivot women into jobs or to keep women out. By describing her career in terms of strong mentoring relationships, she indicates that she has successfully negotiated asymmetrical gender relations. Yet by juxtaposing this characterization of her work history with an incident of discrimination, she warns that access to power cannot be negotiated once and for all. The possibility of exclusion always lurks within a male-dominated profession.

As she narrates her work history, Margaret does not separate discourse about professional work from discourse about inequality. Rather, she speaks about asymmetrical gender relations in order to describe both her professional success (through the support of powerful male mentors) and her subjection (her continual vulnerability to men's greater power). While Ana Martinez and Denise Nelson separate talk about professional work and inequality, Margaret constantly juxtaposes her professional success and her vulnerability as a woman in a male-dominated occupation. And while Ana and Denise wait until

NARRATIVE STRATEGIES

we ask before addressing inequality directly, Margaret integrates discourse about inequality into her work history without prompting from us.

Several questions are left unanswered in this part of Margaret's narrative. What is her experience of race relations in the profession? What is the meaning of her response to the discriminatory situation: "I work very hard not to enter into other people's battles"? What is the "war within myself"? How does discourse about unequal power coexist with discourse about women's nature? Finally, if it is unusual for professional African-American women to have powerful male mentors, how has Margaret managed to cultivate such relationships throughout her career?

Placing the Discrimination Story in the Context of Work History and Life History

After Margaret brought her work history up to the present, I asked a direct question about sex and race discrimination. Although she had already described being denied the assistant superintendency and had briefly mentioned discriminatory treatment at two other points, she had not used the word *discrimination*.[10] Nor had she included race in her story about the assistant superintendency.

SC: Okay let me just move back to *one* more question about *your* experiences
uh and you've already touched on this a bit
it's a question about discrimination (MP: hm hmm)
um [p] and different people say different kinds of things about this but [p]
would you say you've experienced sex discrimination or race discrimination?

My interjection—"and different people say different kinds of things about this"—indicates that I am inviting Margaret to move further into the discursive realm of inequality where ideological struggles abound over what counts as discrimination and how discrimination should be handled. My impulse to qualify the question about discrimination conveys my own self-consciousness in this discursive context, my awareness that when Americans talk about discrimination they often attend to the "different kinds of things" that people say about inequality. My interjection is a subtle instance of disrupted talk, similar to the metastatement example discussed in chapter 2.

In her initial response to my question, Margaret once again juxtaposes the story about being denied the assistant superintendency with her general work history. But this time, she also places these two stories in the broader context of her life history. In addition, she interjects a story about interviewing for her current superintendency in River City, a predominantly Black urban district.

Notice Margaret's pauses as she begins. Until this point, and indeed through much of her narrative, there are remarkably few pauses in her speech. These pauses suggest that she feels a direct question about discrimination requires an especially careful answer.

MP: [p] [softly] That's such an interesting question um [p]
in the profession [p]
I have *never* felt that I was discriminated against because I was Black or a female
except when I went for the assistant superintendency.
I *truly* believed that that was discrimination. (SC: hmm)
And ah ah ah [p]
[louder voice] *more* so than the fact that I *knew* that this guy was a *friend* of that superintendent's
I *TRULY* believed that it was sexual and racial discrimination. (SC: hm hmm)
And that was okay that's what he chose to do [small laugh] because I felt like it was going to wash out in the end anyway but I believe that. (SC: hm hmm)
Other than that
I have to say to you honestly no [p]
I said to the youngsters here in River City when I came here to be interviewed at Carver High School
they were saying
"we sure hope you get this job because you're just so down to earth."

I said "well I want to tell you something.
If I don't get the job
it's because I'm a woman
I don't want you all to forget that" [roaring laugh] (CB and SC:
    [laugh])
I told *all* these *people* in this library and the kids and I just said
"if I don't get it (SC: uh huh)
it's 'cause I'm a woman."
But I [p]
[serious tone] *in* the profession you hear me saying in the profes-
    sion because I'm just let's 'cause in my *life* I've had a lot of it
    (SC: hm hmm)
but in the profession
I *do* not believe that has happened to me. (SC: hm hmm)
Isn't that something? (SC: hm hmm)
[laughs] That's the ‖truth‖ (SC: ‖yeah‖)
I as I said I had these good strong mentors who were always
    they were just ‖*clearing*‖ (SC: ‖yeah‖) the path away for [laugh-
    ing] me all the time. (CB: hm hmm) (SC: right)
It just didn't happen.

Margaret affirms that being denied the assistant superintendency
was a case of sex and race discrimination. She uses the word *discrimination* to refer to the superintendent's actions toward her as a Black
woman rather than to describe the consequences of his choice to hire a
friend. At the same time, she asserts that the incident was an aberra-
tion in her work history. In turn, she emphasizes the aberrant character of her work history when seen in the context of her life story: "*In*
the profession you hear me saying in the profession because . . . in my
life I've had a lot of it."[11] Through this comparison, Margaret points to
the relatively safe and privileged environment provided by the professional world. Unlike life in general, the profession holds out the promise of advancement through connections with powerful men.[12] She
suggests that this privilege is available even to an African-American
woman as long as she is able to negotiate asymmetrical gender and race
relations in the profession.

After reiterating the deviant nature of the discrimination story (being denied the assistant superintendency), Margaret comments, "Isn't

that something? . . . [laughs] That's the truth," suggesting that her experiences might have been otherwise. By hinting at the precariousness of her relatively discrimination-free professional history, she corroborates her earlier conclusion about the discriminatory incident: "That's what happens to women you know." In that earlier excerpt, Margaret indicated that discrimination is not unusual in the collective story of professional women's experiences. Here she explains the almost unbelievable absence of discrimination in her own career history by the presence of "good strong mentors who were always . . . just *clearing* . . . the path away for me all the time."[13]

In the middle of this excerpt, Margaret interjects a story about how she raised the possibility of sex discrimination during the interview process for her current superintendency in River City. At first I was tempted to delete this story because it seemed superfluous to the excerpt as a whole. However, following Elliot Mishler's suggestion that we should listen to stories whose relevance is not immediately evident, I found that this one is integral to Margaret's more general points.[14] She had previously told us that the other final candidate for her current job was a Black man who was overly self-assured when he discovered his competitor was a woman. She also reported that his attitude motivated her to become more competitive. In the above excerpt, she roars with laughter as she describes her conduct during the interview process: "I told *all* these *people* in this library and the kids and I just said / 'if I don't get it . . . / it's 'cause I'm a woman.' " In this predominantly Black urban school district, it makes sense that Margaret would speak about the possibility of sex but not race discrimination. The city leaders as well as the school board that hired Margaret were predominantly Black and male. Moreover, the school board was looking for an African-American superintendent.[15]

Margaret's roaring laughter pulls Colleen and me into her experience of the incident; we laugh along with her.[16] By telling this story, she acknowledges that discrimination in the profession is always a possibility. But her pleasure in telling the story represents the confidence she felt as she spoke about possible discrimination. In Marianne Paget's words, "her manner of speaking reaffirms her meaning."[17] Margaret's confidence and pleasure confirm what she is expressing more generally in response to my direct question about discrimination: she has experienced the profession as relatively free of discrimination, as offering opportunities for upward mobility and for exercising her competence as an educational leader. She tells this story, then, to dispel any doubt the listener might have that her work history has been relatively discrimination-free.

Throughout this excerpt, Margaret expands on the ideas she articulated in her work history: although the professional world is structured by gender and race inequalities, she has been remarkably successful. She clarifies the relationship between the discrimination story, her work history, and her life history by presenting each story in the context of the others.

UNCOVERING LAYERS OF VULNERABILITY AND STRENGTH

At this point, I was ready to move to the next part of the interview, but Margaret wanted to return to the story about being denied the assistant superintendency in Lake City. Here we can see how, in Martine Burgos's words, Margaret "exercises her power upon the person who is ostensibly conducting the interview by derealising [her] interventions; capturing [her] attention, neutralizing [her] will."[18] Margaret exercises her power as a narrator not simply in an interactional sense—by asserting herself to say more—but more deeply by retelling the discrimination story. While her initial response to my question about discrimination confirmed and expanded on her first telling of the discrimination story, here she retells the story in a way that uncovers new layers of vulnerability and strength. In the following excerpt, Margaret describes how Connie Johnson—a white woman administrator in Lake City—threatened to file a lawsuit on Margaret's behalf if the superintendent did not hire Margaret as assistant superintendent.

SC: Okay—
MP: Matter of fact there was a woman in in in in uh Lake City at the
    time her name was Connie Johnson
    who had been a part of um a a an action suit
    a class-action suit against the school district many years before I
    went there
    that dealt with sexual discrimination.

And she was white.
And she sat at [laugh] at the conference table one day
and told the superintendent
she said "I want to know what you all are doing with this assis-
    tant superintendency
and I think you need to know Mr. Smith
that if you don't hire Margaret Parker for that job
we're going to fi file a suit against you because you're going to
    be [laughing voice] right back where you were." (SC and CB:
    [laughing])
I said [laughing] I said [dramatic voice of desperation]
"Wait a minute! Don't file it for ME!" [All: laughing]
And she was expecting discrimination and and
[serious voice] it *did* happen it
it *did* happen (CB and SC: uh huh)
it *did* happen.
But she did not file the suit (SC: hm hmm)
because he got her out of that central office so quick it made her
    head swim
and *that* was discrimination also (CB: uh huh)
towards Connie Johnson
because of her exercising her rights
her freedom of speech. (CB: yeah)

Margaret not only gives us new information about the discrimination story, but she also delves further into the discursive realm of
inequality. She augments her earlier talk about asymmetrical gender
relations by portraying herself in the midst of a struggle about how to
respond to discriminatory treatment. Indeed, she forcefully disagrees
with Connie's notions about how to handle such situations. In this
excerpt, then, Margaret explicitly acknowledges that responding to
discrimination is a highly contested issue. Interestingly, as soon as she
introduces an alternative to her own stance—Connie's offer to sue on
her behalf—she rejects it. Her laughter expresses her confidence in
rejecting an invitation to join forces with a woman experienced in
filing discrimination suits.

Why does Margaret mention that Connie is white when race is not
obviously relevant to this story? I suggest two possible interpretations.

It may be that Margaret heard my earlier direct question about race discrimination as an invitation to be more specific about race as she continued her narrative. It is also conceivable that she mentions Connie's race as a way of highlighting their disagreement about the way to respond to discrimination. Margaret implies that Connie assumed that Margaret would take up her support; apparently Connie did not discuss her tactic with Margaret before publicly declaring her intention to sue. In this respect, the story reminds us of tensions that arise between Black and white women when white women assume they understand Black women's experiences and needs.[19]

Immediately after the previous story, I prompted Margaret to speak about why she refused to take up Connie's offer to file a lawsuit.

SC: But but filing a suit
    it sounds like that's not your way of dealing with it
MP: nope not mine (SC: hm hmm)
    other people can do that all they want to.
    Uuuum they're dead-ended. [p]
    Isn't that sad to say but it's *true*.
    They're dead-ended.
    Because you can *win* the suit
    but you're going to [slaps table] lose the war you know.
    You *have* to try to do it other ways. (SC: uh huh)
    And I guess I just fell into a *good* situation where I had people to
       pave the way for me all the time (SC: hm hmm) you know
    just like when he denied me that position
    I just sat back and let that board fight that out [laugh] (CB: hm
       hmm) you know.

Here Margaret develops her stance on the contentious question of how to respond to discriminatory treatment. In her view, legal action is politically unwise and futile. She argues in favor of an alternative method, but, paradoxically, her method sounds like taking no action: "I just sat back and let that board fight that out." This statement echoes her earlier account of her response to the discriminatory incident: "I work very hard not to enter into other people's battles." By placing herself as the subject rather than the object in each of these statements, however, Margaret conveys that she *chooses* not to get involved, that she *decides* to sit back. Contrary to appearances, then, she does not accept passively whatever comes her way. As Patricia Hill Collins observes about Black women's ways of coming to terms with subjection, "silence is not to be interpreted as submission."[20]

Yet Margaret's decision to sit back is dependent on having others to fight it out for her. In fact, she presents the discriminatory situation as re-creating the pattern in her work history of strong support from powerful men. In this case, the school board paved the way for Margaret by stepping in and fighting on her behalf. Her choice to sit back is effective, then, because she already has a history of strong support from men. Thus, her decision not to take legal action rests on her perception that informal networks—specifically, relationships with powerful men—carry more clout than the legal system, even if one has a justifiable complaint. She is most concerned about winning the war—maintaining her professional position so that she can do her work—and feels it is imperative to gauge others' interest in supporting or hindering her.[21] A lawsuit would threaten her relationships with those who have the power to influence her career.

Although Margaret explains that her decision to sit back is effective because she has the support of powerful men, she leaves unexplicated how it happens that she "just fell into a *good* situation where I had people to pave the way for me all the time." That statement conceals how she has managed to cultivate the relationships she needs in order to be successful.

As she continues, Margaret retells the story of how she handled the discriminatory situation on a day-to-day basis when the man who was hired for the job that should have been hers came to work.

MP: And my people who were working with me were saying
    [whispering] "boy how is she doing it?
    how is she taking it?"
    [return to normal voice] Especially when the guy came on board
    [p]
    and he was introduced to the cabinet as the assistant superintendent
    and everybody's eyes sort of propped on me
    and I'm sitting here
    holding back all of my feelings

'cause I'm *very* pained
no question about that (SC: hm hmm)
um [p] but I went right ahead doing my job
and people'd see him and me standing talking together
they'd see us eating lunch together you know (SC: hm hmm)
and uh that's just who I am. (SC: hm hmm)
That's just who I am.

In retelling this story, Margaret pulls back another layer to show the depth of her vulnerability to asymmetrical gender and race relations in the profession. While she has already named the incident as discriminatory, here she speaks of its deeper consequences. For the first time in her narrative, she describes the pain she felt as a result of discrimination.

In order to understand her pain, I need to summarize what we know about her experience of the discriminatory incident. She is certain that what happened *was* race and sex discrimination; she places her experience in the context of race and sex stratification in the occupation; she connects her experience to other women's experiences; and she feels vindicated by the school board's willingness to fight on her behalf. Thus, her pain is not due to any sense of her own responsibility for her predicament. Neither is it caused simply by the loss of a job opportunity. Rather, the source of Margaret's pain is the experience of subjection itself. She is injured by a white man's abuse of his greater power, which he exercises against her as an African-American woman.

The discriminatory incident, then, requires more than a decision about what to do, about whether or not to file a lawsuit. It also requires a response in relation to the injured self. In response to her pain, Margaret performs what Arlie Hochschild calls "emotional work." When Margaret says, "I'm . . . holding back all of my feelings / 'cause I'm *very* pained / *no* question about that," she describes herself as disguising her pain in her public display and interacting with the newcomer as if nothing unusual were going on. In Hochschild's terms, this is "surface acting."[22] Yet Margaret also claims that her generosity toward the newcomer constitutes more than surface acting. It represents her sense of self, her identity: "That's just who I am. / That's just who I am." Thus, she defines herself as one who *will* act kindly (rather than, say, angrily or resentfully) in such a situation. In that respect, she performs the kind of emotional work Hochschild calls "deep acting."[23]

Kesho Yvonne Scott's notion of Black women's "habits of survival" further illuminates Margaret's emotional work. Habits of survival include "the external adjustments and internal adaptations that people make to economic exploitation and to racial and gender-related oppression. Such habits, first and foremost, are responses to pain and suffering that help lessen anger, give a sense of self-control, and offer hope."[24]

The "war within myself" that Margaret referred to earlier can now be understood as the emotional work she performs in response to the pain of subjection, the habits of survival she has developed for maintaining dignity, self-control, and self-respect in the face of discriminatory treatment.[25] By using discourse about identity—"that's just who I am"—Margaret suggests that her habits of survival are rooted deeply in her strong sense of self. Although she excludes from this narrative stories about the many discriminatory incidents she has encountered in her life—because they are beyond the bounds of an interview focused on her work experiences—we can imagine that Margaret has used the same habits of survival many times throughout her life.

In sum, as Margaret retells the discrimination story, she reveals a deeper sense of her vulnerability than in her earlier recounting of it, and she offers a fuller explanation of her response to discriminatory treatment. In this account, she shows that she takes a firm stand within the contested discursive realm of inequality. She describes herself as confidently choosing to sit back rather than fight, a choice geared toward ensuring her professional success in the long run. She is also confident about performing emotional work because that work is grounded in her strong sense of self. Thus, as Margaret retells the discrimination story, she uncovers not only a deeper layer of vulnerability, but also a deeper layer of strength. Unlike Ana Martinez, who uses the discursive realm of professional work to construct herself as powerful, and unlike Denise Nelson, who is in the midst of reconsidering the source of her strength, Margaret turns to discourse about personal identity—a discursive resource outside the professional world—to describe her strength.

In this part of her narrative, Margaret reveals new layers of vulnerability and strength by explaining her earlier talk about the "war within myself" and about her refusal to fight other people's battles. What is still missing, however, is Margaret's account of *her* part in ensuring that she had people to pave the way for her all the time. So far she has been silent about how she has successfully negotiated relations of power in the professional world.

The Deeper Story:
Gendered Identity and the
Negotiation of Unequal Power

As the interview wound down, Margaret commented, "I would imagine we [women superintendents] all say the same thing don't we?" When women expressed an interest in our interviews with others, we took up the invitation to share some of our thoughts. In response to Margaret's comment, I described the encouragement theme that seemed to run through many of the interviews, including hers.

SC: One of the common themes I was thinking of
wh while you were talking
this notion that a lot of the women we have talked to
have *not* gone out to get administrative positions
but have been [p]
pulled into them by other people
not something we had expected to hear (CB: hm hmm)
because you would expect that the women who get to the top
positions in a male-dominated occupation would have to be
extremely am*bi*tious in order to *get* there (MP: hm hmm)
and then we find they're *not* necessarily (MP: hm hmm)
extremely ambitious (MP: hm hmm) to begin with
they're pulled into it.
MP: You know what?
That's because like my friend Connie
if you show a lot of am*bi*tion towards men
they're threatened. (CB: hm hmm)
So they're going to sure push *you* back. [laugh]

Drawing again on discourse about asymmetrical gender relations, Margaret suggests that a woman's professional success depends on how she negotiates her relationships with men. She explains that men feel threatened by ambitious women like Connie Johnson and respond to that threat by pushing them back. As she continues, Margaret fortifies her argument by describing the upshot of Connie's participation in a class-action discrimination suit. Even though the lawsuit was successful and Connie received a promotion, the long-term consequences were decidedly negative.

MP: One thing we do well in education
  [voice change to low, strong voice]
  we take the stories with us you know.
CB: Right.
MP: We *do* carry them on. [p] [return to regular voice]
  Well Connie all of a sudden lost favor with folk
  and folk began to talk about how she was a troublemaker
  and saying to me as I came in
  "I'd be very careful about Connie Johnson 'cause I don't think
    you're her type."
  You know I mean that's what the *white* boys are telling me
  "be careful of that Connie Johnson
  I don't think you're her type."
CB: "Stay away from her" hm hmm
MP: Yeah you know and I'm trying to figure out what all of this is
    about
  and I ask one of my *Black* administrators
  "what's you know she's *very* nice to me what is this?"
  They said "she's just a little sneaky you have to watch her you
    have to watch her."
  It took a long time for me to get all of that together
  by the time I started getting *women* around me
  and I started hearing all of this *history* (SC: hm hmm)
  I began to realize what it was all about. (CB: hm hmm)

Margaret's comment about "tak[ing] the stories with us" seems to refer to Connie Johnson's reputation as a troublemaker. In a more subtle sense it may also refer to Margaret's need to tell Connie's story in order to tell her own. Margaret argues that powerful men use the label of troublemaker as a weapon against those who resist established relations of power. Her specific references to race reveal how race and gender relations intersect in this story. When Margaret first arrived in Lake City, her relation to Connie was mediated by what "the *white* boys [were] telling me." Suspicious of what they said, Margaret solicited information from one of the Black administrators.[26] But what she heard was no more helpful than what the white men had said. Not until Margaret "started getting *women* around me / and . . . started hearing all of this *history*" did she figure out what the problem was. The history was less about Connie and more about the way powerful men were threatened by Connie's willingness to resist them.

By gathering women around her and bringing Connie's story into her own, Margaret links her experiences to other women's experiences. She uses Connie's story to speak about all women's subjection to asymmetrical gender relations in the occupation. In a certain sense, however, Margaret does stay away from Connie. Because men have the power to thwart women who seek equal power, Margaret perceives Connie's discrimination suit as too risky and ultimately futile. Thus Margaret also uses Connie's story as a point of contrast to her own story about success in negotiating relationships with powerful men.

Margaret finally turns to that deeper story, explaining that her gendered identity provides a basis for negotiating relationships of unequal power.

MP: Now you hear me say
　　"I will not file a suit."
　　You hear me say
　　"I will not get into other people's battles." (SC: hm hmm)
　　You hear me say
　　"all I want to do is do my job"
　　and that's the truth. (SC: hm hmm)
　　Well *men* like that. [laugh]
　　And it's not that I was particularly *groomed* that way for the sake
　　　of *men*
　　but that's just how I turned out (SC: hm hmm)
　　you understand? (SC and CB: hm hmm)
　　And uh [p] when a woman is really *pushing* (SC: hmm)
　　that *scares* them. (CB: hm hmm)

That *scares* them. (SC: hm hmm) [small laugh]
Uh no because we were not reared to believe that we could go as
far as we have gone. (SC: hm hmm)
So we don't um [p] for the most part
we don't go in with those kinds of dreams and aspirations. (CB
and SC: hm hmm)
[softly] We just go in to do our job.

Here Margaret finally reveals how it happens that her work history
has been characterized by the support of powerful men. Men like and
are willing to mentor women who do not push, do not file suits, and
do not get into other people's battles. Men support women like Margaret who just go in to do their jobs. By contrast, men are scared by
and thwart the careers of overtly ambitious women like Connie. Margaret's explanation of her professional success coheres with and clarifies her earlier analyses of asymmetrical gender relations in the occupation. Because men control positions of power, women who please
powerful men will reap the privileges of mentorship.

Margaret knows that there is a wide range of discourse about asymmetrical gender relations. Here, more than anywhere else in her narrative, she comes closest to speaking what Mikhail Bakhtin calls the
"double-directed word," which in Jane Hill's description is "discourse
with a sideward glance at the word of another."[27] Unlike her earlier
unequivocal rejection of Connie's offer to file a lawsuit, here Margaret
gives voice to others' objections to her ideas. When she states, "And it's
not that I was particularly *groomed* that way for the sake of *men* / but
that's just how I turned out / you understand?" we can hear her
listening to and struggling against alternative understandings.

Margaret resists the idea that her refusal to make trouble is simply
the result of having been socialized to please men. She also anticipates the objection that her actions are calculated to manipulate men
through feminine wiles. She rejects these ideas by claiming that her
desire just to do her job represents who she is, her identity: "That's just
how I turned out." Even while Margaret acknowledges that her identity has been shaped by gendered socialization—"we were not reared to
believe / that we could go as far as we have gone"—she embraces her
gendered identity and chooses to be the gendered person she has become.[28] Notice that once again Margaret shifts from *I* to *we*, pro-

claiming her identification with other women.[29] These claims echo her statement about women's nature in her first description of how she responded to the discriminatory situation: "*Most* women / just by the nature of ourselves / we will say / 'we'll let this work itself out.' "

Thus, Margaret uses discourse about gendered identity to construct her solid, stable, and strong sense of self. She claims that her identity provides a foundation for her professional demeanor, not only in response to discriminatory treatment but also in her everyday negotiations of unequal power relations. She also claims that her gendered identity is the source of her success in the professional world; through her gendered identity she has managed to cultivate relationships with powerful men. By using discourse about gendered identity, then, Margaret constructs herself as a successful professional woman and an empowered person.

MARGARET PARKER'S NARRATIVE STRATEGY: JUXTAPOSING SUCCESS AND SUBJECTION; UNCOVERING LAYERS OF VULNERABILITY AND STRENGTH

Margaret Parker's narrative strategy includes continual juxtaposition of her professional success and her vulnerability as an African-American woman in a white- and male-dominated occupation. Unlike Ana Martinez and Denise Nelson, Parker does not separate talk about success and subjection; rather, she consistently presents herself as both successful *and* subjected.

This narrative strategy undermines in important ways the disjunction between the discursive realms of professional work and inequality. Parker unsettles the individualistic, gender- and race-neutral character of discourse about professional work by introducing asymmetrical gender or race relations into every discussion of her experiences in the professional world. Beginning with her work history and continuing throughout her narrative, Parker exposes the gendered and racial underpinnings of her subjection and her success. Significantly, she uses discourse about asymmetrical gender and race relations to articulate not only her subjection but also her professional success. She uses this discourse to talk about how she has been successful through powerful men's mentorship, to interpret even the discriminatory incident as an instance of support from men (in the sense that she relied on the school board to fight on her behalf), and to reject the option of a lawsuit because it would threaten her relationships with powerful men. By integrating discourse about inequality and discourse about professional success, then, Margaret Parker undermines the discursive disjunction and presents a cogent narrative of subjection and success.

But there is more to Parker's narrative strategy. As she recounts her experiences over the course of the interview, she retells her stories about professional success and discrimination. When we attend to this movement within her narrative—the slow uncovering of deeper layers of vulnerability and strength—we hear that she begins with what James Scott calls a "public transcript" and ends with what he calls a "hidden transcript."[30] At the beginning of her narrative, when Parker credits powerful male mentors for her professional success, she offers a public transcript, a story that she might tell not only to interviewers but also to her male colleagues and mentors, a story that is wholly acceptable within the professional world because it does not threaten powerful men. But the message we glean when she retells her stories later in the interview is quite different. She slowly uncovers a deeper story about her personal strength in a context of constant vulnerability to men's greater power. This is a hidden transcript, a story that can be told and understood only within a context of trust. When she retells the discrimination story, Parker reveals the pain of discrimination as well as the method she has developed for responding to such treatment. By the end of her narrative, when she finally explains how it happens that *she* has achieved powerful men's support, Parker reveals that underlying that support is her own constant work in cultivating it, work grounded in her gendered identity. She uses discourse about gendered identity, then, to construct her deep personal strength and to portray her ongoing success in negotiating asymmetrical gender relations in the profession.

Contrary to the public transcript she offers first (crediting mentors for her success), Parker's hidden transcript conveys that her professional success is fundamentally the result of her own personal strength and effort. At the same time, she communicates that her success is always precarious because men's power in the profession is pervasive, if not absolute. By moving from a public to a hidden transcript, Parker's narrative represents in a very subtle way the disjunction between the discursive realms of professional work and inequality. Her public transcript—I owe my professional success to powerful men's support—reflects the constraints embodied in the discursive realm of professional work, the constraints on her speech and demeanor in the course of her everyday work. Parker talks specifically about those constraints when she delineates the risks of legal action in response to discriminatory treatment and when she describes her interactions with the man who got the job that should have been hers. In other words, she describes her speech and demeanor within the professional world *as* a public transcript. She carefully avoids any action, like Connie Johnson's, that threatens powerful men's claims to dominance. The hidden transcript that Parker reveals over the course of the interview—I am deeply and persistently vulnerable as an African-American woman in this profession; at the same time I have a deep, solid, strong sense of self that allows me to handle any discrimination I encounter—would never be included in her speech in the professional world. Thus, while Parker's narrative undermines in certain ways the disjunction between the discursive realms of professional work and inequality, her narrative also provides clues that she is more likely to use that undermining strategy in safe contexts outside the professional world than within it. That she moves from a public to a hidden transcript over the course of our four-and-a-half-hour interview suggests that the interview became one such context of trust.

Margaret Parker's narrative is a story about living with multiple versions of her experience. This is a successful professional woman's story about maximizing her efficacy within the professional world by knowing how to say what to whom. It is also a story about the pervasive inequalities that structure the professional world and that constrain her speech. Finally, it is about cultivating personal strength outside the professional world in order to survive within that world. This multilayered narrative is the kind of story a woman tells when she feels that her success is dependent on a public transcript within the professional world, and when she trusts that there are safe places in which she can share her hidden transcript.

6

Using

Professional

Power to

Overcome

Subjection:

KAREN

RHODES

In this chapter I return to Karen Rhodes, the sixty-year-old white woman whose stories introduced chapter 1. During the past ten years, Rhodes has held several superintendencies, all of them in predominantly white, middle-class, small-town districts. In her narrative, she articulates various aspects of her professional power by drawing on discourse about leadership, education, and individualism. At the same time, she continually acknowledges the gender inequalities to which she is subject in her male-dominated profession. Like Margaret Parker, Karen Rhodes integrates stories about professional success and inequality. Indeed, our interview with Rhodes was one of the few in which there was no need to ask a direct question about discrimination because she repeatedly raised the topic herself.

Throughout the interview, Rhodes develops a narrative strategy of using discourse about professional power to describe how she overcomes her subjection and integrates herself into the professional community. This narrative strategy undermines the discursive disjunction between professional work and inequality by stretching professional discourse far beyond its conventional use. Nonetheless, she also reinforces the individualistic character of that discursive realm by couching her efforts to integrate herself into the professional community in individualistic terms. Over the course of her narrative, she communicates her strong desire for integration with her male colleagues and her faith that her professional power and individual strength will aid her in that effort. Her narrative also conveys the isolation she experiences as a woman who struggles alone for that integration.

WORK HISTORY:
CLAIMING LEADERSHIP

When asked about her youthful aspirations, Karen talked about the influence of her family background: "I come by my interest in education very naturally because I come from a long line of preachers and teachers and social workers and people-oriented people." She also mentioned gender-related factors: "I got married very young and went to school . . . and what do you do in the fifties when you're going to school? You become a nurse or teacher." Immediately following these comments, I asked the first in a series of questions about Karen's work history. In this section, I examine Karen's full response to that first question.

SC: Um could you tell us the story of how you got interested in doing administration in education?
How did that happen?
KR: [small laugh] [p] um [p] [speaking slowly and softly]
This is *really* going to sound [p] arrogant
and I don't mean it to be that way but [p]
to tell you the truth I just [p]
you get involved.

Karen begins this story hesitantly and with a disclaimer.[1] Requesting that we not judge as arrogant the self-image she will present, she introduces her story as one of active involvement: "I just [p] / you get involved." Notice the shift from *I* to the impersonal *you*. Suzanne Laberge and Gillian Sankoff explain that when a speaker uses the impersonal *you*, she "assimilates [her]self to a much wider class of people, downgrading [her] own experience to incidental status in the discourse, phrasing it as something that could or would be anybody's."[2] Karen's shift from *I* to the impersonal *you* is a way of connecting her story to those of similarly situated people, perhaps other successful administrators. By minimizing the uniqueness of her story, Karen encourages the listener not to think of her as inflating her importance or accomplishments.

As we will see, Karen's choice of *I* at certain points and the impersonal *you* at other points is significant to what she communicates in her narrative. In order to highlight her frequent use of the impersonal *you* (and to distinguish it from her use of *you* as a personal pronoun) I will mark the impersonal *you* with an asterisk in all excerpts.

KR: [slowly, softly] I'm a person I think who has [p]
strong principles and beliefs
and I was raised that way I guess.
Mainly *you don't grow up in a big family like mine
unless *you you know learn to take a stand
and then stand up for it and and I care.
As I say I come from a family that's always been very very
socially involved and conscious and running for public offices
and things like that and people oriented.
So when *you get into a position
*you start to involve yourself.

Unlike Ana Martinez, Denise Nelson, and Margaret Parker—all of whom grew up in working-class families—Karen describes herself as having acquired in her youth the identity, strengths, and opportunities necessary for leadership. Tacitly acknowledging the effects of her professional, middle-class background, Karen suggests that anyone who comes from a family of preachers, teachers, and social workers would develop a drive (and have access to opportunities) for leadership.

By describing herself as a strong individual who has always been deeply concerned about and actively involved in public service, Karen constructs a positive, powerful self-image. At this point we can begin to understand the meaning of the disclaimer with which she began: "This is *really* going to sound [p] arrogant / and I don't mean it to be that way." A woman who describes herself as a leader, as powerful, sounds arrogant in light of conventional gender ideologies.[3] Although Karen does not make explicit the gendered character of her disclaimer, this interpretation is supported by general cultural knowledge: it is unlikely that a male superintendent would worry about sounding arrogant in telling a similar story. On the one hand, then, Karen presents her story as a counternarrative, as violating the ideology that women are not suited to positions of power.[4] On the other hand, she forestalls derogatory evaluations of her positive self-description by suggesting that anyone with her upbringing would have developed the same strengths. Thus, the impersonal *you* both protects her from the listener's potential disapproval and justifies her self-description.[5]

Nonetheless, Karen does not completely bury her story in a generic account. By alternating between *I* and the impersonal *you*, she simultaneously tells her own story and shows how her story is like others'.

KR: [speaking quickly] First of all I got involved with the union.
I think you'll find that this is *very* very common.
Most people who are administrators have some kind of background where they got involved with the teachers' union.
I was no different.
I was president of my union as I was teaching in a couple different schools
and I got involved in negotiations
and being on negotiating
which gets *you very *into* finding out what the other side of the field fence is all about.

Although Karen speaks almost entirely in the first person here—she uses the impersonal *you* only once—she reports that her involvement in union leadership is typical of most who become educational administrators. As she continues, however, she drops the generic story, at least for a while. In the next excerpt her voice gets progressively louder, as if to reinforce her self-assertions.

KR: I think that I began to think
     "well I could do this this and this"
     I wanted all these things for teachers.
     [louder] I can remember going in and being told I couldn't have a
         job you know
     in the city school district cause I had a little *baby* you know. (CB:
         hmm)
     "Oh sorry we don't hire people you know
     unless the kids are at least a year old" you know
     and then [louder] and then I looked at going to medical school
     and I went up to the university and they said
     "oh gee you're married and got kids.
     Well I'm sorry. We wouldn't let *you* into med school." [laughs]
         (CB: hmmmmmm)
     [louder, slowly] So it wasn't *that* but [p]
     that perspective
     seeing how things were *working*
     and that there was another *dimension* to the operation
     [softly but with great emphasis] and quite frankly the fact that
         there are so many *assholes*
     [laughs] *doing* these things
     I kept thinking
     "*god* there's got to be a better way to do this (SC: hmm)
     if *I* were doing it I'd do this this and this."

This excerpt displays several significant features. First, Karen points to specific experiences through which she began to imagine herself as an administrator. As union president she caught a glimpse of administrators' power, which fueled her desire to be in a position where she could improve conditions for teachers. And at the beginning of her career, when she was a young mother experiencing discrimination while looking for a teaching job, Karen developed ideas about what those changes should include.[6]

Narrative Strategies

Second, Karen talks about discrimination in a particular way. Rather than focusing on the discriminatory experiences themselves—for example, on the pain they caused her or how she responded—she emphasizes how the discriminatory incidents had consequences similar to her involvement in the teachers' union. Through both experiences she began to understand how much power administrators have and that many of them abuse it. She began to imagine what she would do if she acquired such power. Thus, Karen acknowledges her experience of gender inequality but chooses not to dwell on it at this point. She is concentrating on telling the story of how she developed a strong sense of herself as a leader.

Third, Karen begins what will become her persistent use of the expression "you know." While Margaret Parker used "you know" very selectively, at points where her meanings were unclear, Karen uses this expression frequently throughout the interview. Because I have found no specific patterns, I suggest that Karen uses this expression in a general way to reach out to Colleen and me as listeners.

Finally, by offering this account entirely in the first person, Karen conveys the intensity of her desire to do the work she believes administrators should do. She also expresses complete confidence in her ability to do that work. Nonetheless, as she concludes this story in the next excerpt, she speaks haltingly again and reintroduces the impersonal *you*.

KR: [speaking more slowly and softly] And I'm fairly [p]
     you know I I tend to be a person
     and I'm not sure why but [p]
     people *look* to me a little bit you know
     or *you if *you're part of the group pretty soon they say
     "well Karen why don't *you* be the one to go in and talk" or
     "why don't *you* go and negotiate" or you know
     so *you get pushed forward a little bit
     and and I began to think you know (SC: hmm)
     "I could do I could do a better job quite frankly than some of
     them." [small laugh]

Although Karen corroborates her sense of her competence by citing the confidence of peers, she seems hesitant to talk about how peers have pushed her forward. She expresses this hesitance by using the impersonal *you* in a way that departs from conventional usage. Most of the time an easy substitution of *one* for *you* indicates that a speaker is using the impersonal *you*.[7] In this case, however, substituting *one* for *you* produces a comprehensible but clumsy sentence: "If one is part of the group pretty soon they say / 'well Karen why don't *you* be the one to go in and talk.' " The impersonal *you* is awkward here because Karen is giving a specific example of how others treat her. It would have been more appropriate if Karen were describing how others treat someone like her in a situation like this one. This linguistic awkwardness signifies her discomfort in describing herself as set apart from her peers. In other words, this use of the impersonal *you* reiterates Karen's disclaimer: although she wants to present herself as the competent leader she is, she also fears sounding arrogant.

In sum, throughout this explanation of how she moved into positions of educational leadership, Karen presents herself as a strong individual with confidence in her leadership abilities. She experiences the professional world as providing resources and opportunities for exercising her competence and her desire to lead, to get things done, to make changes. As a white woman from a professional, middle-class family oriented toward public service, she focuses on the ease of her move into educational leadership. For Karen, becoming an educational leader was neither a process of acquiring a new identity (as it was for Ana Martinez) nor a matter of gaining access through mentors (as it was for Margaret Parker). Despite the relative ease with which she moved into leadership positions, however, Karen's narration of her work history is actually less smooth than that of most women superintendents. On the one hand, she draws easily on discourse about leadership, competence, and public service—discourse that belongs to the realm of professional work. On the other hand, there is an undercurrent of tension in her use of these discursive resources. The source of that tension seems to lie in Karen's recognition that others might find fault with her assertion of professional power. By introducing her work history with a disclaimer, she conveys both her desire to speak forthrightly about her competence and her fear that her candid speech will be criticized as arrogant. By shifting between *I* and the impersonal *you*, she indicates both that she wants to tell her own story and that she needs to connect herself to other educational administrators in order to protect herself from criticism. This pervasive tension suggests that Karen is highly aware of and attentive to the gendered inequalities that structure the world of professional work.

EDUCATING MEN ABOUT SEXISM

As she brought her work history up to the present, Karen plunged into the discursive realm of inequality by discussing women leaders' responsibility to educate the sexist men with whom they work. This discussion was not prompted by any direct question on our part but arose as we talked about the small number of women administrators in education.

KR: As I say there are some female superintendents
and and one gal who had her Ph.D.
and was out doing it before I was
Nancy Smith and Nancy didn't *last* you know (CB: hm hmm)
but Nancy was always having a you know
if they if anybody said *anything* to her when about being female
and stuff like that
I mean it was right away [slaps her knee] "let's get em" you know
and be hostile.
Oh god you know
things don't change
*your *your job kind of when *you come in is to *educate* people
to what it means to be a woman
and to *laugh* when they when they do those kinds of things
and *not* to make the situation *worse.*
It's to make them *aware* but do it in such a way that *you don't
make them so damn defensive that *you *can't* promote change.

Karen takes a stand on the disputed issue of how women in positions of power should respond to sexist treatment. Drawing on discursive resources provided by her profession, she treats the problem of sexism in the workplace as an educational matter. In this context, she uses the impersonal *you* to include all women leaders in the educational task she outlines. If women seek to change sexist attitudes, the method has to be one that makes people aware but not defensive. Karen introduces her educational stance by criticizing as hostile, ineffective, and ultimately self-destructive another woman superintendent's confrontational response to sexism. After all, "Nancy didn't *last*" as a superintendent. By using educational discourse to solve the problem, Karen presents sexist men as ignorant and women leaders as the ones who know better, as the educators, as the leaders. She argues that men can and will change their attitudes if women teach them well. Although she is working in a male-dominated occupation and workplace—contexts that she recognizes as making her vulnerable to sexism—Karen gives herself and other women the responsibility of educating their male colleagues.

As she continues, Karen describes the male-dominated administrative teams and school boards in the districts where she has held superintendencies. She talks about the feedback she has received from many of the men, who, although initially skeptical about working for and with a woman, have learned to respect her leadership.

KR: *All* the time "*oh* man we were scared we were going
we thought you were going to be just a bitch" you know (SC: hmm)
and and I *am* sometimes. [laughs loudly] (CB and SC: [laugh])
That's beside the point [laughs] you know.
But "we wouldn't be able to talk to you
and and you wouldn't get things you wouldn't you know
you wouldn't get things done" (SC: hmm)
and you know "we were afraid the staff wouldn't accept you"
a lot of that from the board members
you know that the staff wouldn't accept a woman leading them
and stuff like that but (SC: hm hmm)
oh a lot of feedback on that.

Here Karen draws on discourse about socially constructed gender differences to characterize the sexist attitudes she has encountered. While women leaders are confronted by the culturally pervasive stereotype that women are bitchy, unapproachable, and incompetent administrators, men face no corresponding stereotypes. Karen suggests that men's willingness to share their initial misgivings demonstrates that their fears have been overcome and that the stereotypes have dissipated. In short, she argues that her educational method for dealing with sexism works.

Karen also shows her sense of humor, which could be part of her educational stance; she laughs loudly as she acknowledges that "I *am* [a bitch] sometimes." By using *I* in a simple declarative sentence, Karen reveals her comfort with this ironic self-characterization. Nonetheless, she immediately qualifies that pronouncement—"That's beside the point [laughs] you know"—and asserts her broader point: the problem lies in sexist interpretations of women's actions, not in the actions themselves.

When I prompt Karen to say more about how men who are initially apprehensive overcome their fears of working for a woman, she offers the example of how she has already managed to transform her relationship with Joe, the assistant superintendent in her new district. (At the time of our interview, Karen had been in her current superintendency for less than a month.) On the day of the annual meeting (attended by school administrators, the school board, and community members), Karen shared with Joe her concern about whether the school board would pass the proposed budget. She claims that her willingness to show her vulnerability, her worry about failure, "seemed to break a barrier between us." She concludes the story:

KR: That sort of thing starts to happen.
     But *you have to [p]
     you know it's up to *me* to make them trust me too
     and I know that (SC: hm hmm)
     and I [p]
     and *you *want* to *forget* and just operate
     as a as a manager and as a superintendent
     but *you are insensitive I think if *you don't
     and *you and I have to remind myself
     "Karen step back a minute" you know
     that these they have never had this experience before you know
     and so I kid them
     you know I said
     "which one of you guys is going to make sure I got an extra pair
          of nylons" or something or "I'm not going to get a run" or you

know they come in off the street [laughing as she talks] and smell hairspray in the superintendent's office for a while or something you know. (SC: [laugh])
*You've got to start including them.

As in her work history, Karen alternates between explicating this educational method through *I* and telling a more general story through the impersonal *you*. When she uses *you*, she connects herself to other women, acknowledging that they share the problem of sexism and expecting that they share the responsibility for educating men. When she uses *I*, Karen focuses on how *she* puts this educational method into practice.

In this excerpt, Karen develops two salient features of this educational stance. First, it requires effort. Although she would rather forget that gender is an issue so that she could do her work without the burden of having to attend to the difference that gender makes, she argues that a gender-neutral perspective ignores the gendered reality of the situation. By taking the men's point of view—reminding herself that working for a woman is a new experience for most men—she puts her educational method into action. Second, Karen argues that the educational stance works by including men. Her examples of inclusion—showing her vulnerability; kidding them about her need for a supply of nylons (for her many public appearances); commenting on the smell of hairspray in her office—are all related to conventional feminine identity. These examples suggest two possible interpretations. On the one hand, when Karen invites her male colleagues to think of her as a woman, they may become more comfortable with her presence in the workplace as a leader. As Barbara Reskin argues, "Social differentiation is achieved through norms that set dominant and subordinate groups apart in their appearance . . . or behavior. . . . Because of the centrality of differentiation in domination systems, dominant groups have a considerable stake in maintaining it."[8] According to this view, men feel more comfortable when a woman leader behaves in conventionally feminine ways because gender differentiation reminds men of their dominance in society at large. In other words, Karen may be the boss in this context, but she is still a woman. If that is the upshot of her method, we might doubt that Karen is promoting the change she seeks in men's attitudes.

On the other hand, we could interpret Karen's jokes about nylons and hairspray as a way of including men as she constructs a feminine appearance for the public. According to this interpretation, she aims to teach men not only that stereotypes about women leaders are socially constructed, but also that feminine identity itself is socially constructed. Thus, men learn that the appearance created by nylons and hairspray is not naturally feminine. In Simone de Beauvoir's words, Karen teaches them that "one is not born, but rather becomes, a woman."[9]

In either case, by using discourse about education, Karen presents herself as a teacher, as one who uses her power to help others learn. Rather than focusing on how sexism in a male-dominated workplace excludes her, she treats sexism as a problem that calls on her responsibility and competence as an educator.

At this point, Colleen prompts Karen to say more about what men are really worried about when a woman is in charge.

KR: Women as as as authority figures are very threatening I think to
        a lot of them
      and they *don't know* how to relate to it
      it's not their *fault* quite frankly you know (SC: hmm)
      sure it is because they've built the system and a network and
        they've kept us out.
      But here in this office in particular
      I can't single these guys out and say
      "you bastards you know now that I'm here I'm going to"
      ppfff *nonsense* you know. (SC: hm hmm)
      So I think *you have they're afraid of women as authority fig-
        ures
      because they don't know how they're supposed to react
      or how that they should accept them.
      The other thing is that the perception about *women* is that
      [p] *men* you know are *decisive* [pounds fist on table]
      and they're *action oriented* [pounds table]
      and they're *aggressive* [pounds table] you know
      and *assertive* [pounds table] and stuff like that
      women are just *bitches* you know
      if *you* become like that.

So that's a perception that *you have to *worry* about or be *aware*
   of
when *you *deal* with people (CB: yeah)
when *you come across to them.
So *you have to let them know that the decision-making process
   is you know is going to be there.
They're all going to have input into it you know.
And I *think* that's probably the best
the best thing that happens when they get women.
Women I think have a management style
most of them that *I* know
now *some* are not
but but *most* that I know are much more open.
They are much more willing to lis
we're better listeners quite frankly I think than a lot of guys are.

This time Karen uses discourse about socially constructed gender differences to explain that men feel threatened because of their culturally instilled ignorance of and fears about women leaders. The culture invites positive evaluations of men but negative evaluations of women who are decisive, action oriented, aggressive, and assertive. In addition to this cultural explanation, Karen points to men's dominance of positions of power as a related source of the problem: "They've built the system and a network and they've kept us out." Yet because cultural and structural inequalities are systemic, she argues that she cannot blame the particular men with whom she works. She defends a "no-fault concept of institutionalized discrimination" that fixes responsibility on the culture and society at large.[10]

As before, Karen rejects a confrontational and angry stance toward the sexism she faces on an everyday level in her workplace. Although she acknowledges that she is subject to men's use of gendered stereotypes in their interpretations of women leaders' actions, she assumes responsibility for doing something about the problem. Once again, she makes room for educational discourse by treating men as ignorant.

At the end of this excerpt, Karen turns to a description of her management style, which she suggests most women use: giving others input in the decision-making process, listening, being open.[11] This leadership style corresponds closely to her method for educating male colleagues. Listening well and soliciting others' ideas have the same effect as being inclusive and encouraging trust; both defuse men's tendency to interpret women's actions as threatening or bitchy. Moreover, both are unlikely to elicit the criticism that she is arrogant.

In this part of her narrative, Karen uses discourse about socially constructed gender differences to speak directly about sexism she encounters in her male-dominated profession. When she uses educational discourse to treat sexism as a matter of ignorance, she simultaneously asserts her power vis-à-vis her male colleagues and situates herself among them as their teacher. Moreover, when she discusses sexism as a problem that all women leaders face—by using the impersonal *you* throughout these excerpts as well as *we* and *us* in the previous one—she expresses her connection to other women.[12] Interestingly, the only woman Karen names (Nancy Smith) is one whose confrontational stance she criticizes. Karen rejects that stance because it is ineffective; it alienates a woman from those she leads. As in her work history, she exhibits confidence in the efficacy of her leadership abilities.

Finally, by defending a no-fault explanation of sexism and by proposing an educational stance to remedy it, Karen takes a stand within a contentious ideological terrain. Just as she is confident about her competence for educational leadership, she is confident about the efficacy of her educational method. She argues that educating men about sexism is pivotal to women's success as educational leaders, to their integration into a male-dominated profession.

Taking Legal Action
against Blatant Discrimination

Not long after discussing her educational stance, Karen mentioned for the first time her successful discrimination case against some of the most powerful men in public education in her state. Given her insistence that educating sexist men is crucial to women's success in the superintendency, it is interesting that Karen decided that *these* discriminatory actions required the direct resistance of legal action. Also, recall that as part of her work history, she mentioned discrimination she encountered as a young mother looking for a teaching job. In that context, she focused less on the experience of discrimination itself and more on learning about educational administrators' power. By contrast, Karen clearly tells this story of discrimination as a story about subjection and resistance.

She brought up her legal case as she talked about her collegial relations with people in school districts across the state.

SC: So people keep track of where you go.
KR: Oh *yeah.* [loud laugh]
    You should have seen when I won that lawsuit.
    Did I get the letters from all over the state. [loud laugh]
    That was so funny.
SC: ‖Tell us about that.‖
CB: ‖Now what was yeah‖
    what happened?
KR: I sued Richard Stuart
    and Rockville School District
    over a job.
    It was I should let you see the file if I could find it.
CB: That'd be great.
KR: It's it's *so* amazing 'cause it was so *blatant* I guess.

Karen's laughter introduces this as a story of successful resistance. She takes pleasure in her victory, in her triumph over a powerful group of men. Here she names Richard Stuart, a man who carries a great deal of influence in the profession and who was retiring from the Rockville superintendency at the time of the incident. By using *I* in these declarative statements—"I won that lawsuit. Did I get the letters. . . . I sued Richard Stuart"—Karen clearly presents this as *her* story rather than as a story any woman educational leader might tell.

According to her account, Karen had applied for the superintendency in Rockville, was told by the search consultant that she was second on the short list, and discovered later that a man further down on the list was offered the job after the top candidate turned it down. On the advice of her sister, a lawyer, Karen filed a complaint with the Equal Employment Opportunity Commission (EEOC), the federal agency responsible for investigating charges of sex discrimination.[13] She eventually won a substantial out-of-court settlement, which, she said gleefully, "paid for a lot of college for my kids."[14] (Although Karen refers to her legal action as a lawsuit, her EEOC complaint was investigated and settled without an actual lawsuit.)

In the following excerpt, *they* refers to Richard Stuart (the retiring superintendent in Rockville), Bob Nicholson (the search consultant for the vacancy), and Jim Green (president of the Rockville school board).

KR: They just skipped conveniently skipped over me
and went down and started finding everybody else
and reranked everybody and all that kind of stuff (SC: hmm)
in order to get one of the [superintendents] who was in big
trouble in his district
Frank Snow nice guy
one of the good old guys
but he was in deep shit trouble with his board and the community and all that kind of stuff.
Anyway he's been friends with the people in Rockville
and they wanted to find him a job is what it is (CB: hm hmm)
so they went [imitating the sound of shuffling through papers]
"ch ch ch ch ch ch
FRANK YEAH HEY." [loud laugh] (SC and CB: [laugh])

Karen describes these powerful men as deliberately altering hiring procedures in order to offer a job to a friend, one of the "good old guys." She depicts Frank Snow, the superintendent who was given the job, as nice but unable to keep himself out of trouble in his district. Through her comic rendition of the men's reranking of the short list, Karen ridicules their blatantly discriminatory actions and invites us to laugh along with her.

Despite her enjoyment of this story, she quickly turns to a serious discussion of the discriminatory nature of the incident. In the following excerpt, she describes her relationship with Bob Nicholson, the influential educational consultant hired by Rockville School District to conduct the superintendency search, and who was primarily responsible for reshuffling the short list in order to give the job to Frank Snow. Karen's predominant use of *I* in this and the following excerpts indicates that she is concentrating on telling her own story. It also underscores her sense of personal injury.

KR: And see that's I think what *really* concerned me a lot too
     because I had [p]
     I had worked within the system
     and Bob Nicholson's one of the first guys I ever met down there
     when I went to Odessa [where Karen held her first superinten-
        dency]
     you know I mean what do *you know about school budgeting?
     Squat you know (CB: hm hmm)
     and all of a sudden *"holy mackerel*
     I need some *help* here"
     and I did I called Bob and I said "Bob"
     I said "I'm not smart enough to know *what* it is"
     I said "but something's terribly wrong here
     can you come out?"
     And he did and he spent a couple of days with me out there and
     very nice *very* helpful
     always been felt that I had a *very* good working relationship with
        him and everything.
     [louder voice] But you know it didn't stop *them*
     from going to find you know one of *their* good old guys (SC: hm
        hmm)
     and helping him out
     and I just there's a *time* to take a *stand* man you know?

Karen introduces discourse about institutionalized male dominance
to portray the discriminatory treatment she received. Even though she
was judged the top candidate for the job according to the criteria the
men themselves had set, and although she had worked within the
system as evidenced by her story about working with Bob Nicholson
over a difficult school budget problem during her first superintendency, these powerful men passed over Karen and chose to give the job
to a friend in trouble. Karen's use of discourse about male dominance
mirrors that developed by sociologists such as Stanley Lieberson, who
states, "The dominant group . . . uses its dominance to advance its
own position."[15] Karen claims that within this male-dominated occupation both her competence and her relationships with the powerful
have come to naught. As Judith Lorber argues, even if women in male-

dominated occupations reach the friendly circles, they very rarely move into the inner circles of the occupation.[16]

When Karen states, "There's a *time* to take a *stand* man you know?" she draws a line between general cultural sexism and blatant discrimination. While she does not blame the men in her office for what she considers to be their ignorance, she *does* single out and blame her powerful colleagues for knowingly discriminating against her. While she uses discourse about socially constructed gender differences to fault the culture for teaching men that women leaders are threatening, she uses discourse about male dominance to fault these particular men for promoting one of their own at her expense.[17]

Karen's construction of the difference between everyday sexism and blatant discrimination is related to what she expects from others. She presents her relationships with men in the workplace in terms of the development of trust, for which she holds herself responsible. By thinking of them as ignorant, she does not hold them accountable for their sexist attitudes. She treats their sexism as a constraint with which she (and other women in her position) must contend. By contrast, she presents her relationships with Richard Stuart and Bob Nicholson in terms of the violation of already established trust. She already has good working relationships with them; they know her as a colleague. She treats their discriminatory actions not as a matter of ignorance but as an exercise of their dominance.

As she continues, Karen describes her relationship with another powerful man, Stephen Mitchell, her former boss and mentor in another school district. Although Stephen was not directly involved in the discriminatory situation, he carries a great deal of clout in the profession and is close to those who discriminated against Karen. It is here that she speaks most directly about the pain she felt as a result of the discriminatory treatment.

KR: And I called Stephen and I told him what had happened
I think probably the thing that hurt me worse
and I *did* something I *never* should have done
I said to him "you *knew* what was going on"
you know I said "and that hurt me more
you and I sat for many for many hours and talked about"

you know how *his* daughter who is in kind of a a male-dominated
    thing too
she went into medicine
and how tough it was for *her* because of being a female in it
and I said "you *knew* what was going on (CB: hm hmm)
and after we talked about all the things that your daughter you
    know you just" [p]
and I know darn well there wasn't a thing he probably could have
    done about it in his position (CB: right) and everything
and I shouldn't have I shouldn't have bitched at *him*
but it *hurt* me that he'd been my superintendent
I'd been his assistant superintendent (SC: yeah)
for a couple of years and everything else you know
and he just and he didn't he wasn't *straight* up with me . . .

CB: So Stephen didn't tell you what was really ‖going on‖
KR: ‖no no‖ he said "I'll check into it and I'll get back to you" you
    know and whatever else (CB: hmm)
and he just he just smoothed it *all* over (SC: hmm)
and really was *very* evasive and didn't tell me anything
and didn't help and and
let the system go on
and *that* hurt me a lot.

Karen depicts Stephen Mitchell's behavior as a betrayal. Although
she acknowledges that he could not have rectified the situation, she
faults him for evasiveness and failing to offer support. Given the history of their relationship, especially their conversations about the
problems his daughter has faced as a woman in the male-dominated
field of medicine, Karen expected that Stephen would at least be honest
with her. Instead, according to Karen, he chose to cover up his friends'
discriminatory actions, thus affirming his loyalty to them rather than
her.

As in Margaret Parker's description of the experience of discrimination, it is not primarily the loss of a job opportunity that constitutes
Karen's pain but rather her subjection to institutionalized male dominance. She has portrayed herself as a competent educational leader
who is well integrated into the network of professional colleagues. This
conception of herself is violated by discriminatory treatment, by her

vulnerability to men's abuse of their greater power. She depicts the powerful men as excluding her *because* she is a woman. By using discourse about male dominance, Karen argues that she has been judged not as an individual but as a member of "a group that is generally accorded a lesser status."[18]

Unprompted by us, Karen expresses concern about how the EEOC complaint might lead others to label her a troublemaker, and she explains why she decided "to take a stand" despite this concern.

KR: I'd be *crazy* if I didn't think that I
     you know wasn't worried (CB: hm hmm)
     about that impacting on *me* (SC: hm hmm)
     or being looked on as a troublemaker
     you know *all* those things *you think about (CB: right)
     and you know and and the reasons that *so* many people don't take
       any action
     I thought "no this is not right." (SC: hm hmm)
     [exasperated voice] *They're arrogant as hell.*
     Why should they be able to *do* that and get away with it?

Karen is not only hurt but also angered by the injustice she has suffered. In Marilyn Frye's words, "to be angry you have to have some sense of the rightness or propriety of your position and your interest in whatever has been hindered, interfered with or harmed."[19] Certain that she has been wronged, Karen defends herself by drawing on discourse about individuals' legal rights as well as more general discourse about individualism. She calls on the legal system to be accountable to itself, to the rights and protections it guarantees to each individual. She also conceives of her legal action as an individual act of resistance to the arrogant men who control the powerful informal network in her occupation. By so resisting, Karen knows she risks the label of troublemaker; she acknowledges the fears that prevent most people from taking legal action against discriminatory treatment. But backed by certainty that she is right, she refuses to be intimidated by the potential hazards to her career. Pointing to her willingness to take such a risk (and others' fear of doing so), Karen presents herself as an unusually strong and self-reliant individual.

This self-portrayal echoes Karen's earlier statements about growing up in a family where she learned "to take a stand / and then stand up for it." In that context she presented her individual strength as a way of asserting her leadership within the professional community. Here she uses her individual strength to claim her rightful place within the professional community that has discriminated against her.

Throughout this story about discrimination, Karen clearly portrays herself as subject to gender inequality in her male-dominated profession. The pain she describes represents injury to her sense of self as a powerful, well-integrated, educational leader. But while this is a story about subjection, it is also a story about successful resistance to discriminatory treatment. Drawing on familiar discourse about legal rights and individualism—discourse that belongs not only to the professional world but also to American culture generally—Karen takes on the group of powerful men who discriminated against her and wins. She defends the stance she takes within the contested discursive realm of inequality by convincing us that the men's actions were discriminatory, by arguing that she is right to take legal action, and by pointing to the success of her legal action. Nonetheless, she recognizes that the wisdom of such action is debatable and that most women in her situation would not follow her example. While Karen claims that general cultural sexism requires an educational stance that makes men aware but not defensive, she argues that blatant discrimination requires a resistant stance that holds men accountable for the injustice of their actions.

In this part of her narrative, Karen focuses primarily on her relationships with powerful men in the profession. In a less explicit way, however, she also continues to portray her connection to and separation from other women superintendents. By using discourse about institutionalized male dominance to explain the discriminatory treatment she received, Karen tacitly acknowledges her identification with other women. At the same time, by presenting the discrimination story almost entirely in the first person, she subtly communicates both her sense of personal injury *and* her sense of standing apart from other women during this incident. Given her previous pattern of alternating between *I* and the impersonal *you*, of continually connecting her story to the stories of women leaders generally, Karen's predominant use of *I* in this context suggests that she experienced herself as alone and isolated during the discriminatory incident. Significantly, this story includes no talk about other women's support (or even lack of support), except for a brief mention of her sister's suggestion that she file the EEOC complaint. Furthermore, when Karen points out that most women who experience discrimination do not take legal action, she presents herself as separate from other women, as an isolated but strong, self-reliant woman who demands that the community of male professionals treat her justly.

REINTEGRATION INTO THE
PROFESSIONAL COMMUNITY

In the following excerpt, Karen describes the reaction of her peers—the fifty male superintendents in her region of the state—to the news that she had taken legal action in this case. Here she talks about her interactions with these men at one of their regular regional meetings. (Rockville School District, which denied her the job, is in another part of the state and so those involved in the discrimination case were not present at the regional meeting Karen describes here.)

KR: *You walk in and it's you know fifty guys sitting there
        and you know [imitating deep male voice]
        "hey Karen" you know "how's the lawsuit going?" (SC: [small laugh])
        Geez you know (SC: yeah)
        [imitating male voice]
        "don't hang around *Karen*" you know
        "she'll take you to court."
        And there was that kind of stuff (SC: yeah) and everything
        but they knew I meant *business.* (SC: hmm)
        And and now they most of them say
        "man you know it took a lot of guts to do that." (SC: hm hmm)
        And it *did.*

Karen claims that she has achieved her peers' respect for resisting those who discriminated against her. She underscores her individual strength and courage by asserting that "it *did* [take guts to do that]." By framing her resistance in terms of the familiar discourse of individualism, she marshals widespread support for her resistance. Note that when she criticized Nancy Smith's confrontational response to sexist treatment, she implied that Nancy failed to achieve support for her stance. Here Karen intimates that a resistant strategy cultivates widespread support only under exceptional circumstances, only in cases like her own where the injustice to an individual is clear to all. Through these assertions of her individual strength and courage, she appropriates and reinterprets the troublemaker status. Defining herself as brave enough to take on the powerful men in order to protect her rights, she insists that others—her peers as well as the powerful men—have learned to see her in those terms. Later in the interview, she comments that the powerful men in the occupation "don't think *you should buck the system like that"; yet she believes that as a result of her resistant action they see her as one who "will not back down either."

Without prompting from us, Karen moves on to describe how she has maintained relationships with some of the men involved in the discrimination case.

KR: Makes me feel bad too
and I I talked to Frank Snow about that [the man who was given the job that should have been hers]
I you know 'cause *his* name ended up being in the paper and everything (SC: hmm)
and and how *he* was having trouble with *his* board and all that stuff
and I didn't really want that
I said "Frank I can't tell you how *bad* it made me feel
you know I had no intention of ever having that" (SC: hmm)
"and you know I no hard feelings about your being in that job."
You know poor guy he's been I think moved twice since then.

By expressing sympathy toward Frank, Karen tries to undo whatever damage has been done to their relationship by her legal action. She presents herself in a position of strength vis-à-vis Frank and describes him as victimized by the unintended consequences of her action. Although these perceptions of herself and Frank make sense in the context of her legal victory, they are not an inherent part of it.

Another person might have continued to see herself as victimized despite the legal triumph, or might have cut off relations with those involved in the case.

Karen also speaks about mending her relationship with Richard Stuart, the superintendent who retired from Rockville School District but who is still active in public education.

KR: *Richard* likes to hold a grudge
he's he's kind of vindictive
he gets he gets real crazy and wild
but *I* don't I'm not going to allow that to happen
why should I?
So you know when he whenever he was in the area
or he came to Oakton or something like that
I made a point to to be there
and and to talk to him and stuff (SC: hm hmm)
and he's got a mess of kids and I've got a mess of kids (SC: hm hmm)
and they were all in Europe one summer or something
so we talked about that. (SC: hm hmm)
And you know like the other day when he was here for the superintendents' meeting
I walked in you know and he stops his speech and says
"hi Karen"
"hi Richard how're you doing?"

Mending a relationship with a person against whom one has successfully won an EEOC complaint, especially a person who holds grudges, is certainly a challenge. Nonetheless, Karen describes herself as effective here, too. By taking responsibility for restoring her relationships with these powerful men, she makes use of the educational stance she articulated earlier. The process of breaking down the barriers created by her legal action is like that of encouraging the trust of the men in her office. She describes her attempts to transform these relationships from adversarial to congenial ones, as if, as she stated earlier, "it's up to *me* to make them trust me." By taking responsibility for reintegrating herself into the professional community that discriminated against her, Karen asserts herself once again as an educational leader vis-à-vis her colleagues. With the successful legal case behind her, she expects that others have gained respect for her competence as a professional and as a strong individual.

Nonetheless, Karen gives a subtle hint that she has not fully overcome her experience of subjection. When she describes how she worked at mending her relationships with Richard Stuart and Frank Snow, Karen does not talk about the two men whose actions caused her the most pain: Bob Nicholson, the search consultant who was primarily responsible for reshuffling the short list, and Stephen Mitchell, her former boss and mentor who failed to come to her aid.

Karen Rhodes's Narrative Strategy: Using Professional Power to Overcome Subjection

Throughout her narrative, Karen Rhodes integrates talk about her professional strengths and talk about the inequalities that women educational leaders continually encounter. She develops a narrative strategy of drawing on discourse about professional power and individualism to articulate how she overcomes and resists those inequalities. This narrative strategy organizes her discussion about educating sexist men as well as her story about resisting blatant discrimination. She employs educational discourse to treat men's sexist attitudes as a matter of ignorance and to endow herself with the power to disabuse them of their sexism. When she confronts the limit of educational discourse in the blatantly discriminatory incident, she points to institutionalized male dominance in the profession; and she draws on the broad cultural discourse of individualism to claim that her rights have been violated, to assert her membership as an equal within the professional community, and to portray herself as a strong, self-reliant individual brave enough to take on the powerful informal male network.

While Margaret Parker also integrates discourse about professional work and inequality, Parker's and Rhodes's narrative strategies move in opposite directions. By the end of her narrative, Parker has distanced herself from the discursive realm of professional work as a resource for articulating her strength. She slowly reveals that her deepest strength lies outside that realm in her solid and stable gendered identity. Over the course of her narrative, then, Parker *limits* the value of the discursive realm of professional work; by contrast, Rhodes *expands* its purview. Compared to the other three women whose narratives I have examined, Rhodes exhibits the greatest commitment to that discursive realm, the greatest faith in the efficacy of her professional power and individual strength to overcome her subjection and integrate herself into the professional community.

Unlike Margaret Parker, then, Rhodes includes within the realm of professional discourse her efforts to reduce her subjection. In so doing, her narrative strategy stretches the discursive realm of professional work far beyond its conventional use. She makes discourse about educational leadership and individualism conversant with her interest in educating the sexist men around her, resisting blatant discrimination, and becoming integrated as an equal with her male colleagues. Unlike Ana Martinez, Denise Nelson, and Margaret Parker, Karen Rhodes presents herself as a professional woman who directly confronts the inequality she encounters. Although she clearly prefers an educational rather than a confrontational approach to sexism, Rhodes points to the conditions under which she believes confrontation becomes necessary. Indeed, she is the only one among the four who has taken legal action in response to blatant discrimination. Parker and Martinez tell stories about equally blatant experiences of job discrimination, but each pursues nonlegal, nonconfrontative solutions to the problem. (Among the twenty-seven superintendents we interviewed, only one other woman had taken legal action in a discriminatory situation.) Importantly, Rhodes's EEOC complaint is grounded in her faith that such action will bring her further inside rather than push her to the outskirts of the male-dominated professional world. (Recall Margaret Parker's statement that those who take legal action against discrimination are "dead-ended.")

Rhodes argues that by using her professional power—as a competent educational leader, as a strong, self-reliant individual—she succeeds in overcoming her subjection and integrating herself into the professional community. When she cites her colleagues' comments about how their fears of working for a woman have been overcome, she provides evidence that her educational stance works. And when she points to the reputation she has earned among her immediate colleagues as one who has the temerity to stand up for herself even if that entails legal action, she proves that her resistance to discrimination is efficacious. Moreover, she claims that her educational stance has been effective in restoring her relationships with some of the men involved in the discriminatory situation.

On a general level, Rhodes's narrative strategy undermines the disjunction between the discursive realms of professional work and inequality by integrating talk about her professional strengths and talk about her subjection to pervasive cultural sexism and institutionalized male dominance in the occupation. Specifically, her narrative strategy challenges the gender-neutral character of the discursive realm of professional work by stretching it to include discussion of sexism and ways to remedy that problem. This stretching is most evident in her argument that her responsibility as an educational leader includes educating her sexist colleagues.

But Rhodes's narrative strategy also reinforces the individualistic character of the discursive realm of professional work. This comes to light most clearly when we notice the changes in her use of *I* and the impersonal *you* over the course of her narrative. In her discussion of educating men about sexism, her use of the impersonal *you* indicates her connection to other women. She uses this grammatical form to assert women's collective responsibility as professional educators to educate sexist men. By contrast, in her discussion of blatant discrimination, the impersonal *you* disappears almost completely. Rhodes's shift to an almost exclusive use of *I* corresponds to her use of individualistic discourse in this part of her narrative. In this regard, her discrimination story exhibits the same conflict that characterizes the stories of Emily Abel's interviewees, academic women who have filed discrimination complaints: the "conflict between . . . the individualism that underlies both the legal and educational systems, and the collectivism inherent in any political protest."[20] While Rhodes argues that she has been discriminated against on the basis of gender, and while her use of discourse about institutionalized male dominance shows her identification with other women, she articulates her complaint as an individual protest and her resistance as a matter of individual strength and courage. Although some might interpret her legal action as an instance of "me too!" feminism[21]—as representing an interest in becoming a part of the male-dominated system without attempting to change it—an equally plausible interpretation is that

NARRATIVE STRATEGIES

seeking recourse through the legal system requires individualistic discourse.

Rhodes's narrative communicates her strong desire for full and equal participation in the professional community. It also subtly conveys the cost of the individualistic stance that is required for integration into that community. That cost is separation from other women who might share her experience. In comparison to her detailed stories about specific relationships with male colleagues, the sparse appearance of women colleagues in her narrative is striking. (Rhodes briefly mentions that her sister encouraged her to file the EEOC complaint; she talks about but also distances herself from Nancy Smith; and she mentions conversing with Stephen Mitchell about his daughter.) This sparseness is related, of course, to the fact that women educational leaders have few women peers and that those few are geographically separated from each other. And it is exacerbated by the fact that so few women actually file legal complaints, even when they feel they have experienced blatant discrimination. In turn, these conditions may further encourage Rhodes's use of individualistic discourse to portray her efforts at integrating herself into the male-dominated profession.

Karen Rhodes's narrative is the kind of story a successful professional woman tells when she feels that her professional power and her individual strength are her greatest resources in her struggle against inequality. It is also the story a woman tells when she feels she is alone in that struggle.

The

Larger

Story

Part
THREE

7

Individual

Solutions to

the Collective

Problem of

Inequality

In chapters 3 through 6, I analyzed four women's narratives using methods that diverge from conventional social science ways of listening to interview talk. Rather than searching for themes in the content—cataloging *what* women educational leaders have to say about themselves as accomplished and subjected persons—I attended to patterns in *how* each woman tells her stories, patterns in her manner of speaking, and patterns in her use of settled and unsettled discourses. I focused on how she brings together or separates her experiences of achievement and discrimination. In other words, my analyses centered on each person's narrative strategy in relation to the disjunction between the settled discursive realm of professional work and the unsettled discursive realm of inequality. This method of analysis also altered how I heard the content; it produced a fuller understanding of what each narrator conveys about her ambiguous empowerment in the white- and male-dominated profession of educational leadership.

The four women employ diverse narrative strategies and communicate different experiences. Nonetheless, a certain commonality collects them, and that commonality conveys a larger story. As the title of this chapter intimates, the larger story is about women superintendents' primary commitment to professional work itself and their construction of individual solutions to the collective problem of inequality. Although this larger story will likely strike a familiar chord with many readers who are professional women, it does not circulate widely in our culture. The more commonly heard story is about successful women's co-optation by the white- and male-dominated systems in which they work. In this chapter, then, I give the story about individual solutions to inequality a hearing, distinguishing it not only from the co-optation story but also from the activist story, which is about collective solutions to gender and race inequality. Furthermore, in order to understand the structural and discursive conditions that inhibit women school superintendents from developing activist stories, I return once again to their narratives, this time focusing on how they discuss their relationships with other professional women.

In addition to exploring the character and general implications of this larger story, this chapter reiterates the theoretical and methodological themes of the book. This study has brought to light the disjunction between discourse about professional work and discourse about inequality as a significant cultural phenomenon shaping professional women's work narratives and self-understandings. Beginning with the idea that cultural phenomena are embedded in everyday speech in ways that we tend not to notice, I have sought to expose that discursive disjunction and its effects rather than simply reproduce it in my discussion. Thus, my method of inquiry concentrates on the relation between culture and self-understanding as it is embodied and expressed in talk: how narrators use cultural discourse to make themselves intelligible to themselves and others, and how they struggle with discursive constraints in order to produce meaningful self-understandings.

Before turning to the common pattern and the larger story that collects the four narratives I have examined, let me summarize how each of the four superintendents wrestles with the discursive disjunction and what that wrestling communicates about her work experiences.

As she recounts her work stories, Ana Martinez highlights her professional competence and excludes experiences of subjection related to her ethnicity. By sharply separating talk about achievement and discrimination, her narrative strategy reproduces the discursive disjunction. Indeed, this narrative strategy preserves more than others do the settled character of the discursive realm of professional work. Nonetheless, by telling us that she is leaving subjection out, Martinez draws our attention to the problematic character of professional discourse. She informs us that when she makes conventional use of that discursive realm, she is not telling the whole story. Thus her narrative conveys her sense that the professional world makes no room for her stories about subjection, and it communicates her isolation as a Hispanic woman professional.

Denise Nelson's narrative strategy also reinforces the discursive disjunction by separating the story of her ambition from the story of her experience of sex discrimination. However, as she lets go of discourse about ambition in her account of leaving the superintendency, she begins to unsettle the individualistic character of the discursive realm of professional work. Nelson shows how professional discourse conceals the family supports upon which successful professionals usually depend, and she argues that the strong sense of self that professionals develop is countered by costs to their family relationships. When she finally speaks directly about her past experience of sex discrimination, she begins to recast her work stories to include the inequality she has encountered. Her narrative communicates how difficult it is for a successful professional woman to let go of discourse about ambition and how painful it is to acknowledge and articulate the self as subjected.

Margaret Parker's narrative goes further than Martinez's and Nelson's in unsettling the discursive realm of professional work. She continually juxtaposes her professional success and her subjection, and she introduces inequality into every discussion of the profession. Parker presents the profession as a world of inequality. Over the course of her narrative, she slowly reveals that her deepest strength lies not in discourse about professional work but in discourse about her solid and stable sense of self, particularly in her gendered identity. Parker's narrative communicates the pervasiveness and depth of both her vulnerability and her personal strength as an African-American woman in educational administration.

Karen Rhodes's narrative strategy stretches the discursive realm of professional work far beyond its conventional use. She draws on discourse about educational leadership and individualism to articulate how she overcomes everyday sexism, resists blatant discrimination, and integrates herself into the professional community. While her narrative conveys her faith in the efficacy of professional power, it also communicates her isolation as a woman struggling alone for equal treatment in the professional world.

THE LARGER STORY

Despite their diversity, these narrative strategies exhibit a common pattern: they partially dismantle and partially preserve the individualistic, gender- and race-neutral character of the discursive realm of professional work. All four women use discursive resources provided by the professional world to articulate their strengths, resources that are not available to those in other occupational contexts (for example, people in working-class jobs). These superintendents embrace their competence and accomplishment and genuinely enjoy their success. Although Margaret Parker's deepest sense of personal strength lies outside the professional world, she speaks confidently of her competence as an educational leader. And even as Denise Nelson detaches herself from discourse about ambition, she defends her professional accomplishments. By embracing the discursive resources provided by the professional world, these educators overcome the gendered and racialized prohibition against women's achievement in a white- and male-dominated world, a prohibition that paralyzed the narratives of accomplished women in earlier generations, as Carolyn Heilbrun and Patricia Meyer Spacks have shown.[1] Through that embrace, women superintendents claim their achievements as individuals, just as their white male colleagues do.

At the same time, all four women declare that their competence and success within the professional world is not the whole story of their work experiences. In one way or another, they acknowledge their experiences of gender or race discrimination and recognize that gender and race inequalities affect what happens to them as professionals. Unlike their white male colleagues, they are alert to the possibilities of sexist or racist treatment.

While they use a range of specific discourses to recount experiences of discrimination, these educators share a general orientation to the discursive realm of inequality. In recognizing their subjection to gender and race inequalities, they acknowledge that they share similar experiences with other women; and thus they express, implicitly or explicitly, identification with women generally or with women of their race or ethnicity. Every expression of that collective identification challenges, in greater or lesser degrees, the individualistic, gender- and race-neutral character of discourse about professional work. Hence, these educators undermine that settled, individualistic discursive realm to the extent that they interject into their work narratives their collective identification with other women and their acknowledgment of collective subjection. Margaret Parker's narrative displays this undermining clearly when she uses *we* to connect herself to other professional women and when she introduces gender or race asymmetries into every discussion of the profession. Similarly, Karen Rhodes integrates stories of subjection into her narrative about professional success and uses the impersonal *you* to indicate women leaders' collective responsibility to educate the sexist men with whom they work. When Denise Nelson expresses her desire for conversation with women who have had experiences like hers, she clearly exhibits her collective identification with other women. And when she recasts past experiences as discrimination, she begins to integrate subjection into her work narrative. Even Ana Martinez's narrative hints at this undermining. Although she excludes stories of subjection related to her ethnicity, she conveys her identification with other women of color by acknowledging that racial and ethnic inequities exist. Moreover, by telling us that she is leaving out stories of subjection, she invites us to hear her narrative as partial and to imagine the stories that she would tell under different circumstances, stories in which her acknowledgment of the collective character of subjection might become more explicit.

Despite their recognition of subjection and their expressions of collective identification, these educational leaders partially preserve the individualistic character of the discursive realm of professional work.

Individualism is reflected not only in each woman's discussion of her professional competence and accomplishments, but also in how she presents her response to sex or race discrimination. None of these four superintendents draws on her identification with other women as a source of support for collective action in response to discriminatory treatment. In these narratives, collective identification is limited to understanding the collective nature of subjection. In responding to discriminatory treatment, all four women construct individual solutions. Martinez looks for the professional advantages in men's treatment of her as a white, middle-class, good old boy; Nelson leaves the superintendency to take a less demanding but higher-paying job; Parker relies on powerful male colleagues' support; and Rhodes seeks individual recourse through the legal system. With the exception of Nelson, whose decision to leave the superintendency indicates a partial withdrawal from her professional commitment, these educators' actions are aimed at ensuring their integration within the profession.

This pattern—the partial dismantling and the partial preservation of professional discourse—collects the four narratives and communicates a larger or more general story about women educational leaders' work experiences. That story is about their primary commitment to professional work itself, to what they need to do in order to do their work well. That commitment includes finding ways to deal with discrimination they encounter so they can get on with their work. The larger story conveys this message: as an educational leader, I have access to professional power that I use to make a difference to children's education in my community. At the same time, as a woman in a white- and male-dominated profession, my power is limited, uncertain, and ambiguous because I am continually subject to gender and racial inequalities. I am well aware that I share that subjection with women in general or with women of my race or ethnicity. Nonetheless, *I* control my response to that subjection. How I respond to discriminatory treatment affects my relations with male colleagues and so is an important component of my professional success, my ability to do my work well. Because I am most interested in making a contribution as an educational leader, I choose to deal with discrimination in a way that is active but not activist, that is individual rather than collective. I struggle in my own way with the inequality I experience in order to preserve the relationships and conditions necessary to carrying out my professional commitment. I seek my own individual solutions to the collective problem of subjection, solutions aimed at maximizing my integration so I can get on with my work.

In this larger story, the individual struggle for equality is essential, but also secondary, to the primary commitment to professional work. While professional commitment is an end in itself, the struggle for equality is a means to that end.

Women who hold positions of power are often accused of being co-opted by the white- and male-dominated systems in which they work. Conventionally, co-optation means securing upward mobility by denying connection to one's gender or racial group, espousing the values of success and individualism in ways that preclude that collective identification. Such accusations arise not only in popular culture, as in characterizations of powerful women who "act like men,"[2] but also in feminist theory. Some contemporary theorists reject earlier feminist analyses on the grounds that the social change they propose amounts to women's co-optation by male-created systems. For example, Mary O'Brien argues that the world Simone de Beauvoir holds out to women in *The Second Sex* is one in which women must imitate men: "There is no way of escape, except by an undignified catch-up scramble along the paths which men have beaten."[3] Likewise, Jean Bethke Elshtain criticizes Betty Friedan's *The Feminine Mystique:* "Her book is a paean of praise to what Americans themselves call the 'rat race': she just wants women to join it."[4]

In the larger story we are hearing now, however, embracing individual achievement does not inevitably produce co-optation. Women educational leaders resist co-optation by the white- and male-dominated system in which they work by treating the struggle for equality as essential to their professional success. At the same time, by constructing individual solutions to the collective problem of inequality, they limit their challenge to that system.

In contemporary American culture, the story of successful women's co-optation—of women acting like men, of caring only for their own success, of denying subjection shared with others—is more fully articulated and more frequently heard than the story that women superintendents (and, I imagine, many other professional women) struggle to tell about their professional commitments and individual solutions to inequality. This is so, in part, because the latter story is easily missed if we do not know how to hear it. As we have seen, women superintendents do not recount that story directly but communicate it indirectly through their narrative strategies. In other words, we hear that "muffled story"[5] not by listening primarily to what they talk about, but by attending to their narrative strategies, how their narratives dismantle and preserve the individualistic character of the discursive realm of professional work. The fact that no concise label is available for this larger story signifies its lack of articulation in the culture, its muffled character.

In order to characterize this larger story more fully, I compare it to two other stories that are sometimes told by or about professional women: the co-optation story and the activist story.

The Co-optation Story

When I asked Denise Nelson a direct question about whether she had experienced sex discrimination, she responded:

> [p] Till two years ago I would have said no
> and yet I *have*
> and some of it's been overt I've just chosen to put blinders on and
>   and go on and not make issue. [p]

By portraying herself as having worn blinders—as having pushed experiences of discrimination out of her consciousness—Nelson describes a co-optation story. (Note that she does not actually *tell* such a story; rather, she points to an earlier time when she would have told one.) The blinders metaphor fits a stance that a number of researchers have identified: some successful professional women deny that they have experienced any form of discrimination.

In reviewing autobiographical accounts given by twelve successful women at a conference on women and success sponsored by the New York Academy of Science in 1972, Arlie Hochschild found that although they talked about male colleagues or teachers who had discouraged their ambitions, they often concluded by denying that they had suffered any discrimination at all. For instance, one woman stated that "her thesis adviser was 'totally unsympathetic to career women' and left her to do her thesis work alone; but she also notes: 'I cannot say that I face any unique problems in the profession because of my sex.' "[6]

Hochschild explains successful women's denial of discrimination in terms of their marginality in a male-dominated world. In order to secure acceptance as competent professionals, they must work against negative stereotypes of women in general—for example, that women cannot think analytically and are not as committed to work as men are (women quit their jobs to have babies; they move when their husbands move). A woman's denial of discrimination is another attempt to disconnect herself from the group *women* in order to identify herself with professionals in general.

Judi Marshall found a similar contradiction in her interviews with women in the male-dominated management levels of book publishing and retailing. When asked directly, many women claimed that being a woman had not been an important factor in their careers; some claimed it had been an advantage. Marshall discovered, however, that at other points during the interviews, many women contradicted these statements with explicit references to working in "a man's world," coping with discrimination, and foreseeing career obstacles. She analyzes such contradictions as "muted awareness": "This group allowed that there are potential disadvantages to being women, but believed that awareness of this increased the likelihood of such disadvantages becoming significant. To cope, their strategy was to disregard these issues in their surface consciousness, and so to mute their awareness of being female."[7]

Like Hochschild, Marshall argues that this strategy required professional women to differentiate themselves from women in general. They sought recognition as individual professionals, recognition that their male colleagues take for granted.[8] The stance of "muted awareness," of denying discrimination, constitutes co-optation in that it attempts to achieve professional success by sacrificing identification and connection with other women.

Wendy Hollway makes sense of co-optation in relation to dominant cultural discourses. "By positioning themselves in these discourses [those that 'do not accommodate any concept of sexism'], women can refuse to admit sexism."[9] In the terms I have developed, the denial of discrimination suppresses the dilemma created by the disjunction between the discursive realms of professional work and inequality. By encouraging gender- and race-neutral speech about individuals' competence, the discursive realm of professional work inhibits discussion of how gender and race matter in the professional world. When women deny discrimination, they embrace professional discourse in ways that attempt to avoid the discursive disjunction.

A co-optation story conveys this message: as a successful professional, I have certain competencies and expertise, and I have access to professional power that I use to make a significant contribution to my field. I chose professional work because I wanted to make those contributions, not because I wanted to prove anything about women in general or to advance a so-called feminist cause. I am aware that some women may experience sexism or racism. However, I have avoided such treatment by fitting in and winning acceptance from my male colleagues. My success is due to my competence, my impeccable professional manner, and my refusal to participate in inflammatory talk about women's issues, inequality, racism, or sexism.

Researchers such as Hochschild, Marshall, and Hollway are generally sympathetic rather than accusatory toward professional women's co-optation stories. They focus on the structural and cultural conditions that encourage such stories: women's marginality in the professions and the culture's perpetuation of negative stereotypes about professional women. Nonetheless, they find such talk problematic and seek ways to push professional women toward fuller consciousness of their situations. To use George Rosenwald's and Richard Ochberg's term, these researchers imply that a "better story" is possible:

> Individuals and communities may become aware of the political-cultural conditions that have led to the circumscription of discourse. If a critique of these conditions occurs widely, it may alter not only how individuals construe their own identities but also how they talk to one another and indirectly the social order itself. Discourse mediates between the fate of the individual and the larger order of things.[10]

When professional women tell co-optation stories, they "display the scars" of the inequitable conditions in which they work.[11] The denial of discrimination represents the wounding experience of marginality. The narrator of a better story, however, reflects on rather than ignores those conditions. Given that discourse about race and gender inequality has achieved some measure of public currency over the last few decades (in tandem with recurrent backlashes against it),[12] successful professional women in contemporary American society are not compelled to tell co-optation stories. Indeed, the larger story that women educational leaders communicate through their narrative strategies is better than the co-optation story. Like the latter, it presents a primary commitment to professional work itself and what is needed in order to do that work well. The difference, however, lies in women superintendents' acknowledgment of their subjection to gender and race inequalities and their collective identification with other women. By describing their experiences of both achievement and subjection, they wrestle with rather than avoid the discursive disjunction. They present their individual struggles against discrimination as essential (if secondary) to their professional commitments.

There is a subtle but significant difference between denying experiences of discrimination (as in a co-optation story) and excluding such experiences from one's narrative. As in Ana Martinez's case, excluding talk about subjection is a strategy that makes sense in some narrative contexts. The careful listener does not get the sense that Martinez is wearing blinders as she narrates her work experiences; rather, her exclusion of subjection signifies that this interview did not provide a safe context for such stories. Furthermore, when Martinez talks about the exclusion, she indicates that she might include stories about her subjection in other contexts. By contrast, a narrator who denies discrimination is paralyzed by her experience of subjection to the point of failing to address it altogether.

This subtle difference between denying and excluding discrimination highlights the value of narrative analysis for interpreting interviews or other forms of self-report. Without careful attention to the patterns in Martinez's narrative as a whole, I might have interpreted her exclusion of talk about subjection as a denial of those experiences; I might have missed her invitation to hear her narrative as partial, her implication that she might tell a different story in another context. In other words, decontextualized strips of talk present interpretive barriers. Listen, for example, to a woman lawyer's response (as cited by Cynthia Fuchs Epstein) to a researcher's question about "problems of advancement in large firms": " 'The only way I can function is to ignore precisely the questions that you've been asking me!' "[13] When heard by itself, this statement sounds like a choice to wear blinders, to mute awareness of gender inequities. Yet it may have arisen in a narrative context that discouraged rather than invited consideration of sex discrimination. In this regard, it is noteworthy that the autobiographical accounts Hochschild analyzed were public presentations at a conference on women and success. It is possible that this narrative context—primarily public and professional—inhibited talk about subjection. In order to interpret women's speech as denying discrimination, as co-opted, researchers need to take the narrative context into account. What sounds like co-opted speech may be a public transcript, a carefully honed account designed to protect the speaker from an audience that she has reason not to trust.[14]

Women superintendents produced the story about individual solutions to inequality in the context of in-depth research interviews. For many (but not all) women, the interview created a safe space, a context in which hidden transcripts about gender and race discrimination could be recounted. Yet the larger story conveys the importance to professional women of public transcripts, ways of speaking and acting in the professional world that do not threaten male colleagues and that do not seriously undermine the discursive realm of professional work. Among the four women whose narratives I examined in depth, Karen Rhodes risks the most overt resistance to institutionalized male dominance by filling an EEOC complaint. Yet even Rhodes offers a hidden transcript during our interview. It is safe to speculate that when she tells most of her male colleagues about her successful legal action, she does not hoot with laughter as she did in announcing it to us during the interview.[15] I imagine that within the professional context she keeps hidden the extent of her pleasure in having successfully resisted institutionalized male dominance. By constructing individual solutions to the collective problem of inequality, women educational leaders produce a better narrative than a co-optation story, but it is a constrained and muffled narrative nonetheless.

The Activist Story

In an activist story, the narrator moves beyond acknowledging collective subjection to gender and race inequalities to drawing on the strength that lies in collective identification and the power that lies in collective action. An activist story presents collective rather than individual solutions to inequality. But this move presupposes a more fundamental shift. Rather than articulating ways to deal with discrimination so one can get on with one's work, an activist story treats the struggle for equality *as* one's work. An activist story brings that struggle itself to center stage.

In *Gender Shock,* Hester Eisenstein compares Australia and the United States in terms of how "the river of the women's movement has changed the landscape" in each country.[16] In so doing, Eisenstein points to the professional contexts in which activist stories have been most likely to develop in each case.

In Australia, she claims, feminism has cut its deepest channels within governmental bureaucracies. "Entry into the public service in state and commonwealth government has . . . been the target of choice for feminist activists since the period of the Labor Government of Gough Whitlam in 1972–75."[17] These activists, known as "femocrats," have achieved positions of power in which their tasks are more or less directly related to issues of concern to women, not only affirmative action but also social welfare generally. Most significant for my analysis is the discursive development that accompanies the femocrat phenomenon: "That feminist sympathies and commitments of the kind that can be documented in a resume have come to be considered a bona fide job qualification in state and federal bureaucracies is one of the more remarkable achievements of the Australian women's movement."[18]

As government bureaucracies have been altered structurally to include jobs oriented toward issues of inequality, the vocabulary for talking about government work has also changed. With feminist activity showing up on their résumés, bureaucrats now speak publicly about feminist work in ways that were precluded in the past. This is not to imply that the femocrat phenomenon is devoid of controversy. Australian feminists debate its meaning and consequences—for example, whether it has produced significant social change or has simply given a greater number of professional women access to positions of power. In any case, it is significant that the debates themselves have moved into the professional world, a move that seriously undermines the disjunction between the discursive realms of professional work and inequality. When it is possible to speak about feminist work as constituting one's professional qualification, about feminist commitments as belonging on one's résumé, then it is possible to articulate the struggle for equality as one's professional work.

Nothing like the Australian femocrat phenomenon exists in the United States. Instead, "one of the most visible and successful effects of the women's movement has been the growth of Women's Studies programmes. These have proliferated across the country and have continued to operate, if not to prosper, during the political backlash of the Reagan-Bush era."[19]

Women's studies programs provide one context in which the struggle for equality constitutes professional work, in which feminist work constitutes professional qualification.[20] The arenas for that struggle include the classroom, research projects, university committees (such as those concerning curriculum, hiring, and tenure and promotion decisions), and professional organizations.[21] That women's studies programs aim for social change—of curriculum, research, theory, academic institutions, and women's lives—is deeply embedded in the various vocabularies justifying their existence. For example, criticism of the androcentric character of conventional curricula, pedagogical practices, and scholarship infuses women's studies rhetoric.

Those who participate in women's studies programs know how explicitly ideologically charged any speech or action is in that context.[22] Debates abound within women's studies programs concerning how much social change they have accomplished; whether they have forgotten their roots in the women's movement; whether they have been co-opted by the institutions that support them; whether feminist scholarship serves all women or only women scholars' individual careers; which feminist ideologies are most desirable or practical; how feminist principles should be translated into action; how women's studies programs can attain their goals within institutions that range from accommodating to hostile; and whether women's studies programs, practices, and theories are exclusive or inclusive of diverse groups of women.[23] Whatever the upshot in any particular case, to the extent that they integrate such debates into their ongoing activities, women's studies programs challenge the disjunction between discourse about professional work and inequality. They provide a site within the male- and white-dominated professional world in which discourse about gender and race inequality unsettles conventional discourse about objective, gender- and race-neutral practices in teaching, research, and theory, as well as in educating, hiring, and evaluating faculty. As in the case of the femocrat phenomenon, the changes are both structural and discursive. Whether integrated into the power centers of the institution or remaining on its edges, women's studies programs have become part of the structure of academic institutions. Moreover, in one form or another, an activist discourse animates and justifies their existence and activities.

Eisenstein argues that the women's movement has been most successful in areas in each country where a "pre-existing channel" had already been cut. Women's studies programs have flourished in the United States but not in Australia because of differences in the two countries' academic institutions. Unlike Australia's "austere and traditional" educational system, higher education in the United States allows some room for interdisciplinary curricula as well as curricula oriented to social change. Likewise, in Australia the women's movement has achieved its most visible success in the area of least resistance. The Labor Government's success in the early 1970s cut a "pre-existing channel" into government bureaucracies.[24]

Eisenstein acknowledges that her general observations ignore other important influences of the women's movement in both countries. It is clear, for example, that her analysis focuses specifically on professional worlds. Nonetheless, her argument helps me to make a significant distinction within the professional world in the United States. Generally speaking, academia, more than many other male- and white-dominated professions, provides structural and discursive conditions that allow the struggle for equality to come to center stage. Thus women academics have greater access than many other professional women to activist discourse that undermines the discursive disjunction between professional work and inequality. In no way do I mean to minimize the ongoing battle to achieve professional recognition, respect, and legitimacy for feminist teaching, research, and theory within specific disciplines as well as in academia generally.[25] Rather, I mean to point out that such a struggle has not emerged to the same extent as an integral part of the public vocabulary of other American professions as it has in academia. While women's studies programs give academics the option of striving to integrate their interest in equality with their professional work, similar opportunities are scant in much of the white- and male-dominated professional world.

A caveat is important here: descriptions of the work educational leaders do (as well as the work that doctors and lawyers do) may include the rhetoric of fighting inequality that others experience, such as students of color and female and working-class students. Fierce debates now rage within the public educational system about the necessity and feasibility of multicultural and gender-fair curricula, separate schools for African-American boys in urban areas, equitable funding for rich and poor school districts, and the applicability to the public school context of laws prohibiting sexual harassment. But that rhetoric rarely extends to consideration of inequality experienced by women and people of color who administer and teach within public schools. In the world of educational administration, some may conclude—as Ana Martinez does—that it is more important to challenge the inequalities facing students than those that permeate the profession. After all, as powerful educational leaders, Martinez and other women have made it into one of the most privileged strata of the labor market. Yet that stance reinforces the professional world's taken-for-granted claim to gender- and race-neutrality, that it is immune to inequalities that pervade the rest of the social world. When professional women fight against the sexism and racism they experience, they reduce the gulf between themselves and the disadvantaged people they serve. Activist discourse, such as that developed by women's studies programs, challenges institutionalized male and white dominance in all areas of concern to the profession—for example, the education, hiring, and evaluation of academics, as well as the curricula, research, and theory created by academics.

An activist story, in any professional context, conveys a message like this: we exercise the competence and power we have as professionals in relation to needed social change. We integrate the struggle for equality into our ongoing, everyday responsibilities. Our competence includes knowledge about how gender and race inequalities infuse the institutions in which we work and the society in which we live. Our power includes access to resources that can be employed in initiating social change. Equally important, we are not alone in this struggle. Success in our professional work, in the struggle for equality, depends on collective action, on a community of colleagues who work together. We know that the nature of the discrimination each of us faces is specific, and we know that the kind of inequality we encounter within the professional context differs from the inequality that others experience, such as students, clients, or patients. We acknowledge our privileged status as professionals, our greater access to power and resources. However, we do not separate ourselves from those we serve by pretending that the professional world is free of sexism and racism while proposing that the worlds that others live and work in are not. We fight the discrimination we face in the professional world as well as that encountered by those we serve. In so doing, we fight both for ourselves and others. Finally, we do not fool ourselves by thinking that we are immune to discriminatory action and speech. We exercise our activism with respect to our own practices as well as the practices of others.[26]

The collective *we* narrates the activist story. Relations among supportive colleagues provide the foundation for collective action directed toward social change. That the struggle for equality *is* one's professional work depends, in part, on collective power.

What would activist discourse in the world of educational administration sound like? It would move beyond the limited focus on less privileged students as suffering inequalities from which the professional world is supposedly immune. It would also move beyond women's individual struggles for fair treatment and access to jobs and opportunities. Instead, it would articulate connections among all forms of inequality within the profession and within the institution of public education: the small number of white women and people of color in leadership positions; sexual and racial harassment faced by students, teachers, and administrators; funding, curricula, and employment policies skewed to the interests of white, middle-class boys and men. If the work of educational administration were to become a struggle for equality in this sense, activist discourse would be central to superintendents' dealings with school boards, community groups, teachers, students, university departments of educational administration (where administrators are educated), as well as with their colleagues. Developing and maintaining such discourse would require a community of like-minded leaders.

Individual Solutions to the
Collective Problem of Inequality

Women superintendents' story about the primacy of professional commitments and individual solutions to the collective problem of inequality makes sense in a context where so few women reach the top of the occupational hierarchy and where those few are geographically dispersed: out of 10,683 K–12 superintendents nationwide, only 594 are women, an average of about twelve women per state.[27] This structural condition—this isolation from each other—certainty inhibits the possibility of developing activist discourse. However, this feature of the profession coexists with an equally significant one. As the number of women has increased slowly in male- and white-dominated professions over the last twenty years, women have organized informal and formal groups for professional and personal support as well as to push for changes within their occupations. This is certainly true of women in public school administration.

Contemporary feminist theorists and researchers identify relationships among women as a critical site of study, a site that conventional social science research has distorted or concealed.[28] While many point to constant conflicts among women of different generations, races, ethnicities, sexual orientations, or social classes, they also treat women's relationships as a site of potential support, consciousness raising, or collective action.[29]

*Women Superintendents' Relationships
with Women Colleagues*

At some point in each interview, Colleen and I asked the superintendents about sources of support. If, in that context, a woman did not talk about professional organizations for women or about women's informal networks, we usually asked a direct question about her participation in such groups. Out of the twenty-seven women we interviewed, all but two spoke about the importance of professional or personal support from either formal or informal women's groups or from relationships with women peers. Nor surprisingly, there was quite a range in how they described seeking and giving that support. A small number have exercised leadership in starting and directing professional organizations for women educational administrators on the state or national levels. (Such professional organizations often include women at all levels of the administrative hierarchy as well as teachers who aspire to administrative positions.) Others spoke of active participation in such groups—for example, giving keynote conference speeches and leading workshops. Those who limit their support of women's organizations to paying membership dues feel that their needs are not met in that context because such organizations generally cater to the interests of women at earlier career stages. In order to address their particular needs as women educators at the top of the occupational hierarchy, many women superintendents turn to informal groups or relationships with women peers. For example, several women talked about making a point of having breakfast or dinner with other women superintendents at regular statewide and national professional conferences. And in one state, the few women superintendents developed a strong informal network among themselves in addition to participating in the statewide professional organization for women in educational administration, which has two hundred members. The small informal group held monthly meetings that were both professional and social in nature.[30] Finally, many superintendents mentioned their efforts to mentor younger women and the fact of not having had a woman mentor or role model themselves. (A few of the younger women we interviewed—those in their thirties—did have women mentors.)

As these educational leaders talked about the importance of professional women's relationships, they interwove either direct or indirect references to ideological struggles rooted in their relationships. For example, they described debates about whether and how women's professional organizations should include men, how such organizations should go about helping women gain greater access to opportunities and upward mobility, and whether achieving greater access for women would lead to social change. They also mentioned ideological issues that emerge in male colleagues' responses to their participation in such groups. For example, many women reported that men warned them about the danger to their careers of being perceived as radical or feminist. While some women asserted that male colleagues openly disapproved of their involvement in even the most informal get-togethers with other women, a few reported that men encouraged such participation. In short, women educators' talk about their relationships with other professional women belongs to the explicitly ideological, unsettled discursive realm of inequality. Presupposed in their various forms of relating is their collective identification as persons who share similar experiences in a male- and white-dominated profession. While mentoring and networking among men are unnoticed, taken-for-granted aspects of the male-dominated professional world, women superintendents who seek any kind of support among themselves inevitably find themselves implicated in one or another ideological debate about inequality in the profession.

This description of the simultaneously significant and contentious nature of women educational leaders' professional relationships corresponds to that offered by many studies of women who work in male-dominated professions.[31]

Overlapping Readings

How does this talk about the importance of women's professional relationships coexist with the story we have heard about individual solutions to the collective problem of inequality? The methods of narrative analysis allow for a strong answer to this question. Close attention to how women superintendents narrate their relations with women peers reveals a significant pattern. Like the rest of the women we interviewed, Ana Martinez, Denise Nelson, Margaret Parker, and Karen Rhodes spoke with varying degrees of enthusiasm about the importance of women supporting other women within the profession. However, all four of them separated that discussion from their specific stories or talk about their own experiences of discrimination. As I analyzed the four narratives, I noticed that when they recounted their own experiences of subjection, they spoke relatively little about other women, especially about other women's support. By relatively little, I mean little in comparison with their talk about women in other parts of the interviews. It bears emphasizing that in chapters 3 through 6, I focused specifically on the parts of the interviews where women offered their work histories and talked directly about their own experiences of discrimination. Although it is not surprising that there would be little talk about other women in their work histories, given the male dominance of educational administration, I was struck by the absence of supportive women from stories about experiences of discrimination.

A woman would need most the support of women peers during those experiences.

This finding has implications for any research based on intensive interviews. If I had limited myself to conventional qualitative methods of analysis, methods that require the dissection of interviews into pieces and the location of themes across interviews, I would have detected only the general pattern articulated earlier: women educational leaders speak with varying degrees of enthusiasm about the importance of relationships among professional women. But I would have missed the juxtaposition of this talk with the absence of supportive women from their stories about their own experiences of subjection. I would not have noticed that their collective identification with women lacks embodiment in stories of support among women when they narrate their own experiences of discrimination. The absence of such stories comes to light when the interviews are heard as narratives, specifically, when different parts of the interviews are heard in relation to each other through overlapping readings.[32] By attending to that narrative juxtaposition, I can offer a fuller interpretation of the place of professional women's relationships in their work experiences and of the conditions that discourage them from developing activist discourse.

Hence, I turn once again to the four narratives that form the core of this book. This time I present them in a sequence that shows a rough continuum from weakly to strongly developed relationships with other professional women. While none of the four mentioned supportive women as they discussed their own experiences of subjection, this absence becomes most poignant in Margaret Parker's and Denise Nelson's narratives because both include (at other points in their interviews) well-developed stories about strong relationships with women colleagues. I begin, then, with Karen Rhodes and Ana Martinez, whose talk about other professional women suggests less well-developed relationships.

The Unfulfilled Desire for
Supportive Relationships: Karen Rhodes

In chapter 6, Karen Rhodes expressed her identification with other professional women by using the impersonal *you* to include them in the responsibility of educating sexist men. Yet the only woman she named as she talked about this collective responsibility was Nancy Smith, the superintendent whose hostile and confrontational response to sexism Rhodes criticized. As she told the story of her EEOC complaint, Rhodes shifted from the impersonal *you* to a predominant use of *I*, a shift corresponding to the discourse of individualism that she used in that part of her narrative. Significantly, she mentioned no women as either supportive or unsupportive as she told the discrimination story, apart from her sister, a lawyer, who encouraged her to file the complaint. She narrated that story as primarily about her subjection to institutionalized male dominance, her individual resistance, and her success in reintegrating herself into the professional community.

Nonetheless, at several other points in the interview, Rhodes spoke about some of the other women superintendents in her state. As she talked about these peers, however, she focused not on her relationships with them but on their professional competence. For example, she repeatedly described Belle Anderson in admiring terms as "a mover and a shaker," and in several different contexts she spoke with great respect of Mary Fuller's leadership abilities. Toward the end of the interview, Colleen asked explicitly about sources of professional support that Rhodes had not already mentioned. She had already talked quite a bit about the professional organization for superintendents (all men except for her) in her region of the state. In response to Colleen's question, Rhodes stated:

KR: [P] I've enjoyed very much watching the the ranks of women grow
and and I I *regret* very much not being able to to have more access to them you know.
But it sure is nice to [p] be someplace where there are one or two other women who are who have experienced some of those same things that *you have you know.

Here Karen speaks of her unfulfilled desire for strong relationships with her few women peers, a desire related to women's common experiences in the profession. But as she continues, she addresses tensions that might arise among them. In the following, she is talking about

Mary Fuller who, like Karen, had just moved into a new superintendency at the time of our interview.

KR: Mary got the job at Canton.
    And I you know it it made me very happy for her
    and I *like* to see her making the same progression. . . .
    It made me *feel* better than if *I* would be the only one that goes
        out and gets a bigger district you know because
    then I think sometimes
    I don't want *them* to think that I feel like I'm [p] better than they
        are or a bigshot or something like that you know.

These statements echo a theme Karen developed in her work history. While she feels confident about her competence for leadership
positions, she fears that others might find her arrogant. In her work
history she spoke of this fear with respect to male colleagues; here it is
in relation to female colleagues. In a competitive and hierarchical profession—some superintendencies are more desirable than others—
Karen is concerned about the way other women perceive her success.
But notice the abstract or hypothetical character of this concern: she
does not speak about specific relationships or actual comments she has
heard. Rather, it seems that she is not close enough to any of her
women peers to know how they feel about her success or to have the
opportunity to discuss issues of competition.

Karen's next statements are among the most emotional of the entire
interview:

KR: But I don't want any distance to grow between us
    I want us to be unified
    and sometimes I think I feel way too strongly about that to tell
        you that truth.
    And I and I get almost emotional about it but [p]
    *you have to have been there I guess and
    *you have to have been lonesome and you know
    like going through the lawsuit and [p]
    been told you know that *you can't do this because
    *you're you know *you've got babies at home or

*you're a woman or
*you have to have *been* there before *you appreciate [p]
where *you are I guess and how much we have to hang together.
And I'd like nothing *better* than to be part of a a good old girls'
network you know.

When she worries about distance growing between herself and women colleagues, Karen tacitly acknowledges the consequences of the individualism encouraged by the professional world. Competition for desirable jobs and scarce recognition presupposes a focus on one's own competence, accomplishments, and success. Similarly, the individualistic stance Karen presented in her discrimination story facilitated her reintegration into the professional community while downplaying her connections with other women. Yet her wistful statements in this excerpt also express Karen's intense identification and her desire for strong relationships with women colleagues. (Notice that she revives the impersonal *you* in this context.) This explicit talk about her unfulfilled desire allows us to hear a new layer of meaning in that earlier discrimination story: given the absence of strong relationships with other women, Karen's only option when confronted by blatantly sexist treatment is an individual solution. This overlapping reading—my interpretation of this talk in relation to her discrimination story—suggests that her individualistic stance is related at least in part to the lack of strong relationships among her women colleagues. The absence of support from other professional women in Karen's discrimination story, then, does not indicate a lack of interest in such support but reflects her sense that women's professional relationships have barely developed at all.

Participating in Women's Organizations
without Receiving Support: Ana Martinez

In chapter 3, we heard Ana Martinez acknowledge the inequities she experiences as a Hispanic woman and thus tacitly confirm her identification with other women of color. She also connected herself to women generally in describing the sex discrimination she experienced in applying for the job of director of special programs in Urbantown. In addition, she declared her identification with people of color generally in such statements as "I should care more than *anybody* . . . what happens to minorities." However, throughout the parts of her narrative that I examined—her work history and her direct answers to questions about discrimination and the meaning of ethnicity in her life and work—Martinez never once mentioned supportive relationships with women colleagues. Indeed, her only direct talk about other women educators was about her privileged status relative to that of darker-skinned women of color.

In the rest of the interview, Martinez talked about relations with other professional women only in response to a direct inquiry about her involvement in professional organizations for women. I asked this question after Colleen had asked a broader question about "sources of professional support that you draw on." In that context, Martinez told brief stories about four men with whom she has established strong collegial relationships. I cite here just one of those stories.

AM: Paul Jones was in [name of city].
    Paul made it well known from the beginning that
    he admired my strength
    the *things* that I'd done in Urbantown
    and so therefore if I needed to know something
    I never hesitated calling calling Paul because I knew Paul.
    The essence of it is that I knew that these people had *confidence* in
        me as a superintendent.
    They had respect and confidence in me
    I felt an equal and I felt that if *I* called them to ask them for advice
    they would not view it as a sign of a weak woman uh you know
    (CB: hm hmm) not knowing what she was doing.

In this and the other three brief stories, Ana describes her strong collegial relationships with these men as based on their forthright admiration of her competence, on a sense of equality they share as professionals. She trusts that they do not interpret her requests for help through gendered stereotypes. Hence, these relationships support Ana's sense of herself as a successful administrator. As she continues, however, she points out that these few relationships are exceptional because the "good old boy system" is "*very* impenetrable." Ana did not mention any women colleagues in this context, so I asked directly about her involvement in professional organizations for women and whether such groups have been important to her.

AM: Well I've supported all of the organizations with my membership
uh in particular
and anytime they ask me to speak.
Um I've been involved in the women's minority uh group [of the national organization for school administrators].
And I try to go and I'm a speaker.
You know I'm a participant and I am a presenter uh whenever I'm asked.
Um we had a uh women's group the [name omitted] group in you know [another region of the country] (SC: hm hmm)
and I was in that.
Um well I uh I've been selected by women's groups for all kinds of awards. (CB and SC: hm hmm)

By listing her involvements in various groups and organizations, Ana evokes an image of active, ongoing participation. However, she does not develop any of these statements by describing specific relationships or particularly important events as she did in her four brief stories about supportive men. Indeed, she presents her relationship to these women's groups as one-sided: she supports them by complying with their requests for help, by offering herself as a model of a successful, visible, powerful woman leader. Although these groups have selected her for many awards, she implies that she gives more than she receives from them. While she reiterates her collective identification with women, especially women of color, she also indicates that nothing further emerges from these groups for her. Ana continues:

AM: Uh I try to mentor women.
Well in fact I probably have a record for hir hiring more women than [laughs] most superintendents.
And I when I went to Grandcity there were eight men who ran the district basically on cabinet.
I expanded cabinet to twenty-four people half men half women half minority half majority.
I've done in essence the same thing here.

People said to me when I made the decision to select the woman
for the assistant superintendent for secondary here
"aren't you afraid people are going to talk?
You've got all women up at the top." (SC: hmmmm)
Nobody ever complained when they were all men. (CB: [laugh])
[exclaiming] When you consider that the majority of the rank
and file are women 70 percent are women
what is so extraordinary (SC: hm hmm) about having this many
women?

Here Ana narrates specific events in which she practiced her commitment to increasing opportunities for women and people of color. This self-presentation echoes her enthusiastic discussion in chapter 3 about her efforts to increase the achievement levels of students of color. In both cases, she portrays herself as the leader of the groups to which she belongs and with which she identifies (women, minorities), as one who is in a position of power to do something about the inequities these groups encounter.

In answering Colleen's question about sources of professional support and my question about her participation in women's organizations and groups, Martinez reinforces what she communicated in the narrative examined in chapter 3. She emphasizes her strengths, achievements, and leadership, and reiterates that her strongest collegial relationships are with men who recognize her competence. While she describes herself as supporting other women and people of color, she receives little support in return. Thus, as before, Ana communicates her isolation as a successful Hispanic woman in a white- and male-dominated context. This overlapping reading suggests that a woman's active participation in women's organizations and groups may coexist with her continued isolation in the profession.

The Limit of Informal
Networks: Margaret Parker

In Chapter 5, Margaret Parker spoke directly about women's collective vulnerability to men's greater power as well as about women's gendered identity. She used *we* several times, explicitly connecting her experience to women educators' experiences generally. In her work history she mentioned that "the network is much stronger now" and named three African-American women whom she calls on from time to time. Nonetheless, as she told and retold the discrimination story (about being denied the assistant superintendency), Parker portrayed herself as living through that experience alone. She did not mention calling on any women for support. While she did talk at length about Connie Johnson's offer to file a lawsuit on her behalf, she used Johnson's story as much to articulate their different ways of handling discrimination as to point out their common vulnerability to white men's greater power. Thus, in Parker's discussions of the discriminatory incident, the only woman who appeared at all is one whose method of handling discrimination she rejected.

It is interesting, then, that Parker recounted stories about strong relationships with women at several other points in her interview. The lively, rich character of these stories underscores a comment she made early in the interview: "Women are my big suit / you know we just make for a good team and we network and we work hard together." For example, she spoke with great pleasure about the informal networking and gatherings of women she initiated when she first moved to Lake City as director of secondary education.[33] With the male superintendent's support, she organized a one-day workshop for women in educational administration, a workshop that provided the impetus for ongoing relationships.

MP: We pulled together *all* the women in Lake City who had an
     interest in upward mobility.
   The most *interesting* and dynamic linkage occurred from that
   in *my* opinion because it didn't stress out anybody
   we *never* formed a formal organization (CB and SC: hm hmm)
   but we knew one another. (SC: hmm)
   And we would pick up the phone
   and then *once* a year
   I would invite *all* the ladies
   'cause I was *the* highest-ranked woman in Lake City in education
     (CB: hm hmm)
   in the *whole area* as a matter of fact. (CB: yeah SC: hm hmm)
   I led the way. (SC: hm hmm)
   Um I would invite these ladies to my home

and *we'd* sit around and talk about all of this stuff
and we'd eat and we'd laugh
and we'd crack jokes about silly things that men do (SC and CB:
   [soft laugh])
and we'd talk about how you come to understand it.
We did that every year ok? (SC and CB: hm hmm)
And then along with that the women would call and say
"Margaret I want to do such and such a thing.
How do you think I should prepare to apply for this?
Or what what do you think what is your—"
Ladies I *tell* you
they *call* me now.
They I they *call* me long distance to say
"Margaret let me tell you what I ran across
what do you think I should do?" (CB and SC: mm hmmm)

Margaret proudly presents her leadership in pulling women together; she portrays herself as a "centerwoman" in this strong informal group.[34] She uses *we* to underscore the collective nature of the
events, and *I* to highlight her leadership. By telling this story as a
habitual narrative—using "we would," "I would," and "we'd"—she
emphasizes the ongoing character of these relationships.[35] As evidence
of the efficacy of her leadership and the strength of the relationships
that developed, she points out that many women still call her for
advice, even though they are dispersed across the country.

Margaret's comments about the time period indicate that this local
network was already in place when she faced sex and race discrimination in applying for the assistant superintendency. How, then, do I
interpret the absence of talk in Margaret's discrimination story about
support from women in this local network? As the highest-ranked
woman in the district, Margaret was in a position to give rather than receive support within that group. However, occupational hierarchies allow those in lower ranks to volunteer some kinds of support for the one
at the top. For example, Connie Johnson's offer to file a lawsuit on Margaret's behalf can be interpreted as a significant token of support. (As a
woman interested in women's professional experiences, it is likely that
Johnson belonged to this group.)[36] Nonetheless, Margaret interprets
that proposal as more harmful than helpful and mentions no others.

While she clearly enjoys women's supportive relationships, the absence from her discrimination story of talk about support from this network and her rejection of Johnson's offer show that she experiences her relationships with lower-ranked women as limited. Margaret may share hidden transcripts with women in this group (for example, "jokes about silly things that men do . . . and . . . how you come to understand it" and perhaps the discrimination story itself), but she does not rely on them in responding to discriminatory treatment in the professional world. When she encounters powerful men's sexism and racism, she depends on the relationships she has cultivated with other powerful men. She rejects Connie Johnson's offer to take legal action because such action violates her conception of how women achieve success in a male-dominated occupation and her own self-conception as a woman who does not push. Margaret's response to discriminatory treatment is an individual solution to a problem that she recognizes as collective.

This overlapping reading suggests that even when a woman has developed strong relationships with professional women of lower rank, she does not necessarily turn directly to those relationships as sources of support when she encounters discrimination in the professional world. For Margaret, this is a matter of institutionalized inequalities. As she stated when describing asymmetrical gender relations in the superintendency, "you can't get nothing from nothing." In other words, when women have little power relative to men's power, women's relationships may produce safe contexts for hidden transcripts; but they do not produce collective strength that can be exercised publicly.

Leading the Struggle for
Equal Access: Denise Nelson

In chapter 4, Denise Nelson described herself as having worn blinders for much of her career, as having ignored or denied the discrimination she herself has faced. Yet when she recast the traumatic experiences of the last two years as a story about sex discrimination, she made explicit her identification with other women. In that recast story, however, her only mention of support received from others was that "many of our astute [p] community members recognized that [sexism] as well." But

Nelson yearned for more: "I guess that's why there would be a certain amount of catharsis to bring together other women who've had ex— similar things happen . . . / and jus— just to talk about it."

Given Nelson's statement that she has looked directly at her own experience of sex discrimination only in the last two years, it is striking that she spoke at length later in the interview about how she had played a leadership role many years earlier in activities aimed at increasing women's access to positions of power within the profession. When Colleen asked her to reflect on "formal and informal networks" and "connections among the women," Nelson told how she, along with several other women educators in the state, formulated a plan that would help women become integrated into the male-dominated network.

DN: Decided the best way to do it in a *formal* way
   would be to go the executive committee of [the statewide professional organization]
   and point to them that *in their bylaws* uh
   they had this statement about women and minorities
   and *we* wanted more recognition
   we wanted *more* women in on committee assignments
   we wanted then to be able to say to them
   "we will actively recruit women for the organization
   but we want some guarantee that we will have women on *programs* and that we'll have women committee members."
   As I was cleaning my office I came across that proposal that
   we we went to before the executive committee and made the
   proposal and uh we we were *well received* . . .
   you know *we* talk about these things *so* much that we believe
   everybody our male counterparts recognize it.
   They don't. (CB: hm hmm)
   And it really took us several years to even
   for the executive dir director to fully begin to understand what
   we were *saying*
   about the uphill uphill battle for women entering administration
   and *why* we felt we needed to be *visible*
   we *needed* to be on *programs* and and so forth
   uh but we *knew* we'd arrived when we when *he* would be out in the

field talking to college classes that *he* was saying the same thing
we were saying to him [slight laugh] so (SC and CB: hm hmm)
we knew we were getting through.

By using *we* throughout this passage—twenty-three times, in fact—
Denise clearly presents this small group of women as engaged in collective activity. Interestingly, her description of the uphill battle for
women generally is echoed in her group's persistent efforts: it took
them several years to convince the executive director that women face
particular obstacles to achieving visibility and power. As she continued, Denise described how this small group of women also initiated
an informal network for women within the statewide professional organization for school administrators, a network that facilitated wom-
en's move into positions of greater power within local, regional, and
statewide education systems. While they managed to acquire funding
from the state department of education for a conference, most of their
activities were more informal:

DN: The whole idea was to to *give* and to *receive* [p]
      meaning that if we had a skill or had something that we could
         offer another *female*
      that we wanted to know about it so that we could put people in
         touch (CB: hmm)
      and to start playing the *same* kinds of games that the *men* played
         [p]
      uh with knowing about positions before they come open
      start *lobbying* and so forth
      so we had to identify some key people
      um which we *did* and and still do.
      One of them was a a person at the state department of education
      so that if you needed to know something about a district
      [low voice, as if telling a secret]
      you could call her and she could give you the *information* (CB:
         hmm) without being known.
      The interesting thing now [p]
      some of the younger fellows [loud, hearty laugh] are also
CB: they want to ‖join the group‖
DN: ‖they want to‖ *right right right.*

Denise's hearty laughter signifies her sense of the informal network's success. That men now seek support from this group of women suggests that the network has acquired at least a modicum of power, an irony Denise enjoys. At this point I asked whether Denise and her peers had ever considered forming a separate organization for women:

DN: We *consciously* did not feel we wanted to do that
    that we *had* to stay *within* the structure
    if it was really going to work. (SC: hm hmm)
    That we needed to have young women meet the power brokers
    [who] in many cases uh were superintendents male superintendents
    who could give you an endorsement or could could open doors
        with boards of education (SC: hm hmm)
    so to *isolate* ourselves we felt was shooting ourselves in the foot.
        (SC: hm hmm)
    So by *design*—
    and we *one* of the things we said to the executive committee
    we we didn't want to raise any red *flags* necessarily
    we wou didn't want to be militant
    but we saw ourselves as administrators that that needed to have a
        better *access*
    and that there was a *whole pool* out here yet
    that were *not* able to to have access (SC: hm hmm)
    and that we really didn't believe that was what they intended and
        would continually point to their own bylaws (SC: uh huh)
    uh so *definitely* worked through the structure.

Denise distinguishes her group's aim from that of possible alternative aims: they sought equal access, not militancy of any sort. By presenting her group as working within the existing structure, as not disrupting even the bylaws of the professional organization, she uses discourse that emphasizes the professionally oriented nature of their activity and rejects discourse that would highlight its potentially activist character.

In these passages, Denise Nelson clearly presents herself as playing a leadership role, along with several other women, in formal and informal activities aimed at increasing women's opportunities for upward mobility. How do I interpret Nelson's participation in these collective activities in light of her earlier portrayal of herself as having worn blinders with respect to her own discriminatory experiences throughout this part of her career? This juxtaposition suggests that professional women may experience fighting for women's equal access in general and coming to terms with their own personal experiences of discrimination as two very different problems. In describing the problem of unequal access, Nelson focuses on men's collective ignorance and their institutionalized but benign neglect of women. By contrast, she presents her own experience of sex discrimination as intentional, malicious, and deeply hurtful. This overlapping reading suggests that a woman can be at once a leader in terms of women's struggle for equal access and blind to the depth and pervasiveness of discrimination that even highly successful women face once they have achieved what may appear to be equal access as individuals.

What about the absence of Nelson's peers from her discrimination story, peers with whom she successfully organized collective activities benefiting younger women? Why don't these peers provide Nelson with the kind of conversation and support she now yearns for? This absence may also be related to the difference between discourse about equal access and discourse about discrimination that cannot be excused as benign neglect. Now that she no longer blinds herself to the reality of even powerful women's continued subjection, Nelson seeks a kind of conversation she knows she has not had, despite her collective activity with women peers. When heard in relation to each other, these disparate parts of her narrative convey that even strong relations and collective activity with women peers may develop without an activist discourse.

CONCLUSIONS:
HOW WE LISTEN; WHAT WE HEAR

My overlapping readings of the four women superintendents' narratives show that their larger story about individual solutions to inequality coexists with a range of talk about relations among professional women. My readings indicate these educators' sense that even the strongest of their relationships with other professional women are limited. For Parker, relations with lower-ranked women provide a safe context for developing hidden transcripts but lack power within the professional world. For Nelson, relations with women peers provide the foundation for requesting equal access but not for demanding radical changes in the profession itself. Given the limits of even the strongest relationships they have cultivated, these superintendents seek individual solutions when personally confronted by discrimination, solutions aimed at reintegrating themselves within the profession. While they recognize the collective nature of their subjection, they also perceive that their relations with other women hold little or no power to effect radical change in the profession.

Thus, these overlapping readings suggest that the development of activist discourse—the transformation of professional work itself into a collective struggle for equality—depends on more than the existence of strong relationships among professional women. While such relations are a potential site of collective resistance to oppression, the actualization of that potential requires structural conditions and discursive possibilities that do not exist in women superintendents' professional world. Note, for example, the important structural difference between relations among women in women's studies programs and relations among women in public school administration. For those who teach in women's studies programs, the everyday work site is constituted, at least in part, by relations among women colleagues. Even if there is no permanent physical site on campus—such as a women's center or a women's studies office—there are periodic committee meetings and events in which the activities of the program are planned and carried out. In addition, feminist academics have opportunities to work together in contexts (meetings, campus events) not specifically related to women's studies. By contrast, in educational administration, relations among women peers are, at best, peripheral to the sites of everyday work. Because women superintendents are geographically dispersed, even their strongest informal networks or professional organizations usually exist outside the everyday workplace.

Moreover, a significant difference holds between the discursive possibilities prevailing in these two settings. Fundamental to women's studies programs is discourse that has radically redefined the content of academic work, discourse that exposes the ideological character of ostensibly gender- and race-neutral pedagogy, research, and theory, as well as the ideological character of conventional practices in educating, hiring, and evaluating faculty. Because this discourse of social change is central to women's studies programs, any women's studies meeting, activity, or event becomes an occasion for its further development, alteration, or dispute. Although feminist discourse of social change has achieved only a precarious foothold within the academic world generally, it is allowed more or less hostile hearings in that broader setting. By contrast, in their professional organizations and informal networks, women educational leaders are more likely to develop discourse (as Denise Nelson does) about women's need for equal access, discourse that does not redefine the content of their professional work, that does not necessarily challenge conventional professional practices, and that does not develop connections among forms of discrimination experienced by students, teachers, and leaders.

A poignant comment by one educational leader illustrates this point succinctly. As she recounted the many forms of discrimination that women in her position face, she stated, "You see if I weren't involved in the business I'm in / I might be radical [laughs] / because I'm tired of it."[37] Like Denise Nelson, this woman has been much more active than most women superintendents in providing leadership in the struggle for equal access to the profession. Nonetheless, she perceives that within the occupational context of educational administration she must choose between a whole-hearted commitment to her professional work and a whole-hearted commitment to fighting inequality. Under such conditions, women's struggle against discriminatory treatment remains a necessary distraction from their primary commitment to professional work itself; that struggle does not blossom into a fullfledged battle against the individualistic, gender- and race-neutral discourse of the professional world. In such a context, no more than an individual struggle against inequality can be achieved. At best, the collective activity of women's informal networks or formal organizations supports women in their individual struggles.

Like most women who work in male- and white-dominated professions in the United States, women educational leaders work in contexts that have been influenced in limited ways by the structural and discursive changes wrought by the social movements of the 1960s and 1970s. For example, legal regulations and policies concerning affirmative action, sexual harassment, and sex and race discrimination begrudgingly allow individuals—or, in the rare cases of class-action suits, groups of similarly situated individuals—to seek redress for unequal treatment. Although they have opened some doors for white women and people of color, these legal changes generally depend on discourse that presents discrimination as a fluke rather than a major flaw in the system, discourse that precludes a redefinition of professional work itself as the uprooting of deep inequities supporting the system.

As I discussed in chapter 1, women educational leaders' narratives provide evidence that the counternarrative of the successful, accomplished professional woman has achieved at least a modicum of acceptance in contemporary American culture. *Counternarrative* is the appropriate term because the dominant script for women's lives continues to emphasize women's selflessness and orientation to domestic concerns. Stories about gender and race discrimination have also achieved a certain amount of public currency. Thus, late twentieth-century American culture makes some room for (although it certainly does not encourage, and in some sectors, it actively discourages)[38] stories about women's professional accomplishments and talk about women's subjection to gender and race inequalities. What it greatly circumscribes, however, is activist talk about resistance to subjection and activist talk about social change. Catherine Kohler Riessman points to a somewhat analogous circumscription in her analysis of one woman's narrative about marital rape: "The culture is increasingly providing women with a language for talking about and reinterpreting sexual abuse." However, "society provides for women's depressed emotions but not for their rage."[39] A survivor of marital violence easily finds cultural discourse for talking about herself as a victim but not for talking about her rage against social conditions that perpetuate such treatment. Similarly, in many parts of the white- and male-dominated professional world, women more easily find words for their subjection than for social change (in the content of their work and in professional structures and practices) that would radically undermine the conditions that produce their subjection in the first place.

The story about individual solutions to the collective problem of inequality is better than the co-optation story in that it shows women superintendents' recognition of the inequalities they encounter. They do not blame themselves for sexist and racist treatment; they do not mistake "public issues of social structure" (gender and race inequalities) for "personal troubles of milieu" (such as lack of competence).[40] At the same time, they treat as an individual matter their responses to the structural problem of gender and race inequality. When a woman superintendent encounters a specific instance of sex or race discrimination, she experiences its effects most forcefully on herself and her own career, even though she knows that the victim could just as well have been another woman.

How might activist discourse begin to take shape under conditions that strongly discourage it? This study points to one answer to that question. While women superintendents' narratives show their understanding of structural constraints, they do not reflect awareness of the extent and depth of the discursive constraints they encounter in the professional world. Here I mean something quite specific. These educators certainly know that they must speak carefully about gender and race inequities if they want to keep their jobs. However, they do not recognize that the need to speak carefully reflects more than white men's control of gatekeeping positions; it also points to the disjunction in American culture between discourse about professional work and discourse about inequality. Of course, this lack of recognition is not particular to this group of women; it is expressed, for example, in my own initial conceptualizations of the research project. As I discussed in chapters 1 and 2, my coresearcher and I conducted our interviews in ways that took for granted that women superintendents would have stories to tell about their achievement and subjection. But like most researchers, we began by focusing on structural rather than discursive conditions as the source of their subjection. We did not recognize how our own talk as well as that of our interviewees was constrained by and oriented to the discursive disjunction. Indeed, the constraints of language are much more intangible, much more taken for granted, than structural constraints. Thus, in general, neither researchers nor professional women take up that discursive disjunction as a topic.

If professional women were to articulate how their stories are constrained by the disjunction between discourse about professional work and inequality, they would begin to understand their own experiences more fully. In other words, professional women need to ask themselves such questions as these: In what contexts do I speak more and less freely about my competence and accomplishments? Are these the same contexts in which I speak more and less freely about my experiences of sex or race discrimination? What narrative strategies do I use to tell my stories? Do I exclude my subjection when I want to highlight my achievements or ambition (as Ana Martinez and Denise Nelson do), or do I integrate stories of success and subjection (as Margaret Parker and Karen Rhodes do)? When I recount experiences of discrimination, what vocabularies do I draw on to understand what happened, to come to terms with the pain of subjection, to decide what action I should take, and to negotiate my relationships with those who discriminated against me? Do I describe myself as struggling alone during such events or do other women appear in these stories? More generally, where do my relationships with women colleagues and my participation in professional women's networks and organizations fit into my stories? By answering such questions, women can understand more fully how the very process of making sense of and communicating their work experiences is constrained by the discursive disjunction. They can identify how their stories preserve or unsettle the individualistic, gender- and race-neutral discursive realm of professional work. Moreover, they can ask themselves what they need in order to develop activist discourse in their particular work contexts. Finally, they can begin to imagine taking the risk to speak about their experiences in ways that radically disrupt the discursive disjunction.

Researchers, too, would benefit from attending to how disjunctive discourses shape speech, their own as well as that of those they study. The methods of narrative analysis provide one significant avenue for such inquiry. Analysis of how people narrate experience (and how interviewers frame their questions) turns attention to discursive features of contemporary culture that we generally take for granted and allows us to explore how culture is embodied, reproduced, and disrupted through actual speech practices. The methods of narrative analysis alter how we listen to talk produced during in-depth interviews and consequently alter what we hear.

In the case of my study, those methods have brought forth the muffled story about professional commitments and individual solutions to the collective problem of inequality. More conventional methods of interpretation might have mistaken these narratives for co-optation stories. If scholars, students, and professional women are to understand the possibilities for social change that privileged women might avail themselves of, we must comprehend the constraints they labor under and how those constraints might be overcome. We can begin by listening much more carefully to professional women's stories as they are told in different contexts: in the popular media, in public presentations, into researchers' tape recorders, behind closed office doors, in the privacy of their homes, and in the safe spaces produced by relationships with those they trust.

Appendix

The

Research

Project

This book is based on materials collected during a collaborative research project that Colleen Bell and I began in 1986. We combined our interests and disciplines (sociology in my case, education in Colleen's) in order to study women in the public school superintendency in the United States. Generally, we were interested in women's experiences in this male- and white-dominated profession and in the processes by which white men's dominance in the profession is reproduced and challenged. Our project could be called a case study in the sense that it focuses on one group of people in a single occupation.[1] We anticipated that women superintendents' experiences would be similar to and different from those of male educational leaders as well as similar to and different from those of women in other male- and white-dominated professions. When we began our project, there were no extensive qualitative studies published of women school superintendents and few of women leaders in any public school administrative position.[2]

In 1986 we conducted a phone survey, with Marilyn Livingston's assistance, of all fifty state departments of education. This survey gave us data on women in the K–12 superintendency by state and revealed that only 2.8 percent of superintendents nationwide were women.[3] In most cases, we were able to find out which school districts were headed by women as well as the women's names. In 1989, we repeated the phone survey, with Martina Thompson's and Mimi Schuttloffel's help, to find out whether there had been changes in the number of women in the superintendency and to ask about race and ethnicity as well as gender. This survey showed that 4.2 percent of K–12 superintendents were women. In the twenty-six states that collected data on race and ethnicity, 8.8 percent of women superintendents were women of color. By 1991, when we conducted a third and final survey, again with Thompson's assistance, 5.6 percent of superintendents were women. In the thirty-nine states then keeping data on race and ethnicity, 7.6 percent of women superintendents were women of color. Effie Jones at the American Association of School Administrators in Washington, D.C., also helped us to identify women of color in various states.

Between 1986 and 1989, Colleen and I conducted intensive interviews with twenty-seven women superintendents in cities, towns, and rural areas across the United States. In choosing interviewees, we sought several kinds of diversity. First, regional diversity: we interviewed women in western, central, southern, and midwestern regions of the country, including both liberal and conservative states. Second, racial and ethnic diversity: our interviewees included one Asian American, one Native American, two Hispanics, three African Americans, and twenty European Americans. Third, diversity of district type and size: we interviewed ten women in rural districts with student enrollments ranging from two hundred to eight hundred, twelve women in small-town or suburban districts with enrollments from eight hundred to eight thousand, and five women in urban districts with enrollments from eight thousand to fifty-four thousand. The women's ages ranged from mid thirties to early sixties, with most in their forties and fifties. At the time of the interviews, twenty were married, and seven were either divorced, widowed, or single. Eight women were childless, eleven had adult children, seven had school-age children, and one had a preschool child. We did not attempt to produce a representative sample of the entire population of women superintendents; we were more interested in selecting a heterogeneous group.

We contacted the women we chose to interview by letter, introducing ourselves and our research project, requesting an interview, and in some cases asking about the possibility of interviewing school board members in the district. We followed up with phone calls to schedule the interview and to get the names and addresses of school board members. Of the thirty women we contacted, twenty-seven agreed to interviews. Two were uninterested in our project for reasons we could not ascertain because we were unable to speak with them personally, and one could not fit her busy schedule to ours.

The interviews consisted of a series of questions about the tasks and problems women superintendents face in their current positions, the professional and interpersonal contexts in which they work, their work histories, the relationship between their personal and professional lives, and the difference that gender and race or ethnicity have made to their work experiences. Although the interviews were structured by these topics, our questions were very open ended. In some cases we spent two or three interviewing sessions with women in order to cover as much of their experience as they were willing to share. We collected anywhere from two and a half to twelve hours of taped interview from each woman. In addition, we invited them for meals whenever possible, in order to converse more casually about their work and experiences. In one state, we were invited to attend an informal gathering of the women superintendents who kept in regular contact with each other for personal and professional support. We also attended the annual convention of the professional organization for women educational leaders in the same state.

From the beginning, we made it clear to the superintendents that we intended to publish writings based on the interviews, although we did not know in advance what form those writings would take. Indeed, the women we interviewed are no strangers to research; two-thirds have earned doctorates and so have conducted research of their own at some point in their lives. All of the women allowed us to tape the interviews and exhibited no discomfort about being recorded. In one case, a woman asked us to turn the recorder off when she described a particular controversy involving a school board member. In addition, several asked us to keep some particular statement or story confidential. The kind of information they felt most sensitive about usually had to do with tensions among specific persons in their communities. Later on, as I began my narrative analyses, I requested and received permission to use specific parts of the interviews, usually the parts in which work histories, discrimination, and relations among women were discussed.

In order to understand the local and professional contexts in which women superintendents work and to hear more than their own perspectives on their work situations, we interviewed school board members in ten of the districts in which we visited women superintendents. Most school boards are composed of lay people elected by their communities; in a few cases, they are appointed by mayors. Their responsibilities include hiring and evaluating the superintendent and working with the superintendent to set school policies. We interviewed school board members in two rural districts, five suburban or small-town districts, and three urban districts, a total of forty-four people: twenty-seven white men, three African-American men, one Hispanic man, one Native American man, and twelve white women. (In 1991, 34.7 percent of school board members nationwide were women, and 3.4 percent were people of color.)[4] Included were interviews with school board members in Ana Martinez's, Margaret Parker's, and Karen Rhodes's districts. We also attended school board meetings in several districts, which gave us an opportunity to observe interactions between women superintendents and their school boards.

While school board members offered us a close look at the local context in which women superintendents work, we also sought the broader perspective of state-level observers. We interviewed eight people (six white men, one African-American man, one white woman) who are administrators in state departments of education or well-known consultants to superintendency searches. Frequently, these consultants are former superintendents or university professors in departments of educational administration. Increasingly, school boards are turning to consultants to aid them in hiring superintendents.

Upon receiving names and addresses from the superintendent, we contacted school board members by letter and then by phone. We organized our interviews with board members around questions about the history of the school district, the current problems facing the district, the hiring process for the superintendency (past and present), and the relationship between the board and the superintendent (past and present). We made our initial contacts with state-level observers either by letter or phone. In these interviews, we asked about how women superintendents and women aspiring to leadership positions fare and how opportunities, career paths, and professional organizations are structured in the state. School board members, consultants, and state department officials served as key informants for us. Given the controversial and political nature of public education, even aside from questions of gender and race inequality, it is not surprising that a few school board members and state-level observers seemed wary of us, despite our promises of confidentiality. Yet most of them had a great deal to say in response to our questions, and several volunteered to give us tours of their schools and communities.

In a less systematic way, whenever the opportunity presented itself, we sought further insight into the contexts in which women superintendents work by interviewing people either closely connected to the superintendent or knowledgeable about the superintendency. We conducted formal interviews with four staff members and nine of the women superintendents' husbands or partners, and spoke informally with several additional state-level observers. Finally, in every district we visited, we picked up publicly available information about the schools, accepted whatever other information anyone offered, and read the local newspapers for clues about the relationship between the schools and the community and for public attitudes toward the superintendent.

Colleen and I conducted jointly every one of the ninety-two taped interviews for this research project. Although collaborative research projects are common, joint interviews are not. What difference did joint interviewing make? Because our fields of study are different— education and sociology—our interests in and approaches to women educational leaders' work experiences differed in some ways. For example, Colleen had much greater knowledge than I did about the everyday realities, such as educational policies and legislation, that shape school leaders' and school boards' work. Her knowledge facilitated rapport and the ease with which the interviews moved into issues of importance to the interviewees. Superintendents, school board members, and state-level observers did not have to provide as much background information as would have been necessary had I been interviewing alone. As a sociologist, I brought to the joint interviews a focus on the relationship between experience and the structural and cultural features of any work context.

It is more difficult, but perhaps more interesting, to articulate what difference it makes interactionally to interview jointly. As anyone who conducts interviews knows, the process of asking questions and listening carefully for hours is quite intense. Interviewing together meant that we could help each other ask and listen. One would pick up on something the other had missed or would ask an unanswered question in a new way. In addition, we helped each other handle awkward moments. In a coauthored article, we examine an interaction in one of our early interviews in which I persisted in asking a gender-related question that I should have dropped. Colleen's response defused the tension and lightened the moment for both the interviewee and me.[5]

In addition, Colleen and I taped what we called *debriefings* as soon as possible after each interview in order to discuss impressions, themes, important stories, what this or that comment was about, and the nature of the interaction. These conversations helped each of us to rethink assumptions about what we had heard. We also worked jointly on field notes, which provided a more formal record than the debriefings of the interview content, setting, and interaction and of our observations at school board meetings or other gatherings.

Furthermore, we collaborated on early data analyses. Both of us had copies of all of the interview transcripts. We worked individually on organizing and coding the material and then shared and reworked what we had come up with as we analyzed one particular topic or another for a paper or presentation. Although we began the organizing and coding processes as soon as possible after an interview was over and transcribed, we found it necessary to sift through the transcripts time and time again as we went along.

We began work on an interview transcript by writing an index, a detailed summary of what the interviewee said, marked by transcript page numbers for easy reference. These indexes have proven extremely useful over the years as the quickest way to find who said what and where she or he said it. Next, we read through the transcript, making notes in the margins on content, emotions, interactions, and whatever else seemed important. When finished with this process, we copied the margin notes onto separate sheets of paper, which we slowly organized around various categories. We developed these thematic categories as we sifted through all of the material; the categories came from the interviewees' words or from our understandings of their words. For each entry on these category sheets (many of which were eventually many pages long), we marked the interviewee's name and the transcript page number so that we could return easily to the original transcript for the fuller context of a statement or idea. (Each category did not necessarily have examples from every interview.) Some of the categories were broad, some narrow; some stood alone, and some had subcategories. These category sheets provided the starting point for analyses of various topics, such as women superintendents' leadership strategies or how school board members and state-level observers reproduce male dominance as they talk about women superintendents' competence.[6]

For example, here is a partial list of categories developed from the interviews with women superintendents: confidence; image; recognition; competence; isolation; family-work interconnections; women's views on gatekeepers or powerful men (subcategories: support from men, incompetent men, men's egos); discrimination (subcategories: specific incidents, need to prove competence, social awkwardness with colleagues, how gender or race intervene in work situations); gender identity; relations among women (subcategories: women's organizations, professional support from or for other women, women hiring women, role modeling or mentoring, attitudes toward or complaints about other women); emotional strategies or strategies of action; career paths (subcategories: aspirations, learning from doing the job, interest in curriculum or pedagogical issues); most difficult tasks; dealing with personal attacks or painful events.

Although we have continued to work together on certain aspects of our research project, Colleen and I also pursued separate interests. I developed a particular interest in how language processes are implicated in the accounts women offer of their experiences. As I described in the text, my interest in the relations among culture, discourse, narrative, and experience led to alterations in my analytic procedures. I shifted my attention away from themes across the entire set of interviews and began to focus on patterns in content and form within individuals' narratives. In other words, I began to listen to how women narrate their experiences, how they draw on and struggle with various discursive resources for articulating their ambiguous empowerment, their contradictory experiences of power and subjection.

Notes

CHAPTER ONE: AMERICAN CULTURE, PROFESSIONAL
WORK, AND INEQUALITY

1. Like all other names of persons whose interviews are discussed in this
book, "Karen Rhodes" is a pseudonym.

2. In 1991, 5.6 percent of K–12 superintendents nationwide were
women, a slight improvement over 4.2 percent in 1989 and 2.6 percent in
1986 (Colleen S. Bell and Susan E. Chase, "The Underrepresentation of
Women in School Leadership," in *The New Politics of Race and Gender*,
1993 Politics of Education Yearbook, ed. C. Marshall [London: Falmer
Press, in press]). See my appendix, "The Research Project," for a discussion
of the surveys on which these figures are based. In 1990, 3.4 percent of
superintendents were African American, Hispanic, Native American, or
Asian American. Of that small percentage, approximately 12 percent were
women (Effie H. Jones and Xenia P. Montenegro, *Women and Minorities in
School Administration: Facts and Figures, 1989–1990* [Arlington, Va.: Office of Minority Affairs, American Association of School Administrators,

1990], 12–14). Jones's and Montenegro's figures are based on reports from thirty-six state departments of education.

3. The following are just a few of the many important articles and books that have made this argument: Marcia Westkott, "Feminist Criticism of the Social Sciences," *Harvard Educational Review* 49 (1979): 422–30; Beth B. Hess and Myra Marx Ferree, eds., *Analyzing Gender: A Handbook of Social Science Research* (Newbury Park, Calif.: Sage Publications, 1987); Sandra Harding, ed., *Feminism and Methodology* (Bloomington: Indiana University Press, 1987); and Margaret L. Andersen, *Thinking about Women: Sociological Perspectives on Sex and Gender* 3d ed. (New York: Macmillan Publishing Company, 1993), esp. chap. 1.

4. The list of important texts on narrative is long and growing; here I mention just a few: W. J. T. Mitchell, ed., *On Narrative* (Chicago: University of Chicago Press, 1980); Paul Ricoeur, *Time and Narrative*, vols. 1–3 (Chicago: University of Chicago Press, 1983); Wallace Martin, *Recent Theories of Narrative* (Ithaca: Cornell University Press, 1986); Elliot G. Mishler, *Research Interviewing: Context and Narrative* (Cambridge: Harvard University Press, 1986); George C. Rosenwald and Richard L. Ochberg, eds., *Storied Lives: The Cultural Politics of Self-understanding* (New Haven: Yale University Press, 1992); Livia Polanyi, *Telling the American Story: A Structural and Cultural Analysis of Conversational Storytelling* (Norwood, N.J.: Ablex Publishers Corporation, 1985); Walter R. Fisher, *Human Communication as Narration: Toward a Philosophy of Reason, Value, and Action* (Columbia: University of South Carolina Press, 1987); David Carr, *Time, Narrative, and History* (Bloomington: Indiana University Press, 1986).

5. For example, Roland Barthes observes that "narrative is present in every age, in every place, in every society" (*Image, Music, Text*, trans. S. Heath [New York: Hill and Wang, 1977], 79). Fredric Jameson describes narrative as "the central function or *instance* of the human mind" (*The Political Unconscious: Narrative as a Socially Symbolic Act* [Ithaca: Cornell University Press, 1981], 13, emphasis in original). And Fisher suggests the following: "Many different root metaphors have been put forth to represent the essential nature of human beings: *Homo faber, Homo economicus, Homo politicus.* . . . I propose that *Homo narrans* be added to the list" (*Human Communication as Narration,* 62).

6. Jerome Bruner, "Life as Narrative," *Social Research* 54 (1987): 15.

7. Carolyn G. Heilbrun, *Writing a Woman's Life* (New York: Ballantine Books, 1989), 37.

8. Barbara Herrnstein Smith, "Narrative Versions, Narrative Theories," in *On Narrative,* 229, emphasis in original.

9. See, for example, Susan Groag Bell and Marilyn Yalom, eds., *Reveal-*

ing Lives: Autobiography, Biography, and Gender (Albany: State University of New York Press, 1990); Bella Brodzki and Celeste Schenck, eds., *Life/Lines: Theorizing Women's Autobiography* (Ithaca: Cornell University Press, 1988); Personal Narratives Group, ed., *Interpreting Women's Lives: Feminist Theory and Personal Narratives* (Bloomington: Indiana University Press, 1989); Mary Gergen, "Life Stories: Pieces of a Dream," in *Storied Lives*, 127–44; Jacquelyn Wiersma, "The Press Release: Symbolic Communication in Life History Interviewing," *Journal of Personality* 56 (1988): 205–38; Marianne A. Paget, "The Ontological Anguish of Women Artists," *New England Sociologist* 3 (1981): 65–79; and Susan Stanford Friedman, "The Return of the Repressed in Women's Narrative," *Journal of Narrative Technique* 19 (1989): 141–56.

10. Nadya Aisenberg and Mona Harrington, *Women of Academe: Outsiders in the Sacred Grove* (Amherst: University of Massachusetts Press, 1988), 6, emphasis in original.

11. Heilbrun, *Writing a Woman's Life*, 17.

12. Heilbrun, *Writing a Woman's Life*, 23.

13. Patricia Meyer Spacks, "Selves in Hiding," in *Women's Autobiography: Essays in Criticism*, ed. E. C. Jelinek (Bloomington: Indiana University Press, 1980), 132.

14. Mary Gergen suggests that the gendered character of women's stories of achievement lies in their orientation to others, the emotional interdependence they express in recounting their success, and the fluid boundary between their public and private lives ("Life Stories," 138). Gergen also makes the unusual suggestion that the story form available to women is much fuller and more complex than that available to men (140).

15. Personal Narratives Group, *Interpreting Women's Lives*, 11.

16. Patricia Hill Collins, *Black Feminist Thought: Knowledge, Consciousness, and the Politics of Empowerment* (Boston: Unwin Hyman, 1990), 95–96.

17. Deborah Tannen suggests that, in general, men and women talk in different ways and in different contexts about their achievements. For men, "self-aggrandizing information is to be used in public to achieve status, appropriately displayed when first meeting people or with people who have, or seem to be claiming, superior status." By contrast, for a woman, "self-aggrandizing information is to be used only in private, appropriately revealed in rapport-talk—conversations with people she knows and trusts, who will not judge her for her pride" (*You Just Don't Understand: Women and Men in Conversation* (New York: Ballantine Books, 1990), 224.

18. Judith Lorber, *Women Physicians: Careers, Status, and Power* (New

York: Tavistock Publications, 1984); Cynthia Fuchs Epstein, *Women in Law* (Garden City, N.Y.: Anchor Press, Doubleday, 1983); Shirley M. Clark and Mary Corcoran, "Perspectives on the Professional Socialization of Women Faculty: A Case of Accumulative Disadvantage?" *Journal of Higher Education* 57 (1986): 20–43; Karen Fullbright, "The Myth of the Double-advantage: Black Female Managers," in *Slipping Through the Cracks: The Status of Black Women*, ed. M. C. Simms and J. Malveaux (New Brunswick, N.J.: Transaction Books, 1986), 33–45.

19. Rosabeth Moss Kanter, *Men and Women of the Corporation* (New York: Basic Books, 1977); Rhetaugh Graves Dumas, "Dilemmas of Black Females in Leadership," in *The Black Woman*, ed. La F. Rodgers-Rose (Newbury Park, Calif.: Sage Publications, 1980), 203–15; Lois Benjamin, *The Black Elite: Facing the Color Line in the Twilight of the Twentieth Century* (Chicago: Nelson-Hall Publishers, 1991).

20. Debra Renee Kaufman, "Professional Women: How Real Are the Recent Gains?" in *Women: A Feminist Perspective*, ed. J. Freeman, 4th ed. (Mountain View, Calif.: Mayfield Publishing Company, 1989), 329–46; Barbara F. Reskin, "Sex Differentiation and the Social Organization of Science," *Sociological Inquiry* 48 (1978): 6–37; and Cheryl Bernadette Leggon, "Black Female Professionals: Dilemmas and Contradictions of Status," in *The Black Woman*, 189–202.

21. Patricia Gerald Bourne and Norma Juliet Wikler, "Commitment and the Cultural Mandate: Women in Medicine," in *Women and Work: Problems and Perspectives*, ed. R. Kahn-Hut, A. K. Daniels, and R. Colvard (New York: Oxford University Press, 1982): 111–22.

22. This has been argued in a number of different ways. See, for example, Alan Blum and Peter McHugh, *Self-reflection in the Arts and Sciences* (Atlantic Highlands, N.J.: Humanities Press, 1984); Richard Harvey Brown, "Rhetoric, Textuality, and the Postmodern Turn in Sociological Theory," *Sociological Theory* 8 (1990): 188–97; Kenneth Burke, *On Symbols and Society* (Chicago: University of Chicago Press, 1989); Albert Hunter, ed., *The Rhetoric of Social Science Research: Understood and Believed* (New Brunswick, N.J.: Rutgers University Press, 1990); Laurel Richardson, "Narrative and Sociology," *Journal of Contemporary Ethnography* 19 (1990): 116–35; Edward M. Bruner, "Ethnography as Narrative," in *The Anthropology of Experience*, ed. V. W. Turner and E. M. Bruner (Urbana: University of Illinois Press, 1986); Ricca Edmondson, *Rhetoric in Sociology* (London: Macmillan Press, Ltd., 1984); Donald N. McCloskey, *If You're So Smart: The Narrative of Economic Expertise* (Chicago: University of Chicago Press, 1990); and Joseph Gusfield, "The Literary Rhetoric of Science:

Comedy and Pathos in Drinking Driver Research," *American Sociological Review* 4 (1976): 16–34.

23. Harold Garfinkel, *Studies in Ethnomethodology* (Englewood Cliffs, N.J.: Prentice-Hall, 1967).

24. See the appendix for further discussion of our selection of interviewees.

25. Everett C. Hughes writes: "A great many people enjoy being interviewed, almost regardless of subject, and one must assume, from the lack of tangible rewards offered, that the advantages must be totally subjective. Here Theodore Caplow's suggestion . . . that the interview profits as a communication device from the contrast it offers to conversation in less formal situations might satisfy us . . .: that by offering a program of discussion, and an assurance that information offered will not be challenged or resisted, self-expression is facilitated to an unusual degree and that this is inherently satisfying" ("Of Sociology and the Interview," in *The Sociological Eye: Selected Papers* [New Brunswick, N.J.: Transaction Books, 1984], 511). See also Susan Krieger, *Social Science and the Self: Personal Essays on an Art Form* (New Brunswick, N.J.: Rutgers University Press, 1991), 152–53; and Susan Krieger, "Research and the Construction of a Text," *Studies in Symbolic Interaction* 2 (1979): 171–72.

26. Alfred Schutz, *The Phenomenology of the Social World*, trans. G. Walsh and F. Lehnert (Evanston: Northwestern University Press, 1967); Garfinkel, *Studies in Ethnomethodology.*

27. My use of the expression *discursive realm* is somewhat different from Michel Foucault's notion of *discursive field*. In her discussion of Foucault, Chris Weedon notes that "discursive fields consist of competing ways of giving meaning to the world and of organizing social institutions" (*Feminist Practice and Poststructuralist Theory* [Oxford: Basil Blackwell, 1987], 35). While Foucault is interested in how discursive fields structure institutions such as law, education, media, and family, I am interested in how discursive realms organize talk about experience. The discursive realm of professional work is narrower than the institution of the economy, and the discursive realm of inequality transcends several institutional boundaries.

28. A few examples: Margaret Wetherell and Jonathan Potter point to "interpretative repertoires" that people use to talk about race relations ("Discourse Analysis and the Identification of Interpretative Repertoires," in *Analysing Everyday Explanation: A Casebook of Methods*, ed. C. Antaki [London: Sage Publications, 1988], 168–83). And Sandra Silberstein describes the "gender ideologies" that shape heterosexual courtship stories

("Ideology as Process: Gender Ideology in Courtship Narratives," in *Gender and Discourse: The Power of Talk*, ed. A. D. Todd and S. Fisher [Norwood, N.J.: Ablex Publishing Corporation, 1988], 125–49).

29. Ann Swidler, "Culture in Action: Symbols and Strategies," *American Sociological Review* 51 (1986): 273–86.

30. Swidler, "Culture in Action," 279.

31. Burton J. Bledstein, *The Culture of Professionalism: The Middle Class and the Development of Higher Education in America* (New York: W. W. Norton and Company, 1976), esp. 86–92; William J. Goode, "Community within a Community: The Professions," *American Sociological Review* 22 (1957): 194–200; Talcott Parsons, "The Professions and Social Structure," in *Essays in Sociological Theory*, rev. ed. (New York: Free Press, 1954), 34–49; Howard M. Vollmer and Donald L. Mills, eds., *Professionalization* (Englewood Cliffs, N.J.: Prentice-Hall, 1966); Philip Elliot, *The Sociology of the Professions* (New York: Herder and Herder, 1972), esp. 126–39; Robert Dingwall and Philip Lewis, eds., *The Sociology of the Professions: Lawyers, Doctors and Others* (New York: St. Martin's Press, 1983); A. M. Carr-Saunders, *Professions: Their Organization and Place in Society* (Oxford: Clarendon Press, 1928); and Wilbert E. Moore, *The Professions: Roles and Rules* (New York: Russell Sage Foundation, 1970).

32. Social scientists generally understand individualism as an ideology that pervades the contemporary Western world. This understanding follows Karl Mannheim's conception of ideology as a system of thought based in specific sociohistorical conditions (*Ideology and Utopia: An Introduction to the Sociology of Knowledge* [New York: Harcourt, Brace, and Company, 1936). According to Swidler's distinction between tradition and ideology, however, individualism falls on the side of tradition precisely because it is so embedded in American culture that it seems an inevitable part of life. I use Swidler's conceptions because they allow for a careful distinction between two kinds of discourse—discourse about professional work and discourse about inequality—in a way that Mannheim's conception of ideology does not (see note 38).

33. Bledstein, *The Culture of Professionalism*, 87–88. Steven Lukes outlines the origins of the concept of individualism in the United States, England, France, and Germany, and discusses relationships among the various meanings attached to it, such as dignity, autonomy, privacy, and self-development (*Individualism* [Oxford: Basil Blackwell, 1973]).

34. Robert N. Bellah et al., *Habits of the Heart: Individualism and Commitment in American Life* (New York: Harper and Row, 1985), 33.

35. A broad literature on the professions addresses the historical processes by which particular professions (or professions in general) lay claim

to expertise, institutionalize their formal knowledge, and protect their right to educate their own members and to administer and evaluate their own practices. See Eliot Freidson, *Professional Powers: A Study of the Institutionalization of Formal Knowledge* (Chicago: University of Chicago Press, 1986); Andrew Abbott, *The System of Professions: An Essay on the Division of Expert Labor* (Chicago: University of Chicago Press, 1988); Everett Cherrington Hughes, "Professions in Transition," in *Men and Their Work* (Westport, Conn.: Greenwood Press, 1958), 131–38; and Bledstein, *The Culture of Professionalism*, 83–86.

36. Bledstein, *The Culture of Professionalism*, 172.

37. Sometimes the presumption of neutrality *constitutes* the gendered or racial character of discourse. See, for example, Catharine A. MacKinnon's critique of objectivity, a supposedly neutral discourse that is gendered in the sense that it silences women's voices ("Feminism, Marxism, Method, and the State: Toward Feminist Jurisprudence," *Signs: Journal of Women in Culture and Society* 8 [1983]: 635–58). I have argued that when professional women express a desire for a gender-neutral relation to their work, they are using a gendered discourse, one that conflates masculinity and neutrality ("Making Sense of 'the Woman Who Becomes a Man,' " in *Gender and Discourse*, 275–95). In addition, women of color have exposed some feminists' supposedly neutral use of *woman* as a racialized discourse that generalizes from the experiences of white, middle-class women to all women, obliterating the experiences of women of color and working-class women (Angela Y. Davis, *Women, Race and Class* [New York: Vintage Books, 1983]).

38. Swidler, "Culture in Action," 279. In using Swidler's distinction between tradition and ideology, I have chosen not to use *ideology* in its more common sociological sense. John B. Thompson calls the latter the "critical conception" of ideology, a conception that links ideology to "the process of sustaining asymmetrical relations of power—that is, to the process of maintaining domination. This use of the term . . . preserves the negative connotation which has been conveyed by the term throughout most of its history" (*Studies in the Theory of Ideology* [Berkeley: University of California Press, 1984], 4). If I had used the critical conception of ideology, I would have described the discursive realm of professional work as ideological because its individualism and its supposed neutrality with respect to gender and race conceal the ways in which such discourse has been used to advantage white men and disadvantage others. I certainly do not dispute that point; indeed my analysis supports it. However, I decided to follow Swidler's distinction between tradition and ideology because it helps me to demonstrate the relatively settled character of actual talk about

professional work and the relatively unsettled character of actual talk about inequality in contemporary American culture. Thus, in following Swidler's usage, I reserve the term *ideology* for discursive realms that exhibit their ideological content explicitly in talk. For an interesting analysis of professionals' narratives that uses the more common sociological understanding of ideology, see Patricia Geist and Monica Hardesty, "Ideological Positioning in Professionals' Narratives of Quality Medical Care," *Studies in Symbolic Interaction* 11 (1990): 257–84.

39. Mikhail M. Bakhtin, "The Problem of Speech Genres," in *Speech Genres and Other Late Essays*, trans. V. W. McGee (Austin: University of Texas Press, 1986), 92.

40. There is a readily accessible demonstration of this history of change in Paula S. Rothenberg, ed., *Race, Class, and Gender in the United States: An Integrated Study*, 2d ed. (New York: St. Martin's Press, 1992), part 5, "How it Happened: Race and Gender Issues in U.S. Law."

41. Marilyn Frye, *The Politics of Reality: Essays in Feminist Theory* (Trumansburg, N.Y.: Crossing Press, 1983), 4.

42. My use of Swidler's distinction does not do justice to her interest in broad cultural explanation. She argues that during settled periods, tradition "provides a repertoire of capacities from which varying strategies of action may be constructed." Although their constraint may not be felt, traditions do constrain in the sense that "alternative ways of organizing action seem unimaginable, or at least implausible." In unsettled periods, when ideologies are prominent, "meanings are more highly articulated and explicit," but are also more directly "in competition with other sets of cultural assumptions" ("Culture in Action," 284).

43. See the appendix for a discussion of early data analyses.

44. While I use *narrative strategies* in the specific sense defined in the text, others use this term in a similar way to refer to a narrator's orientation to cultural scripts. Indeed, a prominent question in the growing literature on women's narratives is how to interpret the nature of the struggle embodied in narrative strategies. For example, scholars offer various interpretations of women's emphasis on selflessness and orientation to others in their life stories. Some argue that the narration of self through identification with some other signifies acquiescence to conventional scripts about women's lives; others suggest that it can be interpreted as subverting those expectations (Personal Narratives Group, *Interpreting Women's Lives*, 20; Mary Gergen, "Life Stories," 127–44; Mary G. Mason, "The Other Voice: Autobiographies of Women Writers," in *Life/Lines*, 19–44; Susan Groag Bell and Marilyn Yalom, "Introduction," in *Revealing Lives*, 9.)

45. William Labov, *Language in the Inner City: Studies in the Black English Vernacular* (Philadelphia: University of Pennsylvania Press, 1972), 359–60.

46. Interestingly, some major social science studies have been based on the experiences of one individual or a small number of individuals—for example, Harold Garfinkel, "Passing and the Managed Achievement of Sex Status in an Intersexed Person," in *Studies in Ethnomethodology,* 116–85; Robert E. Lane, *Political Ideology: Why the American Common Man Believes What He Does* (New York: Free Press, 1962); and Marjorie Shostak, *Nisa: The Life and Words of a !Kung Woman* (Cambridge: Harvard University Press, 1981). Shostak discusses how she used one person's narrative as ethnography in " 'What the Wind Won't Take Away': The Genesis of *Nisa—The Life and Words of a !Kung Woman,*" in *Interpreting Women's Lives,* 228–40. Perhaps anthropology has been more open than sociology to the cultural or general significance of individuals' lives. For example, sixty years ago cultural anthropologist Edward Sapir argued that the study of culture would be enhanced by the study of personality: "There is a very real hurt done our understanding of culture when we systematically ignore the individual and his types of interrelationship with other individuals" ("The Emergence of the Concept of Personality in a Study of Cultures," *The Journal of Social Psychology* 5 [1934]: 411). Yet sociologist Everett V. Stonequist made a similar argument in the 1930s: "The life histories of marginal men offer the most significant material for the analysis of the cultural process as it springs from the contacts of social groups" (*The Marginal Man: A Study in Personality and Culture Conflict* [New York: Charles Scribner's Sons, 1937], 222).

47. Blum and McHugh, *Self-reflection in the Arts and Sciences,* 37. My understanding of both theoretical commitments is deeply indebted to the social theory of Blum and McHugh, whose work integrates the interests of interpretive sociology and continental philosophy. Readers interested in Blum's and McHugh's full development of these and related theoretical ideas should refer not only to *Self-reflection* but also to Alan F. Blum, *Socrates: The Original and Its Images* (London: Routledge and Kegan Paul, 1978); Alan F. Blum, *Theorizing* (London: Heinemann Educational Books, Ltd., 1974); and Peter McHugh et al., *On the Beginning of Social Inquiry* (London: Routledge and Kegan Paul, 1974).

48. George Herbert Mead, *Mind, Self, and Society,* ed. C. W. Morris (Chicago: University of Chicago Press, 1934), 146.

49. McHugh et al., *On the Beginning of Social Inquiry,* 43–44.

50. In describing the use of examples by discourse analysts, Scott Jacobs states that "what people do a lot may be less important than what people

can do, but don't do very often, or what people mean by what they do, whatever it is. The conditions that lead to particular behaviors is [*sic*] of less interest than the kind of knowledge that makes those behaviors sensible or nonsensical in the first place" ("How to Make an Argument from Example in Discourse Analysis," in *Contemporary Issues in Language and Discourse Processes*, ed. D. G. Ellis and W. A. Donohue [Hillsdale, N.J.: Lawrence Erlbaum Associates, 1986], 152, emphasis in original). Interestingly, Ricca Edmondson argues that qualitative sociologists (not just those using the methods of discourse analysis) often use examples that are not representative of their samples in the statistical sense. They do so in order to show, rather than merely describe, what they want the reader to understand. Examples "function rhetorically as signs: signs as symptoms of states of affairs, signs as encapsulating states of affairs in some way which enables the reader to interpret future situations" (*Rhetoric in Sociology,* 52).

51. Blum and McHugh, *Self-reflection in the Arts and Sciences,* 32.

52. Hans-Georg Gadamer, *Truth and Method* (New York: Seabury Press, 1975), 401.

53. Gadamer, *Truth and Method,* 404.

54. Blum and McHugh, *Self-reflection in the Arts and Sciences,* 42.

55. Kenneth Burke, *Language as Symbolic Action: Essays on Life, Literature, and Method* (Berkeley: University of California Press, 1966), 44, emphasis in original.

56. C. Wright Mills writes, "The only source for a terminology of motives is the vocabularies of motives actually and usually verbalized by actors in specific situations" ("Situated Actions and Vocabularies of Motive," *American Sociological Review* 5 [1940]: 910). Peter L. Berger and Thomas Luckmann state, "The most important vehicle of reality-maintenance is conversation" (*The Social Construction of Reality: A Treatise in the Sociology of Knowledge* [New York: Anchor Books, 1966], 152). And Harold Garfinkel shows the myriad ways that talk both takes for granted and produces the commonsense world (*Studies in Ethnomethodology*). Marjorie Harness Goodwin offers an interesting discussion of talk as social action in *He-Said-She-Said: Talk as Social Organization Among Black Children* (Bloomington: Indiana University Press, 1990), chap. 1.

57. This idea has been argued cogently by several authors, including Mishler, *Research Interviewing;* and Charles L. Briggs, *Learning How to Ask: A Sociolinguistic Appraisal of the Role of the Interview in Social Science Research* (Cambridge: Cambridge University Press, 1986).

58. Blum and McHugh demonstrate the incoherence of such an orientation: "Since all 'meaning,' intelligibility, identification, description, etc. depend on linguistic conventions, the demand to isolate a 'domain' or

'realm' of world, reality, etc., external to language asks for a conception of an actor/interpreter who is not originally oriented and who only acquires an orientation empirically. We assume that the type of actor required by this demand is impossible (inexplicable, incoherent) and, more frequently, that the capacity to imagine such an actor itself testifies to what *we* are arguing for. This is to say that the rejection of the assumption that 'the limits of language are the limits of the world' can only occur as another confirmation of that relationship. That is, the relation can only be rejected *intelligibly*" (*Self-reflection in the Arts and Sciences*, 32–33, emphasis in original).

59. Garfinkel, *Studies in Ethnomethodology;* Peter G. Stromberg, *Language and Self-transformation: A Study of the Christian Conversion Narrative* (Cambridge: Cambridge University Press, 1993).

60. Like Garfinkel did twenty-five years ago (*Studies in Ethnomethodology*), Mishler shows how survey researchers develop techniques to eliminate the effects of specific contexts on subjects' responses, and yet how they must reintroduce contextual factors in order to interpret those same responses (*Research Interviewing*, chap. 1). In this sense, everyday speakers are more sophisticated than survey researchers because they know and take into account that innumerable features of the context affect what others tell them.

61. David R. Maines, "Narrative's Moment and Sociology's Phenomena: Toward a Narrative Sociology," *The Sociological Quarterly* 34 (1993): 32. Many others make similar arguments, among them, Mishler, *Research Interviewing;* Catherine Kohler Riessman, *Divorce Talk: Women and Men Make Sense of Personal Relationships* (New Brunswick, N.J.: Rutgers University Press, 1990); and Richard Harvey Brown, *Society as Text: Essays on Rhetoric, Reason, and Reality* (Chicago: University of Chicago Press, 1987).

62. For a range of these differing interests, procedures, and approaches, see Rosenwald and Ochberg, *Storied Lives;* Personal Narratives Group, *Interpreting Women's Lives;* Stromberg, *Language and Self-transformation;* Sherna Berger Gluck and Daphne Patai, eds., *Women's Words: The Feminist Practice of Oral History* (New York: Routledge, Chapman and Hall, 1991).

63. See, for example, Rosenwald and Ochberg, *Storied Lives.*

64. Clifford Geertz, "Making Experiences, Authoring Selves," in *The Anthropology of Experience*, ed. V. W. Turner and E. M. Bruner (Urbana: University of Illinois Press, 1986), 374, 380.

65. For example, Barbara Cox Walkover provides a fascinating discussion of the contradictory discourses about parenting expressed in prospective parents' stories ("The Family as an Overwrought Object of Desire," in *Storied Lives*, 178–91.

66. Colleen Bell helped me to focus on the most important materials in the vast literature on educational administration.

67. National Center for Education Statistics, *American Education at a Glance* (Washington, D.C.: U.S. Department of Education, 1992).

68. Larry Cuban, "Conflict and Leadership in the Superintendency," *Phi Delta Kappan* 67 (1985): 28.

69. Roald F. Campbell et al., *The Organization and Control of American Schools* (Columbus, Ohio: Charles E. Merrill Publishing Company, 1985), 196–97.

70. M. William Konnert and John J. Augenstein, *The Superintendency in the Nineties: What Superintendents and Board Members Need to Know* (Lancaster, Pa.: Technomic Publishing Co., 1990), 10. For a discussion of the particular tasks of the urban superintendent, see Hugh J. Scott, *The Black School Superintendent: Messiah or Scapegoat?* (Washington, D.C.: Howard University Press, 1980).

71. Nancy L. Arnez, *The Besieged School Superintendent: A Case Study of School Superintendent-School Board Relations in Washington, D.C., 1973– 1975* (Washington, D.C.: University Press of America, 1981); Larry Cuban, *Urban School Chiefs Under Fire* (Chicago: University of Chicago Press, 1976); Arthur Blumberg, *The School Superintendent: Living with Conflict* (New York: Teachers College Press, 1985); and Scott, *The Black School Superintendent.* For a comparison of the political aspects of the job in the United States, United Kingdom, and Australia, see Frederick M. Wirt, "The Chief Educational Officer in Comparative Perspective," *Comparative Education Review* 32 (1988): 39–57.

72. Robert L. Crowson, "The Local School District Superintendency: A Puzzling Administrative Role," *Educational Administration Quarterly* 23 (1987): 51.

73. David Tyack and Elisabeth Hansot, *Managers of Virtue: Public School Leadership in America, 1820–1980* (New York: Basic Books, 1982).

74. Konnert and Augenstein, *The Superintendency in the Nineties,* 51.

75. Luvern L. Cunningham and Joseph T. Hentges, *The American School Superintendency 1982: A Summary Report* (Arlington, Va.: American Association of School Administrators, 1982), 23.

76. Tyack and Hansot, *Managers of Virtue,* 257.

77. Freidson, *Professional Powers,* 60.

78. Konnert and Augenstein, *The Superintendency in the Nineties,* 189.

79. "Education Vital Signs" (a supplement to the *American School Board Journal* and *The Executive Educator*), *American School Board Journal* 178 (December 1991): A-11.

80. Michael G. Fullan, *The New Meaning of Educational Change* (New York: Teachers College Press, 1991), 336.

81. Tyack and Hansot, *Managers of Virtue*, 169.

82. See note 2 and the appendix.

83. Although there are 15,400 public school districts in the U.S., not all of them have a K–12 superintendent, hence the much lower number of 10,683 K–12 superintendents nationwide. The exact number of women of color is difficult to determine because only thirty-nine state departments of education reported statistics on the racial composition of the superintendency in 1991 (see the appendix). In those thirty-nine states, there were thirty-five women of color. If women of color were counted in all states, there might be a few more than that, hence my rough estimate of forty-five. (Bell and Chase, "The Underrepresentation of Women in School Leadership").

84. National Center for Education Statistics, *American Education at a Glance*. The predominance of women in teaching positions has changed remarkably little in the twentieth century. In 1900, 74.5 percent of teachers were women. The highest percentage was reached in 1920 with women constituting 84.5 percent of teachers (Kaufman, "Professional Women," 330.)

85. Jill Young Miller, "Lonely at the Top," *School and Community* 72 (Summer 1986): 11.

86. The figure for the United States population is in *Statistical Abstract of the United States: 1992*, 112th ed. (Washington, D.C.: U.S. Bureau of the Census, 1992), 17. The statistic on students is in National Center for Education Statistics, *Digest of Education Statistics* (Washington, D.C.: U.S. Department of Education, 1991). And the statistic on teachers is in National Center for Education Statistics, *American Education at a Glance*.

87. Here is a very partial list of texts in a rapidly growing literature: Charol Shakeshaft, *Women in Educational Administration* (Newbury Park, Calif.: Sage Publications, 1987); Sakre Kennington Edson, *Pushing the Limits: The Female Administrative Aspirant* (Albany: State University of New York Press, 1988); Flora Ida Ortiz, *Career Patterns in Education: Women, Men and Minorities in Public School Administration* (New York: Praeger Publishers, 1982); Myra Sadker, David Sadker, and Susan Klein, "The Issue of Gender in Elementary and Secondary Education," in *Review of Research in Education*, vol. 17, ed. G. Grant (Washington, D.C.: American Educational Research Association, 1991), 285–94; Colleen S. Bell, "Organizational Influences on Women's Experience in the Superintendency," *Peabody Journal of Education* 65 (1988): 31–59; Susan E. Chase and Col-

leen S. Bell, "Ideology, Discourse, and Gender: How Gatekeepers Talk about Women School Superintendents," *Social Problems* 37 (1990): 163–77.

88. The number of women on school boards had been increasing, but in recent years it has decreased. In 1986, 36.6 percent of school board members were women, but in 1991, 34.7 percent were women ("Education Vital Signs," A-10.) The same survey shows that the representation of people of color on school boards is extremely low. In 1986, 4.7 percent of school board members were Black, Hispanic, American Indian, or Asian American; in 1991, 3.4 percent were of color.

89. Scott, *The Black School Superintendent*, 188.

Chapter Two: Settled and Unsettled Discursive Realms

1. Elliot G. Mishler, *Research Interviewing: Context and Narrative* (Cambridge: Harvard University Press, 1986); Peter G. Stromberg, *Language and Self-transformation: A Study of the Christian Conversion Narrative* (Cambridge: Cambridge University Press, 1993). In more general terms, the indexicality of language has been demonstrated and discussed by many, including Harold Garfinkel, *Studies in Ethnomethodology* (Englewood Cliffs, N.J.: Prentice-Hall, 1967); Charles L. Briggs, *Learning How to Ask: A Sociolinguistic Appraisal of the Role of the Interview in Social Science Research* (Cambridge: Cambridge University Press, 1986); and John Heritage, *Garfinkel and Ethnomethodology* (Cambridge: Polity Press, 1984).

2. Wallace L. Chafe, "The Deployment of Consciousness in the Production of a Narrative," in *The Pear Stories: Cognitive, Cultural, and Linguistic Aspects of Narrative Production*, ed. W. L. Chafe (Norwood, N.J.: Ablex Publishing Corporation, 1980), 14–15. Chafe adopts the term *idea unit* to describe these spurts of language. For my purposes, idea unit is too content oriented; I focus on spurts of language because I want to capture the flow of speech.

3. Because I am focusing on content as well as forms of speech, the extremely detailed transcripts used by discourse and conversational analysts are not appropriate for my purposes. My method of transcription is closest to that developed by Catherine Kohler Riessman in *Divorce Talk: Women and Men Make Sense of Personal Relationships* (New Brunswick, N.J.: Rutgers University Press, 1990). For a discussion of how transcribing practices embody theories of language, see Elliot G. Mishler, "Represent-

ing Discourse: The Rhetoric of Transcription," *Journal of Narrative and Life History* 1 (1991): 255–80; and Elinor Ochs, "Transcription as Theory," in *Developmental Pragmatics,* ed. E. Ochs and B. B. Schieffelin (New York: Academic Press, 1979), 43–72.

4. We determined class backgrounds by asking about parents' occupations and educational levels; we also asked women how they would describe their class backgrounds.

5. In discussing the disjunctures between language and women's experience, Marjorie L. DeVault raises the question of how researchers find categories that are meaningful in women's lives ("Talking and Listening from Women's Standpoint: Feminist Strategies for Interviewing and Analysis," *Social Problems* 37 [1990]: 96–116). For example, DeVault wanted to interview women about a part of their lives for which she could find "no concise label," what she called "the work of feeding a family" (99). My interviewing experience differed from DeVault's in that work history is a readily available category that is meaningful in women superintendents' lives. Yet like DeVault, who found that questions about the work of feeding a family invited women to speak "easily and naturally" because it was "a category that organized their day-to-day activity" (99), I found that women superintendents received the request for a work history as an invitation to speak easily and at length.

6. Dorothy E. Smith, *The Everyday World as Problematic: A Feminist Sociology* (Boston: Northeastern University Press, 1987), 188.

7. William Labov, *Language in the Inner City: Studies in the Black English Vernacular* (Philadelphia: University of Pennsylvania Press, 1972), 363. Although specific definitions differ, most researchers use the terms *story* and *narrative* to refer to a linguistically identifiable stretch of talk. For example, Labov defines narrative (or story) as "one method of recapitulating past experience by matching a verbal sequence of clauses to the sequence of events which (it is inferred) actually occurred" (359–60). According to Labov, a fully developed narrative or story includes an abstract that summarizes the whole story; an orientation that identifies "the time, place, persons, and their activity or situation" (364); complicating action, or a description of what happened; an evaluation that "indicate[s] the point of the story" (366); a resolution that describes the termination of the events; and a coda that signals that "the narrative is finished" (365). By contrast, Riessman uses *story* to refer to a temporally ordered narrative but further identifies other kinds of talk as "habitual," "hypothetical," and "episodic" narrative forms (*Divorce Talk,* 78). As I discussed in chapter 1, I find such distinctions useful. Nonetheless, I use *narrative* in a broader

sense to refer to the entire process by which a woman presents her experiences of power and subjection over the course of an interview.

8. Arthur Blumberg found that "orchestrator" is one of the metaphors some superintendents use to describe their work (*The School Superintendent: Living with Conflict* [New York: Teachers College Press, 1985], 36).

9. Labov, *Language in the Inner City,* 359–60.

10. Livia Polanyi, *Telling the American Story: A Structural and Cultural Analysis of Conversational Storytelling* (Norwood, N.J.: Ablex Publishers Corporation, 1985), 12–13, emphasis in original.

11. Elliot G. Mishler, "The Analysis of Interview-Narratives," in *Narrative Psychology: The Storied Nature of Human Conduct,* ed. T. R. Sarbin (New York: Praeger Publishers, 1986), 234–35.

12. Elizabeth Higginbotham and Lynn Weber Cannon, "Rethinking Mobility: Towards a Race and Gender Inclusive Theory," Research Paper 8 (Center for Research on Women, Memphis State University, Memphis, Tenn., 1988); Cheryl Townsend Gilkes, "Going Up for the Oppressed: The Career Mobility of Black Women Community Workers," *Journal of Social Issues* 39 (1983): 115–39; and Paula Giddings, *When and Where I Enter: The Impact of Black Women on Race and Sex in America* (New York: Bantam Books, 1984).

13. See Hugh J. Scott, *The Black School Superintendent: Messiah or Scapegoat?* (Washington, D.C.: Howard University Press, 1980), chap. 2, "Urban Education: Challenges and Deficiencies," for a discussion of the particular problems facing urban superintendents.

14. Judith Rollins, *Between Women: Domestics and Their Employers* (Philadelphia: Temple University Press, 1985), 225. Similarly, John Langston Gwaltney's study of urban Blacks shows how talk about work is shaped by race and class. He cites May Madison, for example, a domestic worker who states, "One very important difference between white people and black people is that white people think you *are* your work. . . . Now a black person has more sense than that because he knows that what I am doing doesn't have anything to do with what I want to do or what I do when I am doing for myself. Now, black people think that my work is just what I have to do to get what I want" (*Drylongso: A Self-portrait of Black America* [New York: Random House, 1980], 173–74, emphasis in original). Riessman discusses the different meanings of work and leisure for professional and working-class people and the relationship between these meanings and experiences of marriage and divorce (*Divorce Talk,* 71).

15. Carolyn G. Heilbrun, *Writing a Woman's Life* (New York: Ballantine Books, 1989), 18.

16. It is possible to argue that the conventions of intensive interviews reinforce the individualistic character of this discursive realm. Such interviews, especially those aimed at evoking life stories, are grounded in the Western notion that the fundamental unit is the individual's life and experience. Many theorists have pointed to the particularity of the Western concept of the individual. For example, George E. Marcus and Michael M. J. Fischer write, "The Samoan language has no terms corresponding to 'personality, self, character'; instead of our Socratic 'know thyself,' Samoans say 'take care of the relationship'; instead of the European image of a rounded, integrated personality, like a sphere with no sides, Samoans are like gems cut with many distinct sides" (*Anthropology as Cultural Critique: An Experimental Moment in the Human Sciences* [Chicago: University of Chicago Press, 1986], 65).

17. See, for example, Jake Ryan and Charles Sackrey, eds., *Strangers in Paradise: Academics from the Working Class* (Boston: South End Press, 1984). Most of the stories in this collection are by white men; social class is the major topic throughout.

18. Elizabeth Higginbotham, "Employment for Professional Black Women in the Twentieth Century," in *Ingredients for Women's Employment Policy*, ed. C. Bose and G. Spitze (Albany: State University of New York Press, 1987), 73–91.

19. For an analysis of the extent to which women superintendents challenge authoritarian and hierarchical notions of leadership, see Colleen S. Bell and Susan E. Chase, "Resistance and Conformity: Women's Educational Leadership" (Paper presented at the annual meeting of the American Educational Research Association, San Francisco, April 1989). In that paper we also discuss the import of women superintendents' career paths to the superintendency. For example, while virtually all superintendents have been teachers, women tend to have more years of teaching experience than their male counterparts.

20. For an analysis of awkward moments produced by these questions in one of our earliest interviews, see Susan E. Chase and Colleen S. Bell, "Interpreting the Complexity of Women's Subjectivity," in *Interactive Oral Interviewing: Essays on Interactional Processes*, ed. K. L. Rogers and E. McMahan (Hillsdale, N.J.: Lawrence Erlbaum Publishers, forthcoming).

21. Karen Brodkin Sacks describes a similar problem with questions posed in sociological terms ("What's a Life Story Got To Do With It?" in *Interpreting Women's Lives: Feminist Theory and Personal Narratives*, ed. The Personal Narratives Group [Bloomington: Indiana University Press, 1989], 88).

22. Similarly, in her study of women managers, Judi Marshall asked "whether being a woman had been important in any way" only after she had asked about work history, future plans, and hindering and helping factors ("Exploring the Experiences of Women Managers: Towards Rigour in Qualitative Methods," in *Feminist Social Psychology: Developing Theory and Practice*, ed. S. Wilkinson [Philadelphia: Open University Press, 1986], 199).

23. Marilyn Frye and Peggy McIntosh (among others) have articulated an alternative discourse about how being white shapes experience (Frye, "On Being White: Thinking Toward a Feminist Understanding of Race and Race Supremacy," in *The Politics of Reality: Essays in Feminist Theory* [Trumansburg, N.Y.: Crossing Press, 1983], 110–27; and McIntosh, "White Privilege and Male Privilege: A Personal Account of Coming to See Correspondences Through Work in Women's Studies," in *Race, Class, and Gender: An Anthology*, ed. M. L. Andersen and P. H. Collins [Belmont, Calif.: Wadsworth Publishing Company, 1992], 70–81).

24. Others have developed similar notions. For example, Jane H. Hill analyzes "dysfluencies" that indicate "the necessity of *having to choose a language*" ("The Voices of Don Gabriel: Responsibility and Self in a Modern Mexicano Narrative," in *Dialogical Anthropology*, ed. B. Mannheim and D. Tedlock [Philadelphia: University of Pennsylvania Press, in press], 1 in draft, emphasis in original). Peter Stromberg focuses on the "temporary inability to speak" within Christian conversion narratives ("Ideological Language in the Transformation of Identity," *American Anthropologist* 92 [1990]: 49). R. P. McDermott provides an analysis of inarticulateness as resistance to the status quo ("Inarticulateness," in *Linguistics in Context: Connecting Observation and Understanding*, ed. D. Tannen [Norwood, N.J.: Ablex Publishing Corporation, 1988], 37–67).

25. Dana Jack points out that "meta-statements alert us to the individual's awareness of a discrepancy within the self—or between what is expected and what is being said" (Kathryn Anderson and Dana C. Jack, "Learning to Listen: Interview Techniques and Analyses," in *Women's Words: The Feminist Practice of Oral History*, ed. S. B. Gluck and D. Patai [New York: Routledge, Chapman and Hall, 1991], 22).

26. I certainly do not claim that disrupted talk appears only in talk about inequality. In chapter 4, for example, I discuss an instance of disrupted talk related to Denise Nelson's discussion of leaving the superintendency for a less demanding job. In these interviews, however, disrupted talk appeared most prominently in talk about inequality. In other interviews, disrupted talk may appear elsewhere, as the references in note 24 suggest. The reader should remember that in articulating the disjunction between discourse

about professional work and discourse about inequality, I am not pointing to a grammatical rule but to a pattern in actual talk.

27. Jane H. Hill, "The Refiguration of the Anthropology of Language," *Cultural Anthropology* 1 (1986): 97.

28. Corinne Glesne, "Rapport and Friendship in Ethnographic Research," *Qualitative Studies in Education* 2 (1989): 45–54; Arlene Kaplan Daniels, "Self-deception and Self-discovery in Fieldwork," *Qualitative Sociology* 6 (1983): 195–214; Louis Corsino, "Fieldworker Blues: Emotional Stress and Research Underinvolvement in Fieldwork Settings," *The Social Science Journal* 24 (1987): 275–85.

29. Francesca M. Cancian, "Feminist Science: Methodologies That Challenge Inequality," *Gender and Society* 6 (1992): 623–42; Renate Duelli Klein, "How to Do What We Want to Do: Thoughts about Feminist Methodology," in *Theories of Women's Studies,* ed. G. Bowles and R. Duelli Klein (London: Routledge and Kegan Paul, 1983), 88–104; Maria Mies, "Towards a Methodology for Feminist Research," in *Theories of Women's Studies,* 117–39; Marjorie Shostak, " 'What the Wind Won't Take Away': The Genesis of *Nisa—The Life and Words of a !Kung Woman,*" in *Interpreting Women's Lives,* 228–40; Marjorie Mbilinyi, " 'I'd Have Been a Man': Politics and the Labor Process in Producing Personal Narratives," in *Interpreting Women's Lives,* 204–27. Margery Wolf explores the complexities of feminist concerns about the relationship between researcher and researched in *A Thrice-told Tale: Feminism, Postmodernism, and Ethnographic Responsibility* (Stanford: Stanford University Press, 1992), 117–26.

30. Others have developed the notion that interviews consist of listening and narrating as well as asking and answering questions. For example, DeVault, "Talking and Listening from Women's Standpoint"; Kathryn Anderson and Dana C. Jack, "Learning to Listen"; Mishler, *Research Interviewing,* chaps. 4 and 5.

31. Martine Burgos, "Life Stories, Narrativity, and the Search for the Self," *Life Stories/Récits de vie* 5 (1989): 33.

32. Catherine Kohler Riessman exemplifies this process in her analysis of how a white woman interviewer misunderstood a Puerto Rican woman's divorce story ("When Gender Is Not Enough: Women Interviewing Women," *Gender and Society* 1 [1987]: 172–207). Through a close look at the interview interaction, Riessman shows that the interviewer was expecting a temporally organized account while the interviewee offered an episodic narrative. The interviewer exercised her greater power in the research situation by attempting persistently to impose her sense of how a divorce story should be told. However, Riessman's interpretation empowers the narrator by hearing how and what she was communicating.

1. In order to protect Ana Martinez's identity, I use the term *Hispanic* rather than name her ethnicity specifically.

2. William Labov, *Language in the Inner City: Studies in the Black English Vernacular* (Philadelphia: University of Pennsylvania Press, 1972), 363.

3. Such comments are not uncommon among superintendents. In 1971, 71.4 percent of superintendents surveyed by the American Association of School Administrators said they would choose the career of superintendent in answer to the following question: "If you had to do it all over again what career would you choose?" A decade later, however, only 54.6 percent said they would choose their own profession (Luvern L. Cunningham and Joseph T. Hentges, *The American School Superintendency 1982: A Summary Report* [Arlington, Va.: American Association of School Administrators, 1982], 25–26).

4. Sakre Kennington Edson reports that many women aspirants to school administration "credit their spouses for being among the first to encourage them to pursue administrative careers" (*Pushing the Limits: The Female Administrative Aspirant* [Albany: State University of New York Press, 1988], 85). But she also points out that women frequently speak of marital tensions arising from the increased demands on their time related to administrative work (103).

5. Valentin N. Volosinov, *Marxism and the Philosophy of Language*, trans. L. Matejka and I. R. Titunik (New York: Seminar Press, 1973), 115–23. As Alan Rumsey explains, scholars generally interpret reported speech or direct dialogue (as distinct from indirect dialogue) as a storytelling device used to dramatize events by "import[ing] features of the projected speech situation into the projecting one" ("Wording, Meaning, and Linguistic Ideology," *American Anthropologist* 92 [1990]: 347).

6. Gail Jefferson calls this "volunteer" laughter; we laugh at the story even though Ana has not laughed first ("A Technique for Inviting Laughter and Its Subsequent Acceptance Declination," in *Everyday Language: Studies in Ethnomethodology*, ed. G. Psathas [New York: Irvington Publishers, 1979], 81). Our laughter in the earlier excerpt is also volunteer laughter.

7. Flora Ida Ortiz, *Career Patterns in Education: Women, Men and Minorities in Public School Administration* (New York: Praeger Publishers, 1982), 110–17.

8. Michael Agar and Jerry R. Hobbs, "Interpreting Discourse: Coherence and the Analysis of Ethnographic Interviews," *Discourse Processes* 5 (1982): 7.

9. Carolyn G. Heilbrun, "Non-autobiographies of 'Privileged' Women: England and America," in *Life/Lines: Theorizing Women's Autobiography*, ed. B. Brodzki and C. Schenck (Ithaca: Cornell University Press, 1988), 70.

10. Jacquelyn Wiersma, "The Press Release: Symbolic Communication in Life History Interviewing," *Journal of Personality* 56 (1988): 205–38.

11. Wiersma, "The Press Release," 206, 209.

12. Heilbrun, "Non-autobiographies of 'Privileged' Women," 70.

13. Howard S. Becker and James W. Carper, "The Development of Identification with an Occupation," *The American Journal of Sociology* 61 (1956): 289. They also demonstrate how these social-psychological mechanisms interact with the characteristics of specific occupations.

14. Mary Gergen, "Life Stories: Pieces of a Dream," in *Storied Lives: The Cultural Politics of Self-Understanding*, ed. G. C. Rosenwald and R. L. Ochberg (New Haven: Yale University Press, 1992), 138.

15. Rosabeth Moss Kanter, *Men and Women of the Corporation* (New York: Basic Books, 1977); Judith Lorber, *Women Physicians: Careers, Status, and Power* (New York: Tavistock Publications, 1984); Cynthia Fuchs Epstein, *Women in Law* (Garden City, N.Y.: Anchor Press, Doubleday, 1983).

16. In order to protect Ana Martinez's identity, I have excluded the nature and details of this serious crisis as well as Ana's handling of it.

17. Eliot Freidson, *Professional Powers: A Study of the Institutionalization of Formal Knowledge* (Chicago: University of Chicago Press, 1986), 211.

18. Everett Cherrington Hughes, "Mistakes at Work," in *Men and Their Work* (Westport, Conn.: Greenwood Press, 1958), 93.

19. Freidson, *Professional Powers*, 212, 219.

20. Ortiz might interpret this statement as evidence that Ana was expected to be a "warrior," to perform great feats in order to resolve problems within a largely Hispanic school district (*Career Patterns in Education*, 112). For another discussion of tensions experienced by Hispanic administrators, see A. Reynaldo Contreras, "Spanish-surnamed Administrators," *Emergent Leadership* 3 (1979): 33–47.

21. Many of the women superintendents we interviewed reported that they had earned reputations for being tough because of their willingness to make difficult decisions that their predecessors had avoided. This perception of women's leadership represents an interesting twist on gendered expectations. It may be that in a male-dominated professional context, women need to work harder to prove themselves and so adhere more strictly to the standard for excellence—in the case of the superintendency, being tough—than men do. Again, Ortiz might suggest that Ana is being recruited to yet another difficult assignment in an ethnically diverse district (*Career Patterns in Education*, 110–15).

22. George C. Rosenwald and Jacquelyn Wiersma, "Women, Career Changes, and the New Self: An Analysis of Rhetoric," *Psychiatry* 46 (1983): 218.

23. In the previous section, I mentioned only one instance where Ana recites direct dialogue with colleagues: "The male superintendents tell me / 'Ana, in Urbantown you had more experiences in six years than most superintendents have in thirty years.'" However, there were several stories in Ana's work history that included direct dialogue with supportive colleagues.

24. Wiersma, "The Press Release."

25. Public school districts in the United States are racially and ethnically segregated. Educational administrators of color (both men and women) are likely to serve in districts that have substantial populations of students of color (Ortiz, *Career Patterns in Education*, chap. 5; Elizabeth Higginbotham, "Employment for Professional Black Women in the Twentieth Century," in *Ingredients for Women's Employment Policy*, ed. C. Bose and G. Spitze [Albany: State University of New York Press, 1987], 74–75, 78, 84). This pattern characterizes the careers of the women superintendents we interviewed. All of the white women work in predominantly white districts (0 to 20 percent students of color, usually on the lower end). With one exception, the women of color work in districts with a large minority or majority of students of color (35 to 98 percent).

26. Pat Parker, "For the White Person Who Wants to Know How to Be My Friend," in *Making Face, Making Soul, Haciendo Caras: Creative and Critical Perspectives by Women of Color*, ed. G. Anzaldua (San Francisco: Aunt Lute Foundation Books, 1990), 297.

27. For analyses of tensions between white women and women of color, see Marilyn Frye, "On Being White: Thinking Toward a Feminist Understanding of Race and Race Supremacy," in *The Politics of Reality: Essays in Feminist Theory* (Trumansburg, N.Y.: Crossing Press, 1983), 110–27; Angela Y. Davis, *Women, Race and Class* (New York: Vintage Books, 1983); Paula Ross, "Women, Oppression, Privilege, and Competition," in *Competition: A Feminist Taboo?* ed. V. Miner and H. E. Longino (New York: Feminist Press, 1987), 209–20; Gloria Anzaldua, "Haciendo caras, una entrada," in *Making Face, Making Soul*, xv–xxviii.

28. Charles L. Briggs, *Learning How to Ask: A Sociolinguistic Appraisal of the Role of the Interview in Social Science Research* (Cambridge: Cambridge University Press, 1986), 108.

29. For an analysis of this interview, see Susan E. Chase and Colleen S. Bell, "Interpreting the Complexity of Women's Subjectivity," in *Interactive Oral Interviewing: Essays on Interactional Processes*, ed. K. L. Rogers

and E. McMahan (Hillsdale, N.J.: Lawrence Erlbaum Publishers, forth-coming).

30. Elizabeth Higginbotham and Lynn Weber Cannon, "Rethinking Mobility: Towards a Race and Gender Inclusive Theory," Research Paper 8 (Center for Research on Women, Memphis State University, Memphis, Tenn., 1988), 23; Cheryl Townsend Gilkes, "Going up for the Oppressed: The Career Mobility of Black Women Community Workers," *Journal of Social Issues* 39 (1983): 115–39.

31. Clara Rodriguez suggests that biculturalism is different from as-similation in that a bicultural person retains "Puerto Rican-ness, while absorbing that which is considered useful or necessary American-ness" ("A Cost-Benefit Analysis of Subjective Factors Affecting Assimilation: Puerto Ricans," *Ethnicity* 2 [1975]: 74). Similarly, Irene I. Blea describes a bicultural Chicano as one who "does not get caught in and between two cultures, but moves well between both." Blea argues that the one drawback of biculturalism is burn out. "They work too hard to obtain equality, and experience tiredness and frustration" (*Toward a Chicano Social Science* [New York: Praeger Publishers, 1988], 35).

32. The conflicts experienced by upwardly mobile people of color, which are due to pressures from the professional world as well as from the ethnic community, are described by Higginbotham and Cannon, "Rethinking Mobility," 35, 40–41; several essays in Cherrie Moraga and Gloria Anzaldua, eds., *This Bridge Called My Back: Writings by Radical Women of Color* (New York: Kitchen Table, Women of Color Press, 1983); Richard Rodriguez, *Hunger of Memory: The Education of Richard Rodriguez* (New York: Bantam Books, 1982); John Edgar Wideman, *Brothers and Keepers* (New York: Holt, Rinehart, and Winston, 1984); and Leanita McClain, "The Middle-class Black's Burden," in *A Foot in Each World: Essays and Articles by Leanita McClain*, ed. C. Page (Evanston: Northwestern University Press, 1986), 12–15.

33. See the appendix for a description of our interviews with school board members and other gatekeepers to the superintendency.

34. Patricia Hill Collins describes "extended families, churches, and African-American community organizations" as realms of "relatively safe discourse" for African-American women (*Black Feminist Thought: Knowledge, Consciousness, and the Politics of Empowerment* [Boston: Unwin Hyman, 1990], 95). The question of what conditions produce safe spaces within the context of interviews is a complex one. Interestingly, in dis-cussing interviews she conducted with Puerto Ricans, Clara Rodriguez points out that "the people in the ghetto areas certainly seemed to be more at ease with their re-telling [of experiences of discrimination]" than the

professionals ("A Cost-Benefit Analysis of Subjective Factors Affecting Assimilation," 77).

Chapter Four: Letting Ambition Go and Reconsidering Discrimination: Denise Nelson

1. By describing herself as living the life her mother would have loved to live, Nelson offers a good example of the "profound emotional interdependency" Mary Gergen finds in accomplished women's autobiographies ("Life Stories: Pieces of a Dream," in *Storied Lives: The Cultural Politics of Self-understanding,* ed. G. C. Rosenwald and R. L. Ochberg [New Haven: Yale University Press, 1992], 138).

2. In their discussions of stratification, structural functionalists treat the desire for upward social mobility as conformity to the society's stratification system (see, for example, Seymour Martin Lipset and Reinhard Bendix, *Social Mobility in Industrial Society* [Berkeley: University of California Press, 1963]; Pitrim A. Sorokin, *Social and Cultural Mobility* [New York: Free Press, 1959]). By contrast, Max Scheler analyzes the desire for social mobility—embodied by the "arriviste"—as indicating a lack of self-esteem (*Ressentiment* [New York: Free Press, 1961]). In my dissertation, I argued that both formulations fail to distinguish between vulgar forms of social climbing and an alternative understanding of ambition as "appetite, as a desire for what the world has to offer" (Susan E. Chase, "The Theory and Practice of Ambition," [Ph.D. diss., York University, 1987], 40). Denise Nelson expresses that appetite here as well as throughout her work history.

3. A notion of naive self-confidence seems to belong to the youthful stages of ambition. "The [appetitious] actor energetically pursues what the world has to offer, and is confident in an unselfconscious way about his [*sic*] own energetic pursuits" (Chase, "The Theory and Practice of Ambition," 51). I deliberately used the male pronoun in the first two chapters of my dissertation in order to discuss ambition as a gendered discourse.

4. American discourse about ambition includes an array of figures—the social climber, the self-made man, the artist striving for immortality, and the activist striving for social change—all of whom are engaged in activities that develop the self by orienting to others in particular ways. "The various forms of self-interest embodied in ambition—self-regard, self-expression, self-delight, and self-love—are inconceivable without the simultaneous desire for the regard, evaluation, appreciation, or recognition of others" (Chase, "The Theory and Practice of Ambition," 9).

5. In this regard, Denise's work history is more like Ana Martinez's than Margaret Parker's (chapter 5) and Karen Rhodes's (chapter 6). The latter two women include much more discussion of inequality in their work histories.

6. Marvin B. Scott and Stanford M. Lyman show how accounts are required and offered for "untoward" or deviant behavior ("Accounts," *American Sociological Review* 33 [1968]: 46–62). Deviant action within the professional world includes moving down the occupational ladder, taking a job with less remuneration, or taking a job in a less prestigious institution or location.

7. Colleen Bell's notes about her first phone contact with Denise include Denise's comment that she was leaving the superintendency after many years. I mention this to show that Denise topicalized her leaving even before Colleen and I interviewed her.

8. Denise's story about these traumatic events is an example of what superintendents call "war stories" (Arthur Blumberg, *The School Superintendent: Living with Conflict* [New York: Teachers College Press, 1985], 5–6). As Blumberg argues, superintendents face "the necessity of having to live daily with conflictual or potentially conflictual situations in which the superintendent plays a focal role as decision maker, mediator, or simply as a human lightning rod who attracts controversy" (1).

9. Scott and Lyman define accounts as either "explanations" or "justifications" of untoward behavior, and delineate the socially intelligible uses of each ("Accounts"). Although Denise both explains and justifies her decision, her account is more like those offered by Catherine Kohler Riessman's interviewees who sought to make sense of their divorces in a culture that values marriage (*Divorce Talk: Women and Men Make Sense of Personal Relationships* [New Brunswick, N.J.: Rutgers University Press, 1990], 14–16, 23, 64–65). When a speaker offers a justification or an explanation, she or he is usually seeking another's acceptance of that interpretation of an action. By contrast, a speaker who makes sense of an action treats the matter as open to the process of interpretation.

10. William Labov discusses the use of negatives as a way of "compar[ing] the events which did occur to those which did not occur" (*Language in the Inner City: Studies in the Black English Vernacular* [Philadelphia: University of Pennsylvania Press, 1972], 381).

11. Lewis A. Coser, *Greedy Institutions: Patterns of Undivided Commitment* (New York: Free Press, 1974). Greedy institutions "seek exclusive and undivided loyalty and they attempt to reduce the claims of competing roles and status positions on those they wish to encompass within their boundaries. Their demands on the person are omnivorous" (4).

12. For an analysis of that ideology, see Susan E. Chase, "Making Sense of 'The Woman Who Becomes a Man,'" in *Gender and Discourse: The Power of Talk*, ed. A. Todd and S. Fisher (Norwood, N.J.: Ablex Publishing Corporation, 1988), 275–95.

13. Among the superintendents Blumberg interviewed (twenty-four men, one woman), the most commonly mentioned stressful situations were "planning and presenting the budget; dealing with incompetent teachers; making decisions about expelling youngsters from school; and developing satisfying relationships with the news media" (*The School Superintendent*, 125). Although Blumberg does not include it in this list, decisions about layoffs would certainly rank high among stress-producing situations.

14. Kathleen Gerson convincingly demonstrates that women's choices are related to the structure of opportunities and constraints they face in the workplace and at home (*Hard Choices: How Women Decide About Work, Career, and Motherhood* [Berkeley: University of California Press, 1985]). Thus, Gerson might focus on the difficulties Denise faced at work, despite Denise's argument that more is involved. I suggest, however, that by theorizing choice as shaped primarily by conditions, Gerson foregoes a stronger understanding of how persons actively develop interest or desire in one or another aspect of life.

15. Those who write about the superintendency often mention the connection between short terms of office and the immense difficulties of the job. For example, Michael G. Fullan states, "The task of the district administrator is to lead the development and execution of a system-wide approach that explicitly addresses and takes into account *all* these causes of change at the district, school, and classroom levels. In addition to doing this for specific policies, it is also the district administrator's task to increase the basic capacity of the system to manage change effectively. No wonder there is such a high turnover rate among superintendents!" (*The New Meaning of Educational Change*, 2d ed. [New York: Teachers College Press, 1991], 191, emphasis in original).

16. According to Blumberg, superintendents in general are deeply aware of the political nature of their work and frequently use the metaphor of survival to describe how they get through particular situations or how they manage to keep their jobs in general (Blumberg, *The School Superintendent*, 49–50). He states, "For school superintendents . . . the consequence of making unpopular decisions, regardless of how morally and educationally correct they may have been, can be and not infrequently is the rather abrupt loss of one's job" (8).

17. Blumberg, *The School Superintendent*, 156.

18. Blumberg's chapter on the effects of the superintendency on spouses is titled "Being a Superintendent's Wife" (*The School Superintendent*). It is written by Phyllis Blumberg, who interviewed five women whose husbands are superintendents.

19. Hanna Papanek, "Men, Women, and Work: Reflections on the Two-person Career," *American Journal of Sociology* 78 (1973): 852–72. Rosabeth Moss Kanter discusses the two-person career from the perspective of corporate wives (*Men and Women of the Corporation* [New York: Basic Books, 1977], chap. 5, esp. 111). Arlie Hochschild talks about the two-person career in terms of "backstage support" or "backstage wealth." She "discovered that the higher up the corporate ladder, the more home support a worker had," although among executives men had more support than women (*The Second Shift* [New York: Avon Books, 1989], 255).

20. Hochschild, *The Second Shift*, 18, 157.

21. Rose Laub Coser and Gerald Rokoff, "Women in the Occupational World: Social Disruption and Conflict," in *Women and Work: Problems and Perspectives*, ed. R. Kahn-Hut, A. K. Daniels, and R. Colvard (New York: Oxford University Press, 1982), 39–53. In *The Second Shift*, Hochschild presents the various ways that women resolve this conflict.

22. Hochschild, *The Second Shift*, 208–11. She writes, "Men and women may gradually come to share the work at home more equitably, but now they may be doing altogether less of it. The latent deal between husband and wife is 'I'll share, but we'll do less.' A strategy of 'cutting back' on the housework, the children, the marriage may be on the rise, with correspondingly reduced ideas about what people 'need'" (209). In chapter 12, Hochschild shows how a dual-career couple who have decided to make family life their front stage must struggle against the social tide.

23. Suzanne Laberge and Gillian Sankoff, "Anything *You* Can Do," in *Discourse and Syntax, Syntax and Semantics*, vol. 12, ed. Talmy Givón (New York: Academic Press, 1979), 429.

24. Similarly, Riessman discusses an example of pronoun switching in terms of the narrator's attempt to distance herself from her talk. By using "the impersonal 'you' to describe a distinctly personal perception," a divorced woman "communicate[s] her alienation at the time of the marriage from the self she now perceives herself to be" (*Divorce Talk*, 100).

25. While Denise has previously described the discriminatory treatment as "very very subtle," here she describes it as "overt." We can easily resolve this apparent contradiction when we notice that she uses the word *subtle* to argue that it was the type of sexism that cannot be resisted legally. She uses the word *overt* to indicate that it was directed specifically at her.

1. Elizabeth Higginbotham, "Employment for Professional Black Women in the Twentieth Century," in *Ingredients for Women's Employment Policy,* ed. C. Bose and G. Spitze (Albany: State University of New York Press, 1987), 79; Elizabeth Higginbotham and Lynn Weber Cannon, "Rethinking Mobility: Towards a Race and Gender Inclusive Theory," Research Paper 8 (Center for Research on Women, Memphis State University, Memphis, Tenn., 1988), 33; Kesho Yvonne Scott, *The Habit of Surviving: Black Women's Strategies for Life* (New Brunswick, N.J.: Rutgers University Press, 1991), 149.

2. Emanuel A. Schegloff, Gail Jefferson, and Harvey Sacks, "The Preference for Self-correction in the Organization of Repair in Conversation," *Language* 53 (1977): 366.

3. Margaret's use of repetition in this and later passages resembles repetition in the discourse genre of the African-American sermon (Charles L. Briggs, " 'I'm Not Just Talking to the Victims of Oppression Tonight—I'm Talking to Everybody': Rhetorical Authority and Narrative Authenticity in an African-American Poetics of Political Engagement," *Journal of Narrative and Life History* 3 [1993]: 58–60). For another discussion of the functions of repetition in conversation, see Deborah Tannen, *Talking Voices: Repetition, Dialogue, and Imagery in Conversational Discourse* (Cambridge: Cambridge University Press, 1989).

4. Catherine Kohler Riessman, *Divorce Talk: Women and Men Make Sense of Personal Relationships* (New Brunswick, N.J.: Rutgers University Press, 1990), 84.

5. Rosabeth Moss Kanter, *Men and Women of the Corporation* (New York: Basic Books, 1977), 183. See also Judith Lorber, *Women Physicians: Careers, Status, and Power* (New York: Tavistock Publications, 1984), 99; Shirley M. Clark and Mary Corcoran, "Perspectives on the Professional Socialization of Women Faculty: A Case of Accumulative Disadvantage?" *Journal of Higher Education* 57 (1986): 25–27; Sakre Kennington Edson, *Pushing the Limits: The Female Administrative Aspirant* (Albany: State University of New York Press, 1988), 72–80; Charol Shakeshaft, *Women in Educational Administration* (Newbury Park, Calif.: Sage Publications, 1987), 115–116.

6. Lorber, *Women Physicians,* 7. Karen Fullbright found that among twenty-five Black women managers in the private sector, none "described mentor relationships that were similar to those that successful white man-

agers have" ("The Myth of the Double-advantage: Black Female Managers," in *Slipping Through the Cracks: The Status of Black Women*, ed. M. C. Simms and J. Malveaux [New Brunswick, N.J.: Transaction Books, 1986], 39).

7. Marjorie L. DeVault, "Talking and Listening from Women's Standpoint: Feminist Strategies for Interviewing and Analysis," *Social Problems* 37 (1990): 103.

8. Judith M. Gerson and Kathy Peiss, "Boundaries, Negotiation, Consciousness: Reconceptualizing Gender Relations," *Social Problems* 32 (1985): 326.

9. Gerson and Peiss, "Boundaries, Negotiation, Consciousness," 324.

10. The first of these two brief mentions of discriminatory treatment has been cited previously in this chapter; early in her career, Margaret worked as a school secretary in an urban district where she was told they had "all the Black teachers they need [ed]." The second (not cited) arises in Margaret's description of her first administrative jobs. In one city, she was told that the superintendent of schools "didn't want a woman downtown [i.e., in a central office administrative job], certainly didn't want a Black woman downtown." In both cases, Margaret includes race in describing the discriminatory attitudes she encountered.

11. When she speaks of the many discriminatory incidents in her life, Margaret seems to be speaking of her experiences as a Black woman. The fact that she does not specify whether she means race or sex discrimination, or both, suggests that she does not find it useful or even possible to separate her experiences as a woman and as an African American. Patricia Hill Collins discusses the futility of "additive analyses of oppression" in "Toward a New Vision: Race, Class and Gender as Categories of Analysis and Connection" (Keynote address delivered at the Curriculum Integration Workshop, Center for Research on Women, Memphis State University, Memphis, Tenn., May 1989), 4–5.

12. While I was working on this chapter, Thurgood Marshall resigned from the Supreme Court. A story Marshall told (reported on National Public Radio by one of his law clerks) reminded me of Margaret's distinction between her experiences in the profession and in her life in general. While waiting for a train in a small Southern town where he was working on a case, Marshall was threatened by a white man and told to leave town. The point of the story was that professional status does not necessarily protect a Black person outside of the professional context.

13. As described in note 10, Margaret briefly mentioned two other instances of race and sex discrimination in her work history. Because she related those two instances in the same spirit that she discusses the assis-

tant superintendency incident here—mentorship has been the general pattern; discrimination has been the exception—I have chosen not to treat as particularly significant the fact that she does not mention these two incidents again in this context.

14. Elliot G. Mishler, "The Analysis of Interview-Narratives," in *Narrative Psychology: The Storied Nature of Human Conduct,* ed. T. R. Sarbin (New York: Praeger Publishers, 1986), 234–35.

15. Historically, the majority of Black professional women have worked in the public sector within Black communities, although even some predominantly Black cities have been administered by whites (Higginbotham, "Employment for Professional Black Women in the Twentieth Century," 74–75, 78, 84).

16. In this interaction, Margaret "indicates that laughter is appropriate" by laughing first. We laugh with her in response. (Gail Jefferson, "A Technique for Inviting Laughter and Its Subsequent Acceptance Declination," in *Everyday Language: Studies in Ethnomethodology,* ed. G. Psathas [New York: Irvington Publishers, 1979], 80).

17. Marianne A. Paget, "The Ontological Anguish of Women Artists," *New England Sociologist* 3 (1981): 66. See also Catherine Kohler Riessman, "Worlds of Difference: Contrasting Experience in Marriage and Narrative Style," in *Gender and Discourse: The Power of Talk,* ed. A. Todd and S. Fisher (Norwood, N.J.: Ablex Publishing Corporation, 1988), esp. 171–72; and Peter G. Stromberg, *Language and Self-transformation: A Study of the Christian Conversion Narrative* (Cambridge: Cambridge University Press, 1993), 95–96.

18. Martine Burgos, "Life Stories, Narrativity, and the Search for the Self," *Life Stories/Récits de vie* 5 (1989): 33.

19. Angela Y. Davis, *Women, Race and Class* (New York: Vintage Books, 1983); Paula Ross, "Women, Oppression, Privilege, and Competition," in *Competition: A Feminist Taboo?* ed. V. Miner and H. E. Longino (New York: Feminist Press, 1987), 209–20; Barbara Hilkert Andolsen, *"Daughters of Jefferson, Daughters of Bootblacks": Racism and American Feminism* (Macon, Ga.: Mercer University Press, 1986), esp. chap. 5.

20. Patricia Hill Collins, *Black Feminist Thought: Knowledge, Consciousness, and the Politics of Empowerment* (Boston: Unwin Hyman, 1990), 92.

21. If Margaret had chosen to file a lawsuit, however, she would not have been totally alone; she has informed us that Connie Johnson offered to help her through the legal morass. Thus, Margaret chooses relationships with powerful men (mentors who have paved the way for her; the school board that is willing to fight for her) over a relationship with a woman who

also lacks power. Kesho Yvonne Scott might suggest that Margaret has given up on a "potentially strong alliance" with a white woman (*The Habit of Surviving*, 148).

22. Arlie Russell Hochschild, *The Managed Heart: Commercialization of Human Feeling* (Berkeley: University of California Press, 1983), 33, 37–38.

23. Hochschild, *The Managed Heart*, 33, 38–48.

24. Scott, *The Habit of Surviving*, 7.

25. Collins demonstrates that the themes of dignity, self-respect, and achieving respect from others are predominant in the works of Black feminist thinkers (*Black Feminist Thought*, 107).

26. Although Margaret describes the Black administrator as *they* rather than *he*, the context suggests that she is referring to one or more men (rather than women).

27. Jane H. Hill, "The Refiguration of the Anthropology of Language," *Cultural Anthropology* 1 (1986): 97.

28. For an interesting discussion of "choosing" one's gender, see Judith Butler, "Variations on Sex and Gender: Beauvoir, Wittig, and Foucault," in *Feminism as Critique: On the Politics of Gender*, ed. S. Benhabib and D. Cornell (Minneapolis: University of Minnesota Press, 1987), 128–42.

29. But which women is Margaret referring to? Because she initiated this part of her narrative with the question "I would imagine we all say the same thing don't we?" in which *we* referred to women superintendents, she might be using *we* in that way here. It is also possible that she means Black women educators or Black women educators of her generation.

30. James C. Scott, *Domination and the Arts of Resistance: Hidden Transcripts* (New Haven: Yale University Press, 1990). Scott writes:

> With rare, but significant, exceptions the public performance of the subordinate will, out of prudence, fear, and the desire to curry favor, be shaped to appeal to the expectations of the powerful. I shall use the term *public transcript* as a shorthand way of describing the open interaction between subordinates and those who dominate. (2)

He continues:

> I shall use the term *hidden transcript* to characterize discourse that takes place "offstage," beyond direct observation by powerholders. The hidden transcript is thus derivative in the sense that it consists of those offstage speeches, gestures, and practices that confirm, contradict, or inflect what appears in the public transcript. (4–5, emphasis in original)

1. John P. Hewitt and Randall Stokes, "Disclaimers," *American Sociological Review* 40 (1975): 1–11. They define a disclaimer as "a verbal device employed to ward off and defeat in advance doubts and negative typifications which may result from intended conduct. Disclaimers seek to define forthcoming conduct as not relevant to the kind of identity-challenge or re-typification for which it might ordinarily serve as the basis" (3).

2. Suzanne Laberge and Gillian Sankoff, "Anything *You* Can Do," in *Discourse and Syntax, Syntax and Semantics,* vol. 12, ed. Talmy Givón (New York: Academic Press, 1979), 429. See also Chiasato Kitagawa and Adrienne Lehrer, "Impersonal Uses of Personal Pronouns," *Journal of Pragmatics* 14 (1990): 739–59. I thank Jane Hill for these and other references on impersonal pronoun usage. While sociolinguists are most interested in explicating the rules that govern particular linguistic forms and usages, I am interested in what a speaker communicates by using a specific linguistic form. Karen Rhodes's use of the impersonal *you* needs to be interpreted in conjunction with other aspects of her narrative, in this case, her worry about sounding arrogant. Her persistent shifting between *I* and the impersonal *you* conveys a different meaning than does Denise Nelson's very selective use of the impersonal *you* in chapter 4.

3. There is an interesting difference between Karen Rhodes's and Denise Nelson's talk about arrogance. Recall that as she recounted her work history, Nelson was amused at her earlier naive self-confidence as expressed in her perpetual pursuit of "the next step" in her career. She did not criticize what she called her arrogance, and she did not hesitate to narrate her work history as a story about ambition. By contrast, Rhodes worries about sounding arrogant as she describes her competence and ambition.

4. Personal Narratives Group, ed., *Interpreting Women's Lives: Feminist Theory and Personal Narratives* (Bloomington: Indiana University Press, 1989), 11.

5. Laberge and Sankoff, "Anything *You* Can Do," 430. The reader should notice that Karen uses the present tense in conjunction with the impersonal *you* and the past tense when she focuses on her own story. "One syntactic indicator of generality is a tense change, always from a past tense . . . to the present" (424). On tense changes, see also Kitagawa and Lehrer, "Impersonal Uses of Personal Pronouns," 748.

6. There is a long history of discrimination against married women and mothers in the field of public education. Charol Shakeshaft gives a general outline of that history. In the early 1900s, many school districts had reg-

ulations prohibiting married women from teaching. In 1900, 90 percent of women teachers were single; in 1942, 58 percent of school districts across the United States still would not employ married women (*Women in Educational Administration* [Newbury Park, Calif.: Sage Publications, 1987], 40–43). Although such regulations were being changed about the time Karen Rhodes began teaching, the blatant discrimination she describes was not unusual even after new laws were in effect. Because the American education system traditionally has invested much power in the local school district, changes occurring on the national or state level did not necessarily affect policies, practices, and attitudes on the district level (Patricia A. Schmuck and Spencer H. Wyant, "Clues to Sex Bias in the Selection of School Administrators: A Report from the Oregon Network," in *Educational Policy and Management: Sex Differentials*, ed. P. A. Schmuck, W. W. Charters, Jr., and R. O. Carlson (New York: Academic Press, 1981), 74–76.

7. Kitagawa and Lehrer, "Impersonal Uses of Personal Pronouns," 750.

8. Barbara F. Reskin, "Bringing the Men Back In: Sex Differentiation and the Devaluation of Women's Work," *Gender and Society* 2 (1988): 66, 67.

9. Simone de Beauvoir, *The Second Sex*, trans. H. M. Parshley (New York: Vintage Books, 1974), 301. Judith Butler's discussion of Beauvoir's (and others') distinction between sex and gender demonstrates the difficulty of maintaining the difference ("Variations on Sex and Gender: Beauvoir, Wittig, and Foucault," in *Feminism as Critique: On the Politics of Gender*, ed. S. Benhabib and D. Cornell [Minneapolis: University of Minnesota Press, 1987], 128–42).

10. Reskin, "Bringing the Men Back In," 75.

11. For an analysis of women educational leaders' talk about both participatory and hierarchical forms of leadership, see Colleen S. Bell and Susan E. Chase, "Resistance and Conformity: Women's Educational Leadership" (Paper presented at the annual meeting of the American Educational Research Association, San Francisco, April 1989).

12. It is also possible that Karen uses the impersonal *you* to express a connection with Colleen and me as professional women who also work in a male-dominated profession. Kitagawa and Lehrer suggest that "[a] sense of informal camaraderie is often present with the use of impersonal *you* precisely because the speaker assigns a major 'actor' role to the addressee. In so doing, s/he is letting the hearer into the speaker's world view, implying that the hearer also shares the same perspective" ("Impersonal Uses of Personal Pronouns," 752).

13. The Equal Employment Opportunity Commission was established to administer Title VII of the Civil Rights Act of 1964; Title VII prohibits employers from discriminating on the basis of race, religion, national ori-

gin, and sex. For a description of the complaint process, see Andrea S. Christensen, "Sex Discrimination and the Law," in *Women Working: Theories and Facts in Perspective,* 2d ed., ed. A. H. Stromberg and S. Harkess (Mountain View, Calif.: Mayfield Publishing Company, 1988), 329–47.

14. Karen Rhodes's case was handled during the early 1980s before the Reagan administration effectively thwarted the EEOC. Unlike many women who have filed discrimination complaints with the EEOC, Karen had a generally positive experience with the agency. For a description of academic women's experiences with the EEOC and other government agencies, see Athena Theodore, *The Campus Troublemakers: Academic Women in Protest* (Houston: Cap and Gown Press, 1986), esp. 105–18.

15. Stanley Lieberson, cited in Reskin, "Bringing the Men Back In," 59. Reskin develops the thesis that "men resist allowing women and men to work together *as equals* because doing so undermines differentiation and hence male dominance" (65, emphasis in original). Myra Strober also develops the theory that men act in ways that preserve their privilege and dominance ("Toward a General Theory of Occupational Sex Segregation: The Case of Public School Teaching," in *Sex Segregation in the Workplace: Trends, Explanations, Remedies,* ed. B. F. Reskin [Washington, D.C.: National Academy Press, 1984], 144–56). See also William J. Goode, "Why Men Resist," in *Rethinking the Family: Some Feminist Questions,* ed. B. Thorne and M. Yalom (New York: Longman, 1982), 131–50.

16. Judith Lorber, *Women Physicians: Careers, Status, and Power* (New York: Tavistock Publications, 1984), 13–14.

17. Karen reiterates the idea of institutionalized male dominance in other parts of the interview. She does so, for example, by strongly resisting the notion that the sex segregation of the occupation is the result of women's not seeking administrative positions. Like Karen, most social scientists criticize supply-side explanations of occupational segregation. Conflicting explanations of the persistence of occupational sex segregation were well aired when historians Alice Kessler-Harris and Rosalind Rosenberg were called as expert witnesses for opposite sides of the *Sears vs. EEOC* discrimination case. See Ruth Milkman, "Women's History and the Sears Case," *Feminist Studies* 12 (1986): 375–400; and Jacquelyn Dowd Hall, "Women's History Goes to Trial: EEOC v. Sears, Roebuck and Company," *Signs* 11 (1986): 751–79.

18. Emily Abel, "Collective Protest and the Meritocracy: Faculty Women and Sex Discrimination Lawsuits," in *Women and Symbolic Interaction,* ed. M. J. Deegan and M. Hill (Boston: Allen and Unwin, 1987), 352.

19. Marilyn Frye, *The Politics of Reality: Essays in Feminist Theory* (Trumansburg, N.Y.: Crossing Press, 1983), 86.

20. Abel, "Collective Protest and the Meritocracy," 347.

21. For a discussion of the strengths and limits of humanistic or "me too!" feminism, see Kathy E. Ferguson, *Reversal and Its Discontents: The Man Question* (Berkeley: University of California Press, 1993), 2, 15, 58–60.

Chapter Seven: Individual Solutions to the Collective Problem of Inequality

1. Carolyn G. Heilbrun, *Writing a Woman's Life* (New York: Ballantine Books, 1989); Patricia Meyer Spacks, "Selves in Hiding," in *Women's Autobiography: Essays in Criticism*, ed. E. C. Jelinek (Bloomington: Indiana University Press, 1980).

2. See Susan E. Chase, "Making Sense of 'The Woman Who Becomes a Man,'" in *Gender and Discourse: The Power of Talk*, ed. A. Todd and S. Fisher (Norwood, N.J.: Ablex Publishing Corporation, 1988), 275–95.

3. Mary O'Brien, *The Politics of Reproduction* (Boston: Routledge and Kegan Paul, 1981), 71.

4. Jean Bethke Elshtain, *Public Man, Private Woman: Women in Social and Political Thought* (Princeton: Princeton University Press, 1981), 251.

5. George C. Rosenwald, "Conclusion: Reflections on Narrative Self-understanding," in *Storied Lives: The Cultural Politics of Self-understanding*, ed. G. C. Rosenwald and R. L. Ochberg (New Haven: Yale University Press, 1992), 280.

6. Arlie Hochschild, "Making It: Marginality and Obstacles to Minority Consciousness," in *Women and Success: The Anatomy of Achievement*, ed. R. B. Kundsin (New York: William Morrow, 1974), 195.

7. Judi Marshall, "Exploring the Experiences of Women Managers: Towards Rigour in Qualitative Methods," in *Feminist Social Psychology: Developing Theory and Practice*, ed. S. Wilkinson (Philadelphia: Open University Press, 1986), 205. See also Susan E. Chase and Colleen S. Bell, "Interpreting the Complexity of Women's Subjectivity," in *Interactive Oral Interviewing: Essays on Interactional Processes*, ed. K. L. Rogers and E. McMahan (Hillsdale, N.J.: Lawrence Erlbaum Publishers, forthcoming).

8. In "Making Sense of 'The Woman Who Becomes a Man,'" I argue that the appearance of gender neutrality that professional men take for granted is something they achieve through actions and discourse that conflate professional deportment and masculinity.

9. Wendy Hollway, *Subjectivity and Method in Psychology: Gender, Meaning and Science* (London: Sage Publications, 1989), 45.

10. George C. Rosenwald and Richard L. Ochberg, "Introduction: Life Stories, Cultural Politics, and Self-understanding," in *Storied Lives*, 2.

11. Rosenwald, "Conclusion: Reflections on Narrative Self-understanding," in *Storied Lives*, 284.

12. Susan Faludi, *Backlash: The Undeclared War against American Women* (New York: Anchor Books, 1991).

13. Cynthia Fuchs Epstein, *Women in Law* (Garden City, N.Y.: Anchor Press, Doubleday, 1983), 214–15.

14. James C. Scott, *Domination and the Arts of Resistance: Hidden Transcripts* (New Haven: Yale University Press, 1990).

15. The disruptive character of women's laughter in public—in the presence of powerful men—is portrayed beautifully in Marlene Gorris's radical feminist film *A Question of Silence*.

16. Hester Eisenstein, *Gender Shock: Practicing Feminism on Two Continents* (Boston: Beacon Press, 1991), 14. It is also possible to find examples of activist stories within the working-class world, but that is not my task here. See, for example, Karen Brodkin Sacks, *Caring by the Hour: Women, Work, and Organizing at Duke Medical Center* (Urbana: University of Illinois Press, 1988); and Cynthia B. Costello, *We're Worth It!: Women and Collective Action in the Insurance Workplace* (Urbana: University of Illinois Press, 1992).

17. Eisenstein, *Gender Shock*, 14.

18. Eisenstein, *Gender Shock*, 31.

19. Eisenstein, *Gender Shock*, 13.

20. There are certainly other contexts within the academic world—such as ethnic studies, multicultural studies, and labor studies—in which the struggle for equality may constitute professional work.

21. There is an immense literature on the transformations that have been taking place in the academy over the last twenty years or so. Although women's studies programs have played a major role in that regard, many who work for those changes are involved in other programs. I list here only a few references to this vast literature: the spring/summer 1990 issue of *Women's Studies Quarterly*, devoted to a symposium on curricular and institutional change; Margaret L. Andersen, "Changing the Curriculum in Higher Education," *Signs: Journal of Women in Culture and Society* 12 (1987): 222–54; Susan Hardy Aiken et al., *Changing our Minds: Feminist Transformations of Knowledge* (Albany: State University of New York Press, 1988); Elizabeth Kamarck Minnich, *Transforming Knowledge* (Philadelphia: Temple University Press, 1990); Margo Culley and Catherine Portuges, eds., *Gendered Subjects: The Dynamics of Feminist Teaching* (Boston: Routledge and Kegan Paul, 1985); Jo Anne Pagano, "Teaching Women,"

Educational Theory 38 (1988): 321–39; Elaine Martin, "Power and Authority in the Classroom: Sexist Stereotypes in Teaching Evaluations," *Signs: Journal of Women in Culture and Society* 1984 (9): 482–92; Yolanda T. Moses, "Black Women in Academe: Issues and Strategies" (Publication of the Project on the Status and Education of Women, Association of American Colleges, Washington, D.C., 1989); Bernice R. Sandler, "The Campus Climate Revisited: Chilly for Women Faculty, Administrators, and Graduate Students" (Publication of the Project on the Status and Education of Women, Association of American Colleges, Washington, D.C., 1988); Marilyn R. Schuster and Susan R. Van Dyne, eds., *Women's Place in the Academy: Transforming the Liberal Arts Curriculum* (Totowa, N.J.: Rowman and Allanheld, 1985); Patti Lather, *Getting Smart: Feminist Research and Pedagogy With/In the Postmodern* (New York: Routledge, Chapman and Hall, 1991); Gloria Bowles and Renate Duelli Klein, *Theories of Women's Studies* (London: Routledge and Kegan Paul, 1983). The rhetoric of social change, of course, pervades feminist criticism generally. See, for example, Francesca M. Cancian, "Feminist Science: Methodologies That Challenge Inequality," *Gender and Society* 6 (1992): 623–42; Christie Farnham, ed., *The Impact of Feminist Research in the Academy* (Bloomington: Indiana University Press, 1987); Sandra Harding, ed., *Feminism and Methodology* (Bloomington: Indiana University Press, 1987); Beth B. Hess and Myra Marx Ferree, *Analyzing Gender: A Handbook of Social Science Research* (Newbury Park, Calif.: Sage Publications, 1987).

22. See, for example, Joan D. Mandle, "Political Correctness and the Feminist Movement," *SWS Network News* 9 (September 1992): 3; and Pauline B. Bart's response to Mandle in "Ain't I Gender," *SWS Network News* 10 (June 1993): 14.

23. Maxine Baca Zinn et al., "The Costs of Exclusionary Practices in Women's Studies," *Signs: Journal of Women in Culture and Society* 11 (1986): 290–303; Esther Ngan-Ling Chow, "Teaching Sex and Gender in Sociology: Incorporating the Perspective of Women of Color," *Teaching Sociology* 12 (1985): 299–311; Margaret L. Andersen, "Moving Our Minds: Studying Women of Color and Reconstructing Sociology," *Teaching Sociology* 16 (1988): 123–32; Elizabeth Higginbotham, "Integrating All Women into the Curriculum" (Publication of the Research Clearinghouse and Curriculum Integration Project, Center for Research on Women, Memphis State University, Memphis, Tenn., 1988); Patricia Hill Collins, "Toward a New Vision: Race, Class and Gender as Categories of Analysis and Connection" (Keynote address delivered at the Curriculum Integration Workshop, Center for Research on Women, Memphis State University, Memphis, Tenn., May 1989).

24. Eisenstein, *Gender Shock*, 14. Thelma McCormack makes a similar argument in describing the successful implementation of a new graduate program in women's studies at York University in Toronto ("Women's Studies: A Threat to Academic Freedom or a Test of It?" *SWS Network News* 9 [December 1992]: 3–4): "Part of our success in getting the programme through our various internal committees was that York has had a long tradition of interdisciplinary studies and educational innovations. Our colleagues, male and female, were not as unfamiliar or suspicious of it as they might have been at a more traditional university."

25. Recent discussion about how feminist thinking has changed the discipline of sociology can be found in the symposium on Dorothy E. Smith's work in *Sociological Theory* 10 (1992): 60–98; the symposium on gendered institutions in *Contemporary Sociology* 21 (1992): 565–95; and Paula England, ed., *Theory on Gender: Feminism on Theory* (Hawthorne, N.Y.: Aldine de Gruyter, 1993). A now classic article on that topic is Judith Stacey and Barrie Thorne, "The Missing Feminist Revolution in Sociology," *Social Problems* 32 (1985): 301–16.

26. Peggy McIntosh, "White Privilege and Male Privilege: A Personal Account of Coming to See Correspondences Through Work in Women's Studies," in *Race, Class, and Gender: An Anthology,* ed. M. L. Andersen and P. H. Collins (Belmont, Calif.: Wadsworth Publishing Company, 1992), 70–81. This article provides a strong model for exercising activism with respect to one's own taken-for-granted privileges in an inequitable world.

27. Colleen S. Bell and Susan E. Chase, "The Underrepresentation of Women in School Leadership," in *The New Politics of Race and Gender,* 1993 Politics of Education Yearbook, ed. C. Marshall (London: Falmer Press, at press).

28. Mary F. Rogers, "They All Were Passing: Agnes, Garfinkel, and Company," *Gender and Society* 6 (1992): 174–76; Kathryn Anderson and Dana C. Jack, "Learning to Listen: Interview Techniques and Analyses," in *Women's Words: The Feminist Practice of Oral History,* ed. S. B. Gluck and D. Patai (New York: Routledge, Chapman and Hall, 1991), 12; Patricia Hill Collins, *Black Feminist Thought: Knowledge, Consciousness, and the Politics of Empowerment* (Boston: Unwin Hyman, 1990), 96–99; Susan E. Chase, "Social Science *for* Women: A Reading of Studies of Women's Work," *Humanity and Society* 13 (1989): 260–63.

29. Angela Y. Davis, *Women, Race and Class* (New York: Vintage Books, 1983); Paula Ross, "Women, Oppression, Privilege, and Competition," in *Competition: A Feminist Taboo?* ed. V. Miner and H. E. Longino (New York: Feminist Press, 1987), 209–20. For a case study that discusses conflict between working-class and professional women, see Linda M. Blum, "Pos-

sibilities and Limits of the Comparable Worth Movement," *Gender and Society* 1 (1987): esp. 390–92.

30. For a description of how one member of this informal network talks about its significance, see Chase and Bell, "Interpreting the Complexity of Women's Subjectivity."

31. Judith Lorber, *Women Physicians: Careers, Status, and Power* (New York: Tavistock Publications, 1984), 62–63, 113–15; Epstein, *Women in Law*, 257–61; Debra Renee Kaufman, "Professional Women: How Real Are the Recent Gains?" in *Women: A Feminist Perspective*, ed. J. Freeman, 4th ed. (Mountain View, Calif.: Mayfield Publishing Company, 1989), 342–43; Lois Benjamin, *The Black Elite: Facing the Color Line in the Twilight of the Twentieth Century* (Chicago: Nelson-Hall Publishers, 1991); Pamela Roby, "Women and the ASA: Degendering Organizational Structures and Processes, 1964–1974," *The American Sociologist* 23 (1992): 18–48.

32. In commenting on an earlier draft of this chapter, Laurel Richardson suggested the term *overlapping readings* to describe my method of interpreting different parts of each narrative in relation to each other.

33. Margaret Parker was much more interested in talking about informal sources of support than about her participation in professional organizations. When Colleen asked about organizations for Black educators, Margaret mentioned a national organization that is "dominated by Black males," which she would like to be active in but has not because of lack of time. When Colleen asked whether she had participated in the statewide organization for women in educational administration when she was at Lake City, Margaret described the organization as "a *good* network for women" and its leaders as "smart enough to not limit themselves to females." She spoke about sitting on panels, speaking at the annual meetings, and receiving the organization's highest award.

34. Sacks, *Caring by the Hour*, 120–21.

35. Catherine Kohler Riessman, *Divorce Talk: Women and Men Make Sense of Personal Relationships* (New Brunswick, N.J.: Rutgers University Press, 1990), 84.

36. Recall Margaret Parker's story about how white and Black male administrators warned her to stay away from Connie Johnson when Margaret first arrived in Lake City. She claims that she understood that warning only when she started gathering women around her. Now we understand this gathering of women around her as a reference to the informal network she initiated. Once Margaret heard the whole history from other women, she realized that the powerful men in the district experienced Connie as a threat.

37. Colleen Bell analyzes this woman's gender consciousness in " 'If I

Weren't Involved with Schools, I Might Be Radical': Gender Consciousness in Context," in *Women Leading in Education,* ed. D. M. Dunlap and P. A. Schmuck (Albany: State University of New York, forthcoming).

38. Faludi, *Backlash.*

39. Catherine Kohler Riessman, "Making Sense of Marital Violence: One Woman's Narrative," in *Storied Lives,* 246.

40. C. Wright Mills, *The Sociological Imagination* (New York: Oxford University Press, 1959), 8. When analyzing individuals' responses to structurally based social problems, sociologists frequently point out that individuals tend to confuse "personal troubles of milieu" and "public issues of social structure."

Appendix: The Research Project

1. Joe R. Feagin, Anthony M. Orum, and Gideon Sjoberg, eds., *A Case for the Case Study* (Chapel Hill: University of North Carolina Press, 1991).

2. See chapter 1, note 87 for a partial list of important studies in this field.

3. A discussion of the tables presenting the number of women K–12 superintendents by state (in 1986, 1989, and 1991) is included in Colleen S. Bell and Susan E. Chase, "The Underrepresentation of Women in School Leadership," in *The New Politics of Race and Gender,* 1993 Politics of Education Yearbook, ed. C. Marshall (London: Falmer Press, at press).

4. "Education Vital Signs" (a supplement to the *American School Board Journal* and *The Executive Educator*), *American School Board Journal* 178 (December 1991): A-10.

5. Susan E. Chase and Colleen S. Bell, "Interpreting the Complexity of Women's Subjectivity," in *Interactive Oral Interviewing,* ed. K. L. Rogers and E. McMahan (Hillsdale, N.J.: Lawrence Erlbaum Publishers, forthcoming).

6. Colleen S. Bell and Susan E. Chase, "Resistance and Conformity: Women's Educational Leadership" (Paper presented at the annual meeting of the American Educational Research Association, San Francisco, April 1989); Susan E. Chase and Colleen S. Bell, "Ideology, Discourse, and Gender: How Gatekeepers Talk about Women School Superintendents," *Social Problems* 37 (1990): 163–77.

Index

women educators, absence from discrimination stories)
legal action against, 140, 159–67, 171
legal action as risky response to, 21–22, 135–36, 141, 144, 165
male dominance and, 162–65, 166, 170
pain or injury associated with, 21–22, 58, 78, 112–13, 116, 118, 119, 137–38, 161, 163–64, 166
past events recast as, 111–17
questions about, in the interviews, 51, 52, 55, 59, 75, 112, 129
reintegration into professional community after legal action against, 167–70
responses to, 57–58, 77–79, 126–27, 128, 134–36, 182
self-conception as affected by, 116–17, 137–38
unprompted talk about, 129, 146
discursive disjunction, 16–17, 27
defined, xi, 11
implications of concept, 33–34
See also disjunction between discursive realms of professional work and inequality
discursive realm
defined, 17
as shaping forms of talk, 59–60
discursive realm of inequality, xii, 20–23, 38, 49–58
and discrimination talk, 21, 49–58, 104, 116, 124–25, 153
and disrupted talk, 51, 53, 54–55, 81, 83, 101, 130
and group membership, 20–21
historical changes in, 21
ideological or unsettled character of, 20, 22–23, 51, 59, 129, 232 n. 38
and self-conscious talk, 16–17, 20, 51, 59, 142
discursive realm of professional work, xi, 17–20, 38, 40–49, 58–59
gender and race neutrality of, 19
historical changes in, 18–19
individualism in, 18–19, 147, 152, 166, 167–68, 170, 171–72, 200, 231 n. 38, 241 n. 16
traditional or settled character of, 17, 22–23, 48, 117
and unselfconscious talk, 16–17
and women's empowerment, 58, 91, 92, 117, 152, 180

and women's silence, 92
and women's work histories, 40–49, 58–59, 74–75, 98–99, 117, 124, 152 (see also work histories of women superintendents)
disjunction between discursive realms of professional work and inequality, 38, 58–62, 178
femocrats' challenge to, 189–90
narrative difficulties and, 79
disrupted talk
defined, 51
examples of, 53, 55, 80–84, 101, 130
Dumas, Rhetaugh Graves, 228 n. 19

Edmondson, Ricca, 228 n. 22, 234 n. 50
Edson, Sakre Kennington, 237 n. 87, 244 n. 4, 252 n. 5
"Education Vital Signs," 236 n. 79, 238 n. 88, 264 n. 4
Eisenstein, Hester, 189–91
Elliot, Philip, 230 n. 31
Elshtain, Jean Bethke, 183
England, Paula, 262 n. 25
Epstein, Cynthia Fuchs, 187, 228 n. 18, 245 n. 15, 263 n. 31
ethnomethodology, x, 15, 25, 29

Faludi, Susan, 260 n. 12, 264 n. 38
family
desire for time with, 102–3
influence of, 147, 148
support from, 95, 100, 108–9, 121
Farnham, Christie, 261 n. 21
Feagin, Joe R., 264 n. 1
feminism. See women's movement
femocrats, 189–90
Ferguson, Kathy E., 259 n. 21
Ferree, Myra Marx, 226 n. 3, 261 n. 21
Fischer, Michael M. J., 241 n. 16
Fisher, Walter R., 226 nn. 4, 5
Foucault, Michel, 229 n. 27
Freidson, Eliot, 35, 73, 231 n. 35
Friedan, Betty, 183
Friedman, Susan Stanford, 227 n. 9
Frye, Marilyn, 165, 242 n. 23, 246 n. 27
Fullan, Michael G., 237 n. 80, 250 n. 15
Fullbright, Karen, 228 n. 18, 252 n. 6

Gadamer, Hans-Georg, 29
Garfinkel, Harold, 14, 30, 229 n. 26, 233 n. 46, 235 nn. 59, 60, 238 n. 1
Geertz, Clifford, 32

Geist, Patricia, 232 n. 38
gender
    identity shaped by, 142–43, 144, 157,
        179
    narratives shaped by, 9
    socialization shaped by, 142–43
Gergen, Mary, 71, 227 nn. 9, 14, 248 n. 1
Gerson, Judith, 127–28
Gerson, Kathleen, 250 n. 14
Giddings, Paula, 240 n. 12
Gilkes, Cheryl Townsend, 240 n. 12,
    247 n. 30
Glesne, Corinne, 243 n. 28
Gluck, Sherna Berger, 235 n. 62
Goode, William J., 230 n. 31, 258 n. 15
Goodwin, Marjorie Harness, 234 n. 56
Gusfield, Joseph, 228 n. 22
Gwaltney, John Langston, 240 n. 14

Hall, Jaquelyn Dowd, 258 n. 17
Hansot, Elisabeth, 35, 236 n. 73, 237 n. 81
Hardesty, Monica, 232 n. 38
Harding, Sandra, 226 n. 3, 261 n. 21
Harrington, Mona, 8
Heilbrun, Carolyn G., 7, 8, 11, 48, 70, 180
Hentges, Joseph T., 236 n. 75, 244 n. 3
Heritage, John, 238 n. 1
Hess, Beth B., 226 n. 3, 261 n. 21
Hewitt, John P., 256 n. 1
Higginbotham, Elizabeth, 240 n. 12,
    241 n. 18, 246 n. 25, 247 nn. 30, 32,
    252 n. 1, 254 n. 15, 261 n. 23
Hill, Jane H., 142, 242 n. 24, 243 n. 27
Hobbs, Jerry R., 244 n. 8
Hochschild, Arlie, 137, 184–86, 188,
    251 nn. 19, 20
Hollway, Wendy, 185–86
Hughes, Everett Cherrington, 73, 229 n.
    25, 231 n. 35
Hunter, Albert, 228 n. 22
husbands
    absence of, 77, 78
    support from, 67–68, 108–9
    perspective of, on the superintendency,
        107

impersonal *you*, 112, 116, 148–49, 151–
    53, 156, 159, 166, 171, 197–98, 251 n. 24
individualism, 18–19, 119, 167–68, 170,
    182, 183
inequality
    individual solutions to, xiii, 33, 182–
        83, 194–97

questions about, in the interviews, 49–
    51
    See also discursive realm of inequality
interviews, intensive
    coding of, 23, 222–23
    interaction during, 11, 61, 92–93, 117,
        219–20
    tension during, 82
    transcripts of, method of displaying,
        38–39
    and trust, 145, 188

Jack, Dana C., 242 n. 25, 243 n. 30, 262 n.
    28
Jacobs, Scott, 233 n. 50
Jameson, Fredric, 226 n. 5
Jefferson, Gail, 244 n. 6, 252 n. 2, 254 n. 16
Jones, Effie H., 218, 225 n. 2

Kanter, Rosabeth Moss, 125, 228 n. 19,
    245 n. 15, 251 n. 19
Kaufman, Debra Renee, 228 n. 20, 237 n.
    84, 263 n. 31
Kitagawa, Chiasato, 256 nn. 2, 5, 257 nn.
    7, 12
Klein, Renate Duelli, 243 n. 29, 261 n. 21
Klein, Susan, 237 n. 87
Konnert, M. William, 236 nn. 70, 74, 78
Krieger, Susan, 229 n. 25

Laberge, Suzanne, 112, 148, 256 n. 5
Labov, William, 25, 41, 240 n. 9, 244 n. 2,
    249 n. 10
Lane, Robert E., 233 n. 46
language as constitutive of meaning, 29–
    31
Lather, Patti, 261 n. 21
Leggon, Cheryl Bernadette, 228 n. 20
Lehrer, Adrienne, 256 nn. 2, 5, 257 nn. 7,
    12
Lewis, Philip, 230 n. 31
Lieberson, Stanley, 162
Lipset, Seymour Martin, 248 n. 2
Lorber, Judith, 162, 227 n. 18, 245 n. 15,
    252 nn. 5, 6, 263 n. 31
Luckmann, Thomas, 30
Lukes, Steven, 230 n. 33
Lyman, Stanford M., 249 nn. 6, 9

MacKinnon, Catharine A., 231 n. 37
Maines, David, 31
Mandle, Joan D., 261 n. 22
Mannheim, Karl, 230 n. 32